DATE DUE

BRODART, CO.

Cat. No. 23-221-003

SHAKESPEARE THE HISTORIES

Shakespeare:
The Histories

Graham Holderness

St. Martin's Press
New York

St. Martin's Press, Scholarly and Reference Division, 175 Fifth Avenue, New York, N.Y. 10010

First published in the United States of America in 2000

This book is printed on paper suitable for recycling and made from fully managed and sustained forest sources.

Printed in Hong Kong

ISBN 0–312–22713–2

Library of Congress Cataloging-in-Publication Data
Holderness, Graham.
Shakespeare—the histories / Graham Holderness.
p.   cm.
Includes bibliographical references and index.
ISBN 0–312–22713–2 (cloth)
1. Shakespeare, William, 1564–1616—Histories.   2. Historical
drama, English—History and criticism.   3. Great Britain–
–History—1066–1687—Historiography.   4. Literature and history–
–Great Britain—History.   5. Kings and rulers in literature.
I. Title.
PR2982.H594   1999
822.3'3—dc21   99–39444
                                                                  CIP

In memory of my father

Eric Holderness
1928–80

Behold, I shew you a mystery:
We shall not all sleep,
but we shall all be changed

1 Corinthians, XV.51

Note on the Text

The text of Shakespeare's plays used for most quotations and references is that of Peter Alexander's *Complete Works*, first published 1951.

Contents

List of Plates

Acknowledgements

Virtually all the writing in this book is new (it was completed between July 1996 and September 1998), and the approach taken differs considerably, as should be immediately apparent, from much of my earlier work on Shakespeare's history plays. Some of the material has been recently but previously published: Graham Holderness and Carol Banks, 'Bravehearts: images of masculinity in Shakespeare's history plays', *Parergon*, n.s., 15: 1 (July 1997), 138–59; Carol Banks and Graham Holderness, 'Shakespeare Rescheduled', *Boxed Sets: television representations of theatre*, ed. J. Ridgman (Arts Council/John Libby Media/University of Luton, 1998), pp. 173–86; and Graham Holderness, 'Shakespeare's "whole History": drama and early modern historical theory', *Rethinking History*, 3: 1 (Spring 1999), 21–52. I am grateful to the editors and publishers concerned for permission to reprint this material. The examples of joint authorship cited here indicate the extent to which this work has been developed collaboratively. I am grateful to Professors Kiernan Ryan and John Russel Brown for some lively and enlightening lunches, and to Professor Dennis Brown and Dr Beverley Southgate for help with the historiographical theory. My editor Margaret Bartley has provided highly valued moral support.

Introduction: The Histories

Gather up the fragments that remain, that nothing be lost.

John, VI.12

I

Dick. They are all in order, and march toward us.
Cade. But then are we in order when we are most out of order.

(*HVI2*, 4.2.183–4)

As the plebeian rebels Dick Butcher and Jack Cade observe the advance of the king's forces in *Henry VI, Part Two*, they contrast the straight line of loyalist power and authority, marching 'all in order' against disorderly insurrection, with their own ragged rout of rebellious commoners. Just as Cade's rebellion is subjugated by the forces of law and order, and dissidence subjected to a rule of regular linearity associated with masculine and patriarchal sovereignty; so in the first 'collected works of Shakespeare', the First Folio of 1623, the history plays were lined up chronologically in an integrated linear sequence, modelled on the dynastic succession of English kings. Here, as Virginia Woolf put it, 'the history of England is the history of the male line' (Woolf, 1958: 76).

This apparent linearity was not, however, the pattern of their original composition: for the plays appear to have been written and performed, like Cade's rebels, 'out of order'. In the Folio text the three parts of *King Henry VI* and *Richard the Third* seem to constitute the self-evident unity implied by their common description as the 'First Tetralogy'. But the same can hardly be said for the plays in their original conditions of publication, where they appeared, often in variant textual forms, as *The First Part of the Contention betwixt the two famous Houses, of Yorke and Lancaster* (1594); *The True Tragedy of Richard Duke of York* (1595); *The Tragedy of Richard the Third* (1597); and *The First Part of King Henry the Sixt* (1623).

It also seems highly improbable that in the theatre of their origin these plays were ever performed as a 'sequence', as 'tetralogies', or in

1

chronological order. On the contrary, recent research indicates that each play was independently and individually shaped by contemporary cultural pressures (Marcus, 1988; Taylor, 1989). Even where such a dramatic succession is suggested, the evidence is inconclusive. The Epilogue to *Henry IV, Part Two* promised that 'our humble author will continue the story, with Sir John [Falstaff] in it' (*HIV2*, 'Epilogue', 27). But what exactly was meant here by 'story'? It could hardly refer to the already written narrative of history – 'the story of England' – since it was to have featured the unhistorical Sir John Falstaff. It could only therefore have been a continuation of the particular localised '[hi]story' constructed by the play. In the Folio's sequence, although continuity is preserved and the chronological order of events followed, the promise of this particular sequel now lies eternally broken, since Falstaff was, in the event, excluded from the comic adventures of *Henry V*.

When the ten Shakespearean history plays were reordered by the editors of the Folio into a chronological and linear sequence, they became available to be read as a linked, sequential narrative of English monarchical history. To enhance this emphasis some of the plays were given different titles from those that had appeared in the earlier, single, quarto editions: titles which now carried the name of a particular king, and some of which indicated by numerical order that they were parts of a continuing historical narrative. Thus the play that appeared in Quarto with the elaborate and descriptive title –

> The First Part of the Contention betwixt the two famous houses of York and Lancaster, with the death of the good Duke Humphrey: And the banishment and death of the Duke of *Suffolke*, and the Tragicall end of the proud Cardinall of *Winchester*, with the notable rebellion of *Iacke Cade*: *And the Duke of Yorkes first claime unto the Crowne*

– became simply *The Second Part of King Henry the Sixt*, and was placed in sequence between the 'first' and 'third' parts of what had thus become a single tripartite drama. Where the Quarto's title emphasises difference and discontinuity, identifying the division between factions and listing the seemingly unrelated elements of the narrative, the Folio title substitutes the single unifying name of a king.

This orderly grouping of the plays within the First Folio volume, a practice thereby normalised and followed in most collected editions of Shakespeare's plays, was therefore an editorial, rather than an authorial or theatrical, strategy. The act of compilation satisfied the contemporary conditions of printing, particularly those required for the relatively new form of a single author's 'collected works'. But the Jacobean First Folio came into circulation at a time when the idea of printing plays simply to be read, rather than performed, was in its infancy. Drama remained of course very much an audio-visual cultural form, each live performance by its very nature a unique presentation, fluid and unstable, open to free adaptation and interpretation. Once transformed into the linear printed text, words set out in lines on numbered pages in a bound book, this transient art was captured, permanently pinned down in a form now closer to the authoritative chronicles of Tudor history, or to the chapter and verse stability of the Holy Bible.

II

In modern criticism, the symbiotic relationship we now assume between the history plays and the Tudor historical chronicles was formally sealed in the 1940s, in the work of E. M. W. Tillyard and Lily B. Campbell (Campbell, 1947). Tillyard claimed that 'Shakespeare conceived his second tetralogy as one great unit' (Tillyard, 1944, 1980: 234); and that furthermore, if we discount *King John* and *Henry VIII*, it could be said that 'the two tetralogies make a single unit' (Tillyard, 1944, 1980: 147). The continuous action of this integrated 'octology', it was argued, not only imitated the historical narrative of that particular period of English history, but also expressed a distinctive historical interpretation of that period, identifying the deposition of Richard II as a kind of 'original sin' which brought upon the reigns of Henry IV, Henry VI and Richard III a providential curse. It was assumed that the chronological reordering of these plays, secured by the printed format, infiltrated the overall meaning of the series, and transformed a sequence of discrete, independent plays into a unified national epic (see Holderness, 1992: 1–8).

In the theatre the plays continued, despite the Folio's imperious 'act of union', to exist in their disaggregated form, with plays like *Richard III* and *Henry V* used as star vehicles for the great actor-managers, and the *Henry VI* plays virtually forgotten, right up to the twentieth century. Just as the reconstruction of the plays into their sequences was very much a feature of twentieth-century criticism, so in the later twentieth-century theatre, whose conditions of production allowed for the possibility of running plays in sequence across several nights, the spectacle of the plays performed in chronological sequence became a dramatic reality (see Holderness, 1985). The production of the cycle or series then became a characteristic ambition of the post-war subsidised theatre, as exemplified in the Peter Hall–John Barton production of *The Wars of the Roses* (1963) and more recently the Royal Shakespeare Company's *The Plantagenets* (see Sinfield, 1986). The link with television, far better adapted to the logistics of a series than the theatre, is also highly significant in this respect, and is clearly visible in the BBC's adaptations of *The Wars of the Roses* (1964), *An Age of Kings* (1960) and the history productions in the *BBC/Time-Life Television Shakespeare Series* (see Holderness, 1986). These initiatives can be contrasted with what continues to be the disaggregating effect of the cinema, which tends instead to extricate individual plays from their metanarrative context, as exemplified by film versions such as those of Laurence Olivier (*Richard III* and *Henry V*) and Kenneth Branagh (*Henry V*).

III

The tripartite division of Shakespeare's plays into comedies, tragedies and histories also derives from the posthumously published 'First Folio' — *Mr William Shakespeares Comedies, Histories and Tragedies* — of 1623. When the plays were originally published, in cheap quarto format through the 1590s and early 1600s, they were by no means so clearly identified and distinguished by genre. The original title pages would offer a play as a 'comical history', or a 'tragical history', or even just as biography, as the 'Life and Death of' the central character. Even in the Folio's contents, biographical titles are given to most of the 'history' plays — for example *The Life and Death of King John* (and also to one of the tragedies — *The Life and Death of Julius Caesar*). Virtually all of the plays designated as 'histories' in the Folio contents page were not so called on their initial publication; and the titles given individually to plays in the Folio all, with the single exception of *The Famous History of Henry the Eight*, omit the word 'history' altogether.

And yet the category of historical drama, the 'history play', has seemed, certainly to modern criticism, the simplest and least controversial of the three major forms established by the Folio. Very early in the day twentieth-century criticism began to reclassify those plays which would not fit very easily into the standard categories, even inventing new types such as the 'problem plays', the 'Roman plays', or the 'late romances' (Tillyard, 1949; Traversi, 1963). *The Tempest* and *The Winter's Tale*, now firmly settled as tragi-comic 'late romances', are classified in the Folio as comedies, while their companion piece *Cymbeline King of Britain* is designated a tragedy. Modern discussions of the tragedies have found them to be also histories; some comedies now seem compounded of a mixture of tragedy and romance (Holderness, Potter and Turner, 1988).

The history plays, by contrast, have appeared relatively easy to define and relatively stable in their occupation of a single discrete genre. There are obvious reasons for this. Where comedy and tragedy are very ancient forms, with ancestries going back thousands of years, the 'chronicle' play, based on incidents from English history, was quite a new, late sixteenth-century form, dating directly from historical narratives such as those of Holinshed (1587, 1965) and Halle (1548, 1809), narratives which were themselves of very recent origin. Where comedies and tragedies tended to derive their plots from fictional narratives, history plays, written in close relation to historiography, were (and are) considered as dealing with matters of 'fact' rather than of 'fiction'. Henry V existed, the battle of Agincourt took place: Orsino and Othello are invented characters, their destinies fabricated from airy nothings to which the drama gave a local habitation and a name.

Every sixteenth-century historical drama, even when written and performed singly (as was, for instance, Marlowe's *Edward II*) very obviously formed, already before its composition, part of a larger narrative scheme, the 'history of England'; and it was perhaps only a matter of time before someone thought of linking several plays into a series, so that the drama (necessarily composed of short 2–3-hour performable units) would begin to imitate the ceaseless continuity and grand comprehensive sweep of the historical narrative. That particular 'English' historical narrative was clearly more extensive, and arguably more central to sixteenth-century culture, than any other available historigraphy; and so the Shakespearean history plays can be read as constructing a more integrated metanarrative than those plays that address other historical times and places. This distinction too is one initiated by the Folio: the plays defined by the Folio as 'histories' are those that deal with English history, and with the history of fairly recent times. So the 'Roman' plays, derived in exactly the same way from older historical texts, or plays like *Macbeth* and *King Lear*, derived from the same historical texts as the 'histories' proper, are not acknowledged as 'histories' in anything like the same sense.

Problems are nonetheless raised about the security of the generic category 'history play'. If what distinguishes a 'history' play from other types of drama is its derivation from a historical narrative, then why are plays such as *Antony and Cleopatra*, *Macbeth* and *King Lear* not 'histories'? The question of historical period is a matter of content and chronology, not one of genre and form; and is in any case open to dispute. The reign of Henry VIII was certainly to Shakespeare recent history, but was the reign of King John?

Further, it is argued that the Elizabethans saw the civil wars of the fifteenth century as their own history, or the pre-history of their present (Tillyard, 1944; Campbell, 1947). But when history becomes important in a particular present, chronological distance does not act as an impediment to perceived contemporary relevance. The more remote mediaeval pasts of both England and Scotland (the subject-matter of *Macbeth*) became, almost by historical accident, of immediate contemporary significance on the accession of James I (Holderness, Potter and Turner, 1988); and it could further be argued that the political histories of Greece and Rome were more thoroughly known and studied, and even perhaps more influential in the later seventeenth century, than the histories of feudal and mediaeval Britain.

The 'Shakespearean history play' is by this categorisation deemed to represent a single homogeneous generic model. But there were many types of historical drama in the Renaissance, as there were many forms of historical writing. The two other history plays that fall outside the tetralogies (*King John* and *Henry VIII*) differ very substantially in style, and it can be demonstrated that each 'belongs' more to the particular cultural moment of its production (e.g. in the case of *Henry VIII*, as Leonard Tennenhouse has shown [Tennenhouse, 1986], to the conventions of the court masque) than to other plays in the 'Shakespearean' history cycles. The two 'tetralogies', even considered as unified cycles, in any case differ substantially from one another in style; and within the sequences, individual plays differ as radically one from another. The four plays of the 'second tetralogy' could for example easily be identified as belonging to different genres – lyrical tragedy, popular comedy, patriotic chronicle (or satire) – as well as to an interrelated series.

Notwithstanding these objections, there are certain strong reasons for separating the history plays from other categories. One is their unique integration into groups, series, narrative sequences, particularly the two 'tetralogies' *Henry VI–Richard III*, and *Richard II–Henry V*. Within each sequence, the individual plays are not only chronologically sequenced, but explicitly interrelated by flashbacks, predictions, cross-referencing. The Folio of course assembled an even larger historical narrative, first by printing the plays not in the order of their composition or production, but in the order of their historical chronology; and second by adding the two 'outlying' dramas, *The Life and Death of King John* and *The Famous History of Henry the Eight*, to form preface and sequel to the great dramatic mini-series of English history.

Lastly, there remains a further context marking an apparently clear theoretical distinction between the history plays and other categories. 'Shakespeare's comedies' and 'Shakespeare's tragedies' were, as aesthetic or critical categories, subsequent constructions. The plays in each group belong together because each is thought of as an exercise in the same repertoire of conventions, not because they are explicitly interrelated one with another, or because they appear to be part of a planned sequence – there is no *Malcolm* to follow *Macbeth*; and when Falstaff did reappear, in *The Merry Wives of Windsor*, he had crossed generic boundaries from history to comedy. The history cycles, by contrast, suggest that the integrated series, imitating the continuity of historical narrative, was a deliberate, planned and intended method of composition. The first publication in the *Henry VI* sequence (actually a version of what we know as *Henry VI, Part Two*), appearing as *The First Part of the Contention of the famous Houses, of Yorke and Lancaster*, suggested by its title other parts to follow. This need not necessarily mean that when *Richard II* was written, there was a clear 'intention', on the part of the 'author', or of the acting company, of following it up with plays on Henry IV and Henry V. What is certain however, is that as the *Henry IV* plays and *Henry V* were written and produced, they were very obviously designed to take their place in a series with the other elements of the tetralogy. *Hamlet* and *Antony and Cleopatra* clearly both belong to the category of tragedy, but do not fit together as do *Henry IV, Part Two* and *Henry V*.

IV

Contemporary opinions of the history plays thus seem to revolve around two apparently polarised positions:

(i)   that 'Shakespeare's history plays' formed from the outset a
       unified, cohesive, organic totality of dramatic and historical
       writing (though the individual plays have often been disag-
       gregated, in criticism and theatrical practice, for particular local
       reasons) (Tillyard, 1944, 1980; Kernan, 1970);

(ii)   that 'Shakespeare's history plays' were from the outset a diversi-
       fied, discontinuous, fragmentary series of historico-dramatic
       explorations, each individually and independently shaped by
       contemporary cultural pressures (though the individual plays
       have often been integrated, in criticism and theatrical practice,
       for general ideological reasons) (Marcus, 1988; Taylor, 1989).

What does it mean to think of Shakespeare's history plays as, on
the one hand, an integrated compilation of elements designed to
compose a grand historical narrative; and on the other, as a discrete
collection of dramatic exercises, differing radically one from another
in form and style, and linked to one another only by the contingency
of common contents? It can be argued, particularly from textual
evidence, that from the very outset these plays functioned in an
essentially disaggregated way, each individually shaped by particular
local pressures and fashions in convention and style; each enacting
not only discrete and singular dramatic structures, but radically different visions of history. From there it can be argued that all attempts,
from the First Folio onwards, to compose or recompose the plays into
cycles, sequences, tetralogies, can be identified as acts of reconstruction, ideological appropriations of an inherently discomposed, disaggregated body of texts.

On the other hand, such arguments tend to minimise the complex
but unmistakable internal connections that link the plays together,
not necessarily into a seamless chronological narrative or a unified
generic totality, but certainly into a long, sustained and extra-
ordinarily innovative dramatic meditation on the nature of history.
The large metanarrative of English history is obviously a convenient
frame within which to develop such an inquiry, though the focus in
practice is very often on specific episodes that could be described as
micro-narratives within the larger whole.

Fundamentally, what is at issue here is the changing definition of
'history'. The Shakespearean history plays have traditionally been
framed within Tudor and Jacobean attempts to construct a national
history. Yet more intricate explorations of the contemporary conditions of cultural production indicate that these dramas drew on a

much wider range of generic and narrative possibilities, which were then synthesised to form isolable units of performance, 'plays'. The First Folio grouped the plays into chronicle sequence, and the mid-twentieth century carefully relocated them back into the Tudor narrative of national history. Subsequently however, postmodern notions of the end of history and the fragmentation of all metanarratives into discontinuous, independent 'petit récits' have provided an interpretative context capable of recognising the cultural conditions that produced, in the late sixteenth century, a collocation of volatile and unstable units of performance that appear to have continually thrown into question the apparently stable structure to which they nominally belonged (see Belsey, 1991). Is the traditional concept of a 'Shakespearean historical drama' now capable from this perspective of exposition as one of the great metanarrative signifiers? Should that traditional concept now be replaced by an interest in discrete individual plays and texts as 'petit récits', equally indicative of the real ideological instability of late sixteenth-century culture, and detailing the discontinuity and fragmentation of the postmodern condition?

V

I have tried in the pages that follow to avoid the pressure to distinguish absolutely, or to choose irrevocably, between these two directions in modern criticism. Indeed they no longer seem to me in any sense incompatible. It is certainly true that once the Histories had been collected into compilation and metanarrative, the disaggregated units reorganised into a linear temporal sequence, the overall framework began to prescribe certain interpretative horizons. For instance the compilation of plays into historical sequence turns what may be termed a 'revealed plot' into one which is 'resolved'. Resolved plots, common to much didactic fiction of the nineteenth century, depend on causal enchainment to propel the reader or spectator forward towards a final conclusion or resolution. Revealed plots, where the components of the narrative are randomly arranged, events displayed rather than unravelled, as in much modernist fiction, invite greater participation on the part of the reader or spectator to make connections and assumptions, so the importance of resolution becomes diminished. As Seymour Chatman explains: 'a strong sense of temporal order is more significant in resolved than in revealed plots' (Chatman, 1978: 112). Those editors, critics and directors who arranged the plays into temporal order were seeking to manipulate a resolution, and thereby limiting the greater interpretative liberty permitted by the revealed plot. In terms of historical narrative, the ordering into historical chronology binds the reader/spectator even further, in so far as time is presented in a seemingly 'natural' order, an order which appears to resemble 'real life', and which therefore conceals the artifice of the emplotment, and offers a specific inter-pretation as inevitable, as naturally inscribed.

Structural linearity, which undoubtedly satisfied the printed mode, is not of course necessary to audio-visual performance. Oral art forms (still evident in fairy-tales, nursery rhymes and ballads) depend on human memory for retention and recall, and are therefore structured, like poetry, around balanced patterns, repetitions, antitheses and thematic links (see Ong, 1988). These connections do not move along a horizontal line of causal enchainment, but operate by vertical links, reversals and circular rotations. As I will be showing in the following pages, such non-linear metaphors and figures – circles, intersections, reversals – are characteristic of the ways in which these plays imagine history.

We think of non-sequential structuring as characteristic of mediaeval art and literature, like manuscript and early printed collections of stories still bearing traces of orality. Murray Roston cites the widely read *Legenda Aurea* by Jacobus de Voraigne (c. 1297) as an example of a collection of hagiographies which 'lack any co-ordinating thread or rational order other than their shared didactic purpose' (Roston, 1987: 203). Boccaccio and Chaucer likewise collected disparate narratives into a heterogeneously unified, non-sequential whole, in works such as the *Decameron* and the *Canterbury Tales*. Similar methods of contextual structuring were used in the visual arts of the early Renaissance. The sculptor Ghiberti united his 'continuous narration' (episodes of a story that are disparate in time and place but shown as occurring simultaneously) of Jacob and Esau on 'The Gates of Paradise' in Florence (c. 1452) by means of the architectural perspective of an arched loggia (see Avery, 1970: 51–2). The two- or three-part narrative found in the *Henry IV* and *Henry VI* plays can be compared to grouped visual representations like diptych and triptych paintings. For example the Wilton Diptych (c. 1400), which was to be found at Wilton House, home of First Folio dedicatee the Earl of Pembroke, consists of two separate paintings: an earthly grouping of Richard II, with St John the Baptist and the martyr monarchs Edward and Edmund; juxtaposed with a spiritual revelation of the Virgin, Christ child, and a host of angels. The scenes are not linked chronologically, nor do they share the same scale or the same spatial context. They are simply brought into conjunction thematically, by spatial contingency, in order to position the monarch midway between earth and heaven (see Hawkins, 1982: 278–301).

In another more complex example of pictorial narrative, Piero della Francesca's *Legend of the True Cross* (Arezzo, 1452–66), an apparently random composition of ten scenes is linked in every dimension except the linear (see Brooks, 1992): the fresco narrative, as Perry Brooks describes it, 'abounds with such echoes and reflections – thematic, liturgical and formal – in a dense network that crosses horizontally, vertically and diagonally', so that 'the chronological thread of the story, its succession in history, becomes lost in this web' (Brooks, 1992: unpaginated). It has further been argued that a close relationship existed between the conventions of late mediaeval painting and the *tableaux vivants* of the sixteenth century, not least in terms of shared emblematic and symbolic devices (Kernodle, 1944).

Clearly if we examined the plays in terms of their textual histories (or, in all probability, were there sufficient specific evidence to support an inquiry into their contemporary theatrical life), we could naturally apprehend them as disaggregated, episodic, revealed and unresolved. But with these textual and cultural contexts acknowledged, even the decisive reordering of the plays in the Folio presents no obstacle to our seeing them as interrelated, or interacting, as indicated by Patricia Parker, in non-linear ways:

> reversal ... is repeatedly foregrounded in the plays themselves in ways that suggest a form of design ... what appears as the preposterous estate of sons or offspring who come before fathers ... produces in these histories an inversion that subverts the teleological underpinnings of Tudor providentialism itself. The reversed chronological ordering of the two tetralogies ... undercuts the sense in Hall, for example, of linearity leading toward a punctuating point, historical end or period.   (Parker, 1996: 37)

Parker argues that the word 'preposterous' is a 'key word' within the drama, which, used in the sense of 'a reversal of priority, precedence, and ordered sequence' signals a deliberate questioning of patrilinear inheritance, ostensibly acquired through 'fair sequence and succession' (*RII*, 2.1.199). One of the best examples of this is the way in which Richard of Gloucester, who enters the world 'preposterously', feet forward, justifies his right to the crown by 'lineal true-derived course' (*RIII*, 3.7.200).

Thus a linear temporal framework can be used to explore the little narratives of history just as readily as can a deconstructed, episodic and postmodern form. A totalising framework can indeed be deployed (something that was recognised in relation to the history plays very early on, see Ribner, 1957; Rossiter, 1961) against itself. The separate plays can, for example, be regarded as interconnected in non-linear ways. *Henry VI, Part One* and *Richard III* both appear to be back to front, since each begins with an ending (a funeral) and ends with a beginning (a betrothal). At the beginning of *Richard II* the past is decisively rejected by a breaking of blood-ties within the Plantagenet family; yet the play ends with an image of growth, the new king's future watered by the murdered Richard's unlawfully sprinkled blood (*RII*, 5.6.46). *Henry V* begins with Henry's ascent to power via an inversion of gender priority – descent through the female (*HV*, 1.2.92) – and ends with the prospective birth of Henry VI, recipient of an incontrovertibly direct patrilinear inheritance, yet whose reign has already been represented on 'this same stage' (*HV*, 'Epilogue': 13) as an unmitigated disaster.

VI

In a famous conversation with her antiquary William Lambarde, Elizabeth I compared herself to Richard II: 'I am Richard II. know ye not that?' (Ure, 1961: lix). The occasion of the discussion was a portrait of Richard, which had been discovered by a 'lover of antiquities', Lord Lumley, 'fastened on the backside of a door of a base room'. The queen was asked if the portrait should not be 'put it in order with the Ancestors and Successors' in the Queen's Gallery.

The anecdote models historical method itself. A forgotten, discarded relic of the past, lying abandoned in a 'base room', buried along with the past it commemorates, is discovered by the antiquarian; but then has to be inserted into some larger interpretative scheme or framework before it can reveal its true meaning. Restored to its 'proper' place, reinserted into the lineal succession of Kings and Queens of England, the portrait seems redeemed from its ignoble period of anonymity on the 'backside of a door'. In the same way an early quarto text of a Shakespeare play, roughly and commercially printed and circulated, could be redeemed from its 'base' origins by assimilation into the grand metanarrative of the First Folio. We simply need to remain aware, when addressing the plays reinscribed into their new 'order', together with their 'Ancestors and Successors', of the real nature of their origins: discrete, episodic, localised, even perhaps 'preposterous' like the painting pinned to the backside of a door.

The following analyses of a number of Shakespeare's history plays are not concerned, as some of my previous work on the histories (Holderness, 1985; Holderness, Potter and Turner, 1988) has tended to be concerned, with the historical image contextualised within the proper 'order' of a subsequent historical interpretation. I am not here in search of any grand historical narrative or teleology, whether providential or marxist; but rather engaged in a theoretical attempt to discover, within the totalising grand narrative, the lost portrait pinned to the backside of a base room door. I no longer seek the solid actuality of historical presence, but rather dwell on history's shadows and silences, those lost presences and potentialities that can by their absence disturb and disconcert the present. Hence my method is more concerned with the word than with the concept, with the metaphor than with the theory. I find the ghost more interesting than the living being, and the shadow more illuminating than the substance. My critical language, structured by such 'mighty opposites' (*Hamlet*, 5.2.62) as past and present, absence and presence, male and female, will also be found preoccupied with polarities such as nothing and something, language and silence, substance and shadow, image and reflection, womb and tomb.

VII

Let me take, as a first example, the term 'nothing', which denotes vacuity, the absence of something material or meaningful. Yet this is precisely where the writer, or the production of a literary text, begins:

> as imagination bodies forth
> The forms of things unknown, the poet's pen
> Turns them to shapes, and gives to airy nothing
> A local habitation and a name.
> (*A Midsummer Night's Dream*, 5.1.14–17)

The writer's task is to make something out of nothing, to create substance from absence. Yet most science and philosophy would accept the Epicurean principle that 'nothing can be created out of nothing' (Lucretius, 1951: 31): so the 'nothing' that precedes creative production is not a void, but the material condition from which the text emerges. This is what Marx meant when he wrote:

> The phantoms of the human brain ... are necessary sublimates of mens' material life-processes.   (Marx, 1963: 90)

If it is the 'material' of life that shapes the products of creativity, then what Shakespeare called 'airy nothing' may in fact be, as Pierre Macherey put it, the shadowy hinterland that haunts the text as its invisible but constitutive reality (Macherey, 1978: 82–93). The critic must also begin, like the writer, with 'nothing', in order to expose or explicate meaning from textual absence, by examining the vestiges of that absence, the shadow that hovers at the margins and haunts the text itself.

'Nothing' is what is finally signified by Macbeth's 'poor player', that 'walking shadow' who seeks to present shadow as substance, to emulate vitality by playing on its manifest absence (*Macbeth*, 5.5.24–7). The players are repeatedly referred to as 'shadows', actors whose actions are a counterfeit, or semblance, of the characters and events represented. In *Richard III* Queen Margaret accuses Edward IV's queen, in a figure that metadramatically applies to all the players involved, of such pretence: 'poor shadow, painted queen / The presentation of but what I was' (*RIII*, 4.4.83–4). The players and their actions, the substance of the drama, are shadows of life. But when such shadows are fractured, we may glimpse something of the shaping substance that lies beneath. When the actor playing Richard II – a shadow of a shadow – gazes at his own reflection in a mirror, and in angry sorrow breaks the glass, Bolingbroke observes: 'The shadow of your sorrow hath destroy'd / The shadow of your face' (*RII*, 4.1.292–3). In Richard's reply the shaping substance behind that outward dramatic display is briefly exposed:

> these external manner of laments
> Are merely shadows to the unseen grief
> That swells with silence in the tortur'd soul.
> There lies the substance.   (*RII*, 4.1.296–9)

The substance provoking the action of breaking the mirror is 'grief', which (like the shaping substance of the drama itself) remains 'unseen', nurtured by the unspoken, 'silence'. In addition the language used to describe the 'soul' is that of pregnancy: the soul is imagined as a womb-like space in which grief swells like a growing embryo. Beneath the splintered pieces of a shadow's shadow, we momentarily hear the silence, glimpse the unseen, peer into the heart of nothing.

This language of the female, which as a subtext permeates the history plays in the way that female power (as I will be arguing in Chapter 1) permeated Elizabethan society, is of course traditionally associated with creativity, back to the Greek Muses. But in the early modern period artistic creativity continued to be associated with the muses and with the female body. Sidney opened *Astrophil and Stella* by assuming the female condition, claiming to be 'great with child to speake, and helplesse in my throwes' (Sidney, 1591, 1962: 162). And here there is a close link between woman and 'nothing', since in Elizabethan slang 'nothing' referred to the female genitalia. Woman's sexual difference could be seen as 'no-thing', a lack or absence of what man abundantly possessed. The term provided Hamlet with a source of imaginative speculation when Ophelia, overtly refusing to be drawn into sexual banter over the implications of Hamlet's placing his head 'in' or 'upon' her lap, says: 'I think nothing' (*Hamlet*, 3.2.113). Hamlet extends the bawdy by interpreting her remark contrari-wise, within his own sexual pretext: 'That's a fair thought to lie between maids' legs' (*Hamlet*, 3.2.114). Hamlet's interpretation actually demonstrates Pierre Macherey's theory of literary produc-tion (Macherey, 1978). At one level his linking of Ophelia's lack of thought with the absence designating the female sexual organs, procures a derogatory man-made image of woman as the hollow, mindless vessel, awaiting implantation by the male seed. Yet at the same time his explication confounds that negative description revealing the inadequacies of his own definition. If 'nothing' is a 'fair thought', it is already clothed in semiotic flesh, already a matter of substance. Ophelia's apparent refusal to comment, a silence marked with a word of duplicitous meaning, is pregnant with unrevealed alternatives, presenting an area of shadow or doubt within the text which in turn influences Hamlet's own speech. Hamlet makes the text say what Ophelia doesn't say: from her silence, her ambiguous 'nothing', he produces something distinctively other, which is at once intellectual and sexual, female and powerful, a 'fair thought' that he is unable to detach (as he is unable to detach himself) from the womb of female creativity.

Whilst imaginatively linked to the female, and her reproductive organs, this 'nothing' which precedes and shapes creative production is also the area of textual absence and shadow assigned to the real women of Tudor history, since few of them engross the pages of chronicles or historical play-texts, where male speech and actions predominate. If, as Phyllis Rackin has argued, 'Renaissance historiography constituted a masculine tradition, written by men, devoted to the deeds of men, glorifying the masculine virtues of courage, honor and patriotism, and dedicated to preserving the names of past heroes and recording their patriarchal genealogies' (Rackin, 1990: 147), then it is hardly surprising that women inhabit the absent, shadowy or marginal spaces. On the other hand, the plays repeatedly demonstrate that absence, often referred to as 'nothing', both shapes the drama, and points to deeper levels of meaning within or beyond it. When Ophelia drifts into madness, freed from the social constraint of silence, her bawdy songs recall Hamlet's sexual commentary, and she is again linked with the concept of 'nothing':

> She ... speaks things in doubt,
> That carry but half sense. Her speech is nothing.   (4.5.6–7)

The woman's speech is 'nothing' because it lacks the logical order of masculine discourse. Nonetheless, Horatio admits that 'the unshaped use' of her words 'doth move / The hearers to collection' (4.5.8–9). When Laertes pointedly remarks that 'this nothing's more than matter' (4.5.171), he acknowledges that the contrived text is far from complete, that a woman's words, spoken in the shadowy doubt of insanity, can disclose truths unintelligible to masculine reason.

VIII

> the purpose of playing, whose end, both at the first and now, was and is to hold, as 'twere, the mirror up to nature; to show virtue her own feature, scorn her own image, and the very age and body of the time his form and pressure.   (*Hamlet*, 3.2.21–5)

For centuries Hamlet's definition of 'the purpose of playing': 'to hold the mirror up to nature' served as a model for explaining the relations between history and art. In 1765 Samuel Johnson claimed that 'Shakespeare holds up to his readers a faithful mirror of life and manners' (Johnson in Nuttall, 1983); Lily B. Campbell's book on the history plays was subtitled 'Mirrors of Elizabethan Policy' (Campbell, 1947); and Coppélia Kahn argued that Shakespeare 'makes late mediaeval society a mirror of his own' (Kahn, 1981: 48).

These uses of the mirror image as a model for mimetic reflection and realist art are based on a misunderstanding of what such images meant in their time. The objective of Hamlet's play-within-a-play, *The Murder of Gonzago*, is not simply to reflect reality accurately, but to entrap a guilty conscience:

> The play's the thing
> Wherein I'll catch the conscience of the King.   (2.2.600–1)

Hamlet is likely to have had in mind a perspective mirror, deliberately designed to trick the eye. Mirrors capable of reflecting undistorted images were still a fairly new invention in the sixteenth century; so the mirror is more likely to suggest a fragmented or distorted image than an accurate reflection, as in its most famous usage:

> For now we see through a glass, darkly; but then face to face: now I know in part; but then I shall know even as I am known.
> (I Corinthians, XIII.12)

Thomas Salter, in an instruction manual for woman, *A Mirrhor mete for all Mothers, Matrons and Maidens, intitled the Mirrhor of Modestie* (1579), actually differentiates between the mirror which reflects outward show, and that which reveals a deeper level of being, the inner substance of the person:

> In my judgemente there is nothyng more meete, especially for yong Maidens then a *Mirrhor*, there in to see and beholde how to order their dooyng, I meane not a Christall *Mirrhor*, made by handie Arte, by whiche maidens now adaies, doe onely take delight daiely to tricke and trim their tresses ... no I meane no suche *Mirrhor*, but the *Mirrhor* I meane is made of another maner of matter, and is of muche more worthe than any Christall *Mirrhor*; for as the one teacheth how to attire the outwarde bodie, so the other guideth to garnishe the inward mynde ... (Salter in Trill, Chedgzoy and Osborne, 1997: 45)

In the same way historical narrative and historical drama, though often described as mirrors for viewing the past, were not understood as accurate reflections of what had been: but as instruments of inward inquiry, a means for discerning the true moral character of the person, or the real historical personality of an age. The mirror of the historical drama is an instrument for simultaneously merging and disentangling past and present, there and then, here and now; an instrument that would have been useful to Wordsworth's observer:

> As one who hangs down-bending from the side
> Of a slow-moving boat, upon the breast
> Of a still water, solacing himself
> With such discoveries as his eye can make
> Beneath him in the bottom of the deep,
> Sees many beauteous sights — weeds, fishes, flowers,
> Grots, pebbles, roots of trees, and fancies more;
> Yet often is perplexed and cannot part
> The shadow from the substance, rocks and sky,
> Mountains and clouds, reflected in the depth
> Of the clear flood, from things which there abide
> In their true dwelling; now is crossed by gleam
> Of his own image, by a sunbeam now ...
> Incumbent o'er the surface of past time.
>
> (Wordsworth, 1805, 1971: 153)

Shakespeare's history plays certainly resemble that reflective surface: they peer through the medium of time into the past, seeing its contents with as much clarity and accuracy as contemporary knowledge could afford; and they bear the imprint of their own present, reflected on their surface along with images of the past. They also provide a perspective in which it becomes possible to differentiate past from present; though remaining ultimately, like the observer in the poem, 'perplexed' at the strange interdependence of substance and shadow.

Expect also, as 'incumbent o'er the surface of past time', you read the following pages, to be continually surprised by the sudden apparition, on the water's surface, of something that looks, though apparently an element of the observed landscape, or a detail from times past, unmistakably like a contemporary preoccupation, the present, ourselves.

1

Rainbow and Sword

And God said, This is the token of the covenant which
I make between me and you and every living creature that
is with you, for perpetual generations:
I do set my bow in the cloud, and it shall be for a token of a
covenant between me and the earth.
And it shall come to pass, when I bring a cloud over the
earth, that the bow shall be seen in the cloud:
And I will remember my covenant.

Genesis, IX.12–15

From my office at the University of Hertfordshire, a ten-minute
journey takes me to the Jacobean mansion Hatfield House, built by
Robert Cecil, chief minister to both Elizabeth I and James I; together
with its adjoining mediaeval hall, Hatfield Palace, the only surviving
part of a residence erected in 1496 for the Bishops of Ely, which came
into Henry VIII's possession at the Reformation as a confiscation
of ecclesiastical property, and was used to house his children as a
strange mixture of country retreat and place of exile. At only three
months of age, Princess Elizabeth was brought here in 1553, no doubt
purely for the fresh country air. Her sister Mary, however, was sent
to join her as a punishment for refusing to recognise Ann Boleyn as
the King's lawful wife.

Hatfield Palace was one of several royal residences around London,
and Henry's children were moved around them, together or separ-
ately, according to the tensions of the succession question. In 1553
Elizabeth was here with her brother Edward, both children pursuing
their arduous programme of education. When Edward became king,
Elizabeth was presented at court, and so greatly favoured by the
young king that he gave her the Palace of Hatfield as a present. Later
however, in Mary's reign, suspected by her sister of complicity in Sir
Thomas Wyatt's rebellion, Elizabeth was released from the Tower
where she had been held for questioning, and at her own request
committed in 1555 to a sort of voluntary exile, certainly under

surveillance, at Hatfield. She was still there, sitting of course under the famous Hatfield oak tree, casually reading the Greek New Testament, when the Lords of the Council arrived to inform her that Mary was dead, and she was Queen. She held her first Council meeting in the Great Hall of Hatfield Palace; and it was there that she appointed William Cecil, later Lord Burghley, her principal secretary.

I

In Hatfield House there hang two contrasting portraits of Queen Elizabeth I. In the 'Rainbow Portrait', which dates from the first decade of the seventeenth century, the Queen is depicted in the kind of neo-classical costume used in the elaborate masques then in vogue at the Stuart court. The Latin inscription, *'non sine sole iris'* ('no rainbow without the sun') suggests that ancient symbol of harmony and concord as produced by the sun of majesty. Peace flows from the royal body. The rainbow is the token of a covenant: a communicating link, its arch joins the monarch to her subjects; manifest symbol of popular veneration, its bow disappears into that most secret place, the Queen's virginity. In the portrait Elizabeth manipulates and controls the rainbow in those famous long white fingers, as if social concord were absolutely within her power, wholly at her sovereign discretion. Above all, she is represented here as a deity: while the rainbow as covenant links her to Judaeo-Christian traditions, the masque-like costume, the isolation of the word 'Iris', the wing-like shapes of the ruff, cast her as the Roman goddess Iris, the rainbow, communicator, harbinger of peace.

The 'Ermine Portrait', attributed to Nicholas Hilliard, which is earlier and more contemporary (the date on the sword-hilt is 1585), presents a very different Elizabeth. A much severer figure, encased in a dress so heavily encrusted with jewels that it resembles decorated armour, holds in one hand the olive branch of peace. But the other hand lies close to a heavy, decorative sword, the symbolic state sword of justice.

In one sense these two faces of a Tudor monarch can be considered as reality versus fantasy: monarchy alternately represented and idealised. The 'Ermine Portrait' places the Queen into a room with a contemporary lattice window, while the 'Rainbow Portrait' locates her in the nowhere of romance. But both portraits are political statements defining the monarch as an inclusive figure, capable of

Plate 1   The Rainbow Portrait of Elizabeth I, from Hatfield House, Hertford-shire. Reproduced by courtesy of the Marquess of Salisbury.

both pacification and force, ready like a goddess, or a natural force, to bless or to strike. 'When she smiles', recorded Sir John Harington, 'it was a pure sunshine that everyone did choose to bask in if they could, but anon came a storm from a sudden gathering of clouds, and the thunder fell in wondrous manner on all alike' (Hibbert, 1990: 115). Just as in the 'Ermine Portrait', the sword balances the olive branch, and the fierce, sharp-fanged little ermine represents an aggressively defended purity; so in the 'Rainbow Portrait' the Queen wears on her sleeve a serpent, wise but also deadly, gripping in its mouth a jewel shaped and coloured like a bleeding heart. Her gown is covered with eyes, ears and possibly mouths: symbols, as Frances Yates suggested, of her Fame (Yates, 1975: 216–17); but also representing the vigilant senses of the state, watching, listening, reporting. 'The Queen of England', recorded an ambassador, 'I know not how, penetrates every-thing' (Hibbert, 1990: 112). The eyes of the portrait don't just, as the cliché insists, follow you around the room, but with a quasi-divine omniscience keep you, as subject, permanently under surveillance.

Plate 2   The Ermine Portait of Elizabeth I, by Nicholas Hilliard (1547–1619), from Hatfield House, Hertfordshire. Reproduced by courtesy of the Marquess of Salisbury.

The portraits also offer contradictory representations of gender. The 'Rainbow Portrait' emphasises a feminine beauty: soft eyes, exposed breasts, a cupid's-bow mouth. The other portrait gives Elizabeth much stronger features, sterner eyes, firm mouth and chin; and the body is encased in that virtual shell of precious stones. The jewelled collar worn in the 'Ermine Portrait' resembles a similar piece shown in portraits of Henry VIII, and visualises one of Elizabeth's frequent and favourite assertions: 'Though I be a woman, yet I have as good a courage, answerable to my place, as ever my father had.' One of the most remarkable aspects of Elizabeth's reign is that deep-rooted contradiction between the dynastic principle of succession which, by respecting Henry VIII's will, made both Mary and Elizabeth queens, and a patriarchal culture which was capable of frankly doubting that a woman could actually be a ruler at all: 'there is nothing lacking in her that could be desired in a prince' wrote one admirer of Elizabeth, 'but that she was a woman' (Hibbert, 1990: 112).

Both portraits were the property of, and probably commissioned by, two of the most prominent Elizabethan statesmen: William Cecil, Lord Burghley, who owned the old Palace of Hatfield; and his son Robert, later Earl of Salisbury, who built Hatfield House. The two portraits thus provide, by virtue of their iconography and their historical origin, a set of connections that will be central to the concerns of this book. They link the cultural icons of Elizabethan sovereignty to key personalities of the government that sustained its authority. In their chronology they span precisely the closing years of Tudor power, the period during which the Elizabethan historical drama grew, flowered and died. And in their representations of power they reflect contradictory aspects of Elizabethan politics and culture that will concern us nearly in the following pages: peace and war; mercy and violence; the strength and sweetness of that great culture, its power and its pity.

II

In all her portraits Elizabeth I is represented, whether or not surrounded by the properties of masculine authority, as a woman. She was undoubtedly a female ruler: who nonetheless ruled, within the norms of that patriarchal culture, through the service and the loyalty of men. Her Council was naturally an exclusively masculine preserve. Pre eminent within that Council was William Cecil. But he was not there by accident of birth or by virtue of an illustrious lineage. When Cecil asked the great antiquary William Camden to construct for him a family tree showing the Cecil ancestry hopefully rooted in an ancient and honourable lineage, unfortunately Camden couldn't find his way any further back than William's grandfather, the Welsh squire David Cecil. The family was however distinctly upwardly mobile: by 1547, in Edward's reign, William Cecil was already working for the Lord Protector Somerset; by 1550, under Mary, he was appointed a secretary of state and a member of the Privy Council. From that point on he played a leading role in government until his death.

Cecil's preferment thus had nothing to do with ancestry, but rather with ability, education, ambition and hard work. His marriages linked him less with the nobility than with eminent scholars, or intellectuals who became politicians, and with brilliant women. His first wife was the daughter of Sir John Cheke, the greatest Greek scholar of the age. After her death he married Mildred Cooke, noted by Roger Ascham as one of the two most learned women in England, and whose father was also a leading academic; her sister Anne was the mother of Francis Bacon. So Cecil did not possess the traditional qualification for high office, noble birth; and his necessary competitions for influence at court and in council with patrician favourites such as the Earl of Leicester, were certainly coloured by this fact.

The Elizabethan nobility, though highly educated, still placed a very high priority on the traditional class culture of militarism. They were, like Sir Philip Sidney – 'soldier, scholar, horseman' (Yeats, 1933, 1978: 150) – men of the sword as well as the pen. The exercise of military skills as a social code was institutionalised within the sphere of courtly entertainment, particularly in the famous Accession Day tilts where courtiers jousted for eminence and royal favour. But members of the nobility could also be real soldiers, anxious to acquire genuine military glory in real warfare (though the fact that Sir Philip Sidney was the only member of the Elizabethan aristocracy to die in battle would indicate some degree of caution in their soldiering); or at least, like Leicester who was 'Master of the Horse', would hold quasi-military offices in a domestic context. If denied the violent delights of real warfare, Elizabethan aristocrats would challenge one another to duels, invoking the old feudal principle of satisfaction for defamed honour.

William Cecil's outlook and inclinations were as far removed as possible from that traditional aristocratic investment in militarism or chivalry. In a remarkable document written for his son Robert, Burghley provided ten precepts to guide his moral development. These include advice on how to train and educate Robert's own future children:

> Neither, by my consent, shalt thou train them up in wars; for he that sets up his rest to live by that profession, can hardly be an honest man or a good Christian ... Besides it is a science no longer in request than use; for soldiers in peace, are like chimneys in summer.   (Cecil, 1975: 80)

Significantly the father also warns the son against the dangers of popularity, clearly signalling the potentiality of masculine heroism to constitute a perceived threat to the state:

> I advise thee not to affect or neglect popularity too much. Seek not to be Essex; shun to be Raleigh.   (Cecil, 1975: 82)

In general Cecil's distaste for militarism went with a preference for peace in foreign and domestic policy, though of course military actions of various kinds were found necessary by Elizabeth's Council. 'A reign gaineth more by one year's peace than ten years' war' (Cecil, 1975: 71), he remarked. Like the Queen, Cecil was always inclined towards policies involving caution, realism, economy, and the avoidance of risk. He sought to persuade the Queen to observe these principles; he sought to dissuade her from being influenced by more belligerent voices; and on his death-bed he begged his son to maintain these strategies:

> tend in all thy actions in the state to shun foreign wars and seditions; labour, with thy prince's honour, to reconcile her to all her enemies so far as may stand with honour and safety.
>
> (Cecil, 1975: 107)

'Indeed', writes his descendant, Lord David Cecil, 'it is one of the ironies of history that he should be associated with a heroic period; that the glorious England of Shakespeare and Drake and Sidney should turn out to have been ruled by persons who set so little store on mere glory' (Cecil, 1975: 67).

III

The well-known rivalries within Elizabeth's court between the Cecils and their competitors for place, office, influence, are certainly marked by these class and cultural contrasts. Burghley and Robert Dudley, Earl of Leicester, confronted one another as 'mighty opposites' in the earlier years of the reign; later Robert Cecil had to negotiate his initial position around the growing power of Essex and his supporters and placemen. Ultimately the Cecils were the survivors: Burghley was still in office while Leicester was dying, poor and in royal disfavour; Robert Cecil was instrumental in securing the final elimination of his own greatest rival, Essex.

Essex is a crucial example of the problematic status of aristocratic and masculine militarism within this culture. Though intelligent and learned, a patron of letters and something of a hero to more militant Protestants, his chief motivation throughout his career seems to have been an overweening aristocratic pride, which gave him an irrational conviction of his own worth, and justified him in a jealous contempt of his rivals. He did nothing to conceal his disrespect for other important men, such as Robert Cecil and 'that knave Raleigh'; When his jealousy was provoked, he expressed his contempt as wounded chivalric honour. Charles Blount, a handsome and ambitious soldier — he may be the *Young Man among Roses* in Nicholas Hilliard's famous painting — was given a gold chess queen by Elizabeth, which he wore ostentatiously on his arm at court. 'Now I perceive', observed Essex sardonically, 'every fool must have a favour' (Hibbert, 1990: 225). Such an insult was followed naturally by a duel, in which Essex was slightly wounded. It was Blount, however, who ultimately had the last laugh: after Essex's execution he was given the command of the army in Ireland, disposed his chesspieces more effectively on the board-game of a real war, and fought a campaign which succeeded where Essex had so dismally failed.

Although prominent in the courtly culture of playful chivalry, Essex also had real military ambitions. He had served in the army in the Netherlands at the age of eighteen, and was desperately enamoured of military glory. This ambition was often pursued in direct disobedience of the Queen's orders. Such daring exploits obviously brought Essex popularity, but more prudent friends advised him to seek 'a domestical greatness, like to his father-in-law [Sir Francis Walsingham]' (Hibbert, 1990: 226). From the beginning then, Essex was playing dangerous boys' games: choosing personal glory before loyalty to his Queen, and courting popularity within an armed service whose structure and culture the Queen, as a woman, was unable to penetrate. At the capture of Cadiz he played the warrior's part to perfection, earning the delight of the people as a hero. She preferred military exercises to be conducted as courtly games in her tilt-yards, where courtiers were ritually competing for her own favour. Once such courtiers were abroad or on the high seas, they tended to do what they pleased, rather than follow her instructions. Essex's ambitions to be a military hero, beloved of the populace, were in themselves threatening to the Queen: 'I demand', said Sir Francis Bacon, 'whether there can be a more dangerous image represented to any living monarch' (Hibbert, 1990: 231).

The famous quarrel in which the Queen boxed Essex's ears was closely linked to these military-political tensions. It was proposed that Sir William Knollys, Essex's uncle, should undertake a command in Ireland. Knollys was a useful ally in Essex's rivalry with the Cecils. Essex wanted to send Sir George Carew, a Cecil ally, to get him out of the way. The Queen struck him, and Essex's hand flew to his sword. A soldier's impulse; an aristocrat's gesture; a highly symbolic moment, even in itself an act of treason. When the Queen threw one of her slippers in Sir Francis Walsingham's face, the civil servant by contrast kept both his cool, and his head.

On campaign in France, Essex again displeased the Queen by knighting 21 of his followers, abrogating the power to bestow honours, and like Henry V in Shakespeare's play, binding subjects, in the comradeship of the battlefield, in loyalty to himself. Essex defiantly repeated this exercise in Ireland, in the context of an expensive and unsuccessful campaign against Tyrone and his nationalist army of 'rebels'. The sequel is well known: Essex disobeyed orders, made a truce with Tyrone, contemplated returning to England with his army to protect him, then decided to stake everything on a personal appeal to his sovereign. His career obviously finished, Essex launched his abortive rebellion. Recognising its failure, he and the Earl of Southampton handed over their swords in token of surrender. He was beheaded for treason, by the sword, in 1601.

Essex's career effectively represents the starkest contrast to those of the Cecils. His aristocratic lineage gave him a conviction of his own importance that far exceeded his abilities. The traditional military role of his class survived strongly in him, as a means both of demonstrating status at court, and of courting a popularity beyond the reach of the monarch herself. In seeking advancement and achievement down that road, he chose a dangerous path. Those who remained content with a 'domestical greatness', like Robert Cecil, were not the stars of history, but they were certainly the survivors. It was Cecil who issued the proclamation declaring Essex a traitor; and he also made a notable intervention, described below, into Essex's trial.

So just as Burghley and Leicester represented opposed conceptions of public service, so Robert Cecil and Essex counterpoised diametrically opposite political strategies. Robert, who succeeded to his father's office, and was appointed the Queen's Principal Secretary in 1596, shared his father's views: 'Peace', he wrote, 'is the mother of all honour and state' (Cecil, 1975: 96). Although Robert adopted a somewhat more fashionable style than that of his father, he was also just as far removed from the chivalric display of the tilt-yard, or the prowess and glory of the battlefield. He was after all, like Shakespeare's Richard III, 'not shap'd for sportive tricks' (*Richard III*, 1.1.14), being a 5-foot hunchback with a splay foot. Elizabeth used to call him her 'Elf'. James I styled him, with reference to his short crooked legs, 'my little beagle' (Cecil, 1975: 93–4; *DNB*, IX, 1887: 402). One of the most comical moments of the 6-foot dashingly handsome Essex's courtly career must have been when, in the course of a competition for court position, he challenged Cecil to a duel. Cecil had no need, even if he had possessed the ability, to resort to physical violence to secure his position. He must have felt some of the contempt attributed to Octavius Caesar, challenged in Shakespeare's play to single combat by the old and defeated warrior Antony:

> Yes, like enough high-battled Caesar will
> Unstate his happiness, and be stag'd to th' show
> Against a sworder!   (*Antony and Cleopatra*, 3.13.29–31)

The metaphor of the stage of course forges a link between political and theatrical performances: like Essex, Antony seeks a dramatic dénouement in an old-fashioned style. Cecil, like Octavius, knew that the important thing is to win the war. Robert Cecil's tomb in Hatfield Church was modelled on that of an Italian nobleman: but while the original was supported by four warriors, Cecil's is held up by female figures representing the four cardinal virtues. The sword is there, as it is in the 'Ermine Portrait', not as an emblem of heroism, but as as an attribute of Justice.

IV

This representation of the two great Cecils as essentially learned and pacifistic humanists, loyal but independent-minded civil servants, scrupulous custodians of their sovereign's interests, has the force of a dominant historical tradition: the *Dictionary of National Biography* (*DNB*, IX, 1887: 400–4, 406–12) provides virtual hagiographies of them as two of England's greatest statesmen. And certainly the Cecils were a new breed of politician, brought to power by the Tudor Revolution, firmly Protestant and highly respectable, upwardly mobile and place-seeking, acquiring rather than dissipating wealth, drawing power only from the influence they could exert, by the use of learning, intelligence and diplomacy, over the monarch and others. They belonged in a sense to what Coleridge called a 'clerisy', a new type of secular, humanistic and intellectual politician moving into the vacuum created by the severance of church and state, and the consequent limitation of the church's political authority: in many of his portraits Burghley in his sober-suited black even looks like a kind of secular priest.

But that historical tradition is clearly a sanitised image of these two remarkable men, as agents of peace rather than bringers of war, men of the rainbow rather than the sword. Robert Cecil's double-decker tomb soberly represents the transition from life to death: above, the dignified robed figure of the Lord Treasurer on his marble plinth; below, a skeleton lying on short and musty straw. But the conceit works the other way around too: the mortal remains are transmuted into a permanent memory of Cecil as distinguished statesman, holding the Treasurer's staff, purified in marble, his body straighter than it ever was in life. The Cecils have similarly been straightened out in the process of historical reconstruction. If aristocratic prestige, military glory and chivalric prowess were not the basis of their power, then what was it?

The Tudors had come to power through a bloody civil war, and had succeeded in disarming the nobility responsible for the long-drawn-out conflicts of the 'Wars of the Roses'. Peace at home, and war abroad, became the established pattern of domestic and foreign policy; preserved by Elizabeth and her ministers, and later lost under the Stuarts with the outbreak of the Civil Wars. Under the Tudors, chivalric cults and courtly games to some extent replaced the professional militarism of the old aristocracy. But nonetheless, by any standards, the reign of Elizabeth was a very violent age. There was certainly no repetition of the civil wars of the fifteenth century; nor did England become involved in any long-term and full-scale hostilities abroad. But throughout Elizabeth's reign the English state was involved in military actions of various kinds abroad: in France, in the Netherlands, against Spain. Nearer home there were wars in Scotland and Ireland. Above all, there were significant though ultimately unsuccessful rebellions against Elizabeth's throne, notably the Northern Rebellion of 1569, and Essex's attempted *coup d'état* of 1601. As Catholic opposition gathered and hardened around Mary Queen of Scots from 1570 onwards, the Queen's fear of personal assassination found concrete form in various plots that were discovered and suppressed with extreme judicial ferocity.

As leading government ministers, the Cecils were of course involved in the management of all these initiatives and exercises of state and military violence, though naturally not as generals, but as administrators, organisers, and above all as gatherers of information and intelligence. Though not themselves men of war, they engaged in warfare by other means. Foreign policy was concerned mostly with a careful and diplomatic negotiation and balancing of alliances, with military aid judiciously applied to advance English interests. At home, violence, in the form of torture and public execution, was the means by which civil order was restored or maintained. Tortures such as racking were employed, sometimes on the Queen's personal instructions, to extract confessions and to implicate others. The full severity of the capital punishment for treachery – which involved hanging, followed by castration and disembowelling while the victim was still alive and conscious – was used in, for example, the executions of Antony Babbington and Father Ballard in 1586, under the Queen's explicit instruction to 'protract the extremity of their pains in the sight of the multitude' (vividly and imaginatively described in Burgess, 1993: 90–1). Higher status victims of execution by beheading were the Duke of Northumberland and the Earl of Norfolk following the Northern Rebellion; Mary Queen of Scots in 1569; the Earl of Essex in 1601. The kind of judicial violence required to maintain peace can be seen both as a mechanism of justice, and as a displacement of military force from the battlefield to the domestic arena.

We need to see these exemplary executions not as superfluous relics of barbarism, or as regrettable exigencies adopted under extreme provocation: but as a particular means of exercising and manifesting the royal power in an otherwise peaceful context. Michel Foucault demonstrated the many links between public execution and warfare: 'The right to punish is an aspect of the sovereign's right to make war on his enemies' (Foucault, 1977, 1979: 48). Executions preserved 'something of the battle' (Foucault, 1977, 1979: 51). 'There was still an element of challenge and of jousting in the ceremony' (Foucault, 1977, 1979: 51), where the executioner would be applauded for severing a head with a single blow. Execution was not designed, as it is, where practised in Western societies today, as a means of cancelling out an iniquity and re-establishing moral and social balance; it was not so much that the life of the traitor equalled the threatened life of the sovereign, a death for an attempted assassination. In fact the ritual of punishment was 'carried out in such a way as to give a spectacle not of measure, but of imbalance and excess' (Foucault, 1977, 1979: 49). This excess of force demonstrated the invincible power of the sovereign over the body of his or her subjects.

The symbolic and ceremonial sword of Justice was therefore a real weapon, its power manifested in the axes and cleavers and hooks of ritual public execution. It was exercised as freely and as ruthlessly as occasion demanded by the sovereign acting through her intermediary counsellors (men such as the Cecils) and lesser state functionaries (men such as the executioner). Though symbolically disowned by the state, the executioner was the personal representative of Queen and Council, signing on the subject's body the ugly marks of sovereignty and power. The 'imbalance' produced by such rituals could also have the contrary effect of implicating the sovereign and the state in the crime: the enormity of the punishment swelled to envelop the executioner and his superiors in the enormity of the crime itself. 'The use of torture and other barbarities ... are the shame and indelible reproach that attach themselves to Cecil's conduct of affairs' (*DNB*, IX, 1887: 410). In this way these men of peace exercised violence through the power and machinery of the state.

The other chief basis of the Cecils' power was knowledge, intelligence, significant information. Burghley is probably the chief architect of the original government 'secret service', managed directly by Sir Francis Walsingham, and then after his death by Robert Cecil. This network of paid spies, informers and *agents provacateurs* was set up initially, like MI6, to report on currents of opinion and policy in foreign courts; but was eventually brought nearer home to gather information, like MI5, on potentially treacherous conspiracies and other evidences of domestic sedition. In the course of maintaining surveillance over Mary Queen of Scots, Walsingham used all the now familiar tactics of espionage: intercepting letters, planting false information, forgery, hiding messages in safe drops, communicating in code.

William Cecil was central to these operations.

> Cecil ... kept a small army of spies and informers in his pay, who were the detective police, that he used without scruple to get information when it was needed to keep watch upon the sayings and doings of suspected characters at home and abroad. They were a vile band, and employment of such instruments could not but bring some measure of dishonour upon their employer.
>
> (*DNB*, IX, 1887: 410)

In this respect, of course, men like Burghley and Walsingham were laying some of the foundations of the modern nation-state. They established, through a secret and unaccountable agency of espionage, a third force lying ambiguously between the civil and military powers. In foreign policy, this enabled war to be carried on covertly while maintaining an ostensible 'peace'; and domestically, it made possible the incursion of warlike methods into politics.

Two particular and familiar problems clearly attach to such 'covert operations'. Firstly, they are fully capable of inciting what they aim to discover: Walsingham, for instance, added a forged paragraph to a letter in the hope of entrapping Mary in a more positive incrimination. Secondly, the machinery of a secret service knows no boundaries: though set up to inform on foreign powers, the Burghley–Walsingham service was soon brought home to watch Elizabeth's own subjects. There it began to facilitate the use of closed channels of communication between members of the government, enabling one faction to secure advantage over another, and even to keep knowledge away from the Queen. Members of the Privy Council communicated with one another in secret code, diverting information away from the Queen when they wanted to block her influence. Walsingham once asked the Earl of Huntingdon to supply full information only to himself, and to write a false report deliberately designed to mislead Elizabeth.

When in the later years of Elizabeth's reign Robert Cecil was negotiating, against Elizabeth's explicit instructions, with James VI of Scotland about the succession, he was able to make use of codes and channels established by his father to seek out and punish treachery. As far as Elizabeth was concerned, writing to the King of Scots about the English succession was of course extremely high treason, and could have been fatal for Cecil if discovered. The most dramatic moment of Essex's trial was the point where Essex accused Cecil, who was listening, like Polonius, from behind a curtain, of declaring the Infanta of Spain the rightful heir to the English throne (Cecil did after all receive a secret pension from King Philip). Cecil stepped dramatically out from behind the curtain and in protesting his innocence, drew a broad contrast between himself and Essex.

> 'For wit', he said, 'I give you the pre-eminence ... For nobility also, I give you place — I am not noble, yet a gentleman. I am no swordsman — there also you have the odds ...
> 'The difference between you and me is great: for I speak in the person of an honest man, and you, my Lord, in the person of a traitor.
> 'I stand for loyalty ... you stand for treachery.'   (Cecil, 1975: 115)

Cecil had previously discovered through his spies that Essex was also corresponding with James, perhaps in the hope of enlisting Scots support for a *coup-d'état*. Cecil dutifully reported this to the Queen as further evidence of Essex's treachery. Clearly with Essex gone, Cecil's own communications with James about the succession could be carried on more freely.

V

Let us return now to the Queen whose sovereignty and whose person centred all this complex activity of political diplomacy, war, espionage, loyalty and treachery, reward and punishment. The figure of Henry VIII dominated the popular national consciousness: 'Remember old King Harry the Eighth', called one bystander as Elizabeth was riding to her coronation (Hibbert, 1990: 73). Elizabeth held the throne because she was Henry's daughter, and because Henry had entailed the crown to her in his will. She frequently validated her authority, particularly when it seemed to be challenged, by reference back to Henry. But although she was Henry's legitimised heir, the one thing she was not was his son: she was not a king. The bulky shadow of her father to some extent stabilised her authority, but to another degree provided an image of strong masculine sovereignty to which she could manifestly make no personal claim.

Could a woman really be a ruler? At the beginning of her reign the Archbishop of York argued that she could not be Supreme Head of the church, because she was a woman by birth and nature (Hibbert, 1990: 92). He did not, on the other hand question her right to be monarch, because she was 'by appointment of God, our sovereigne lord and ladie, our king and queen, our emperor and empress'. In so far as she was capable of being a 'lord', a 'king' and an 'emperor', Elizabeth could hold the highest office; in so far as she was a woman, she was unfit to rule. Many questioned whether that 'womanly' nature was compatible with the exigencies of royal responsibility. Burghley himself wondered at times whether she was fit to govern. Why did she not leave important affairs 'to those best capable of understanding them'? Elizabeth's obvious course should have been to marry, thus de-feminising her sovereignty and securing the assumed stability of a male succession. Burghley prayed that 'God would send our mistress a husband, and by time a son, that we may hope our posterity shall have a masculine succession', and he told the Queen that he trusted God would 'direct your Highness to procure a father for your children' (Hibbert, 1990: 80).

Elizabeth's strategies for using her femininity as a source of power are very well known: as the Virgin Queen, she was able at court to manage rituals of service and obedience as romantic games of courtly love; in the country as a whole to present herself as dedicated to the love of her subjects, 'wedded to her England'; and in foreign policy she was able to play the manipulative game of playing candidates for marriage off against one another. In all these contexts she used herself and her female body as an object – of chivalric service, of popular devotion, of dynastic ambition. Femaleness was thus implicitly assumed as passive and subjected; so this strategy did not challenge the patriarchal norms of the age, did not attempt to compete with the memory of male authority in the figure of her father.

At other times, or even at the same time, Elizabeth claimed a masculine authority derived partly from her royal descent, and partly from the office of monarch, which was naturally assumed to be masculine in itself. Thus she would refer to herself as a 'Prince', or invoke her 'kingly prerogative'. Again, this strategy assumes patriarchy as its norm: in order to be powerful, the queen must become a king, the lady a lord, the empress an emperor. These parameters of Elizabeth's sovereignty are well known, and are clearly defined in that great classic of spoof history, *1066 and All That*:

> Although this memorable Queen was a man, she was constantly addressed by her courtiers by various affectionate female nicknames, such as Auroraborealis, Ruritania, Black Beauty ... and Brown Bess.   (Sellars and Yeatman, 1930, 1993: 65–6)

More recently feminist scholars have argued that Elizabeth also represented herself as both female and powerful; or exploited her multiple-gendered image in such a way that male and female characteristics mingled and merged (Hackett, 1995; Marcus, 1988). To a foreign envoy she appeared to command obedience 'as absolutely as her father' (Hibbert, 1990: 70). This masculine side was naturally more prominent in foreign policy. As a woman it was her job to maintain peace: in war, she would still be a woman, but would outdo any man who dared to fight with her.

War, however, was clearly a masculine business: and we have seen how far beyond the Queen's influence was the closed male world of the armed service, how threatening to her own power the men who built their powerbase on militarism. In so far as it was still believed in early modern Europe that rulers ought to lead their troops on the battlefield (the young Henry VIII had taken personal command in France against the wishes of his Council), a female monarch was obviously excluded from such opportunities of demonstrating the capability of command. Elizabeth, or more precisely her publicists, given the crisis of the Spanish Armada, seem to have managed to find an ingenious solution to this problem by inventing the myth of Tilbury.

Whatever actually happened at Tilbury in 1588, a powerful and lasting myth was created of Elizabeth as the warrior queen. Clad (according to what historians now regard as a subsequent invention: see Frye, 1992: 95–6) in armour, she drew charismatically on the strengths of both sexes to encourage her troops. She was depicted as wearing a steel corslet, and preceded by the Earl of Ormond carrying the sword of state. 'Riding about through the ranks of armed men', wrote Camden many years later, 'with a Leader's truncheon in her hand, sometimes with a martial pace, another while gently like a woman, incredible it is how much she encouraged the hearts of her soldiers by her Presence and her Speech' (Frye, 1992: 112). The famous words she is unlikely to have said encapsulate the gender synthesis at which she aimed:

'I know I have the bodie, but of a weak and feeble woman, but I have the heart and Stomach of a king ... I myself will take up Arms, I my self will be your General'.　(Frye, 1992: 98)

At Tilbury in 1588 Elizabeth is represented as more than both man and woman: a composite complex of 'female' gentleness and 'male' courage, but both these virtues elements of her single and irresistible 'Presence': lord and lady, king and queen, emperor and empress; female warrior and invincible 'General', 'weak and feeble woman'.

Elizabeth's ultimate triumph over the destabilising violence of masculine militarism was to appropriate it and to successfully represent herself as excelling the achievements of her own generals and commanders. Fiction or not, this powerful legend was very obviously instrumental in consolidating the Queen's power and facilitating the suppression of those forces of internal dissent that potentially threatened it. By these means Elizabeth was able to remain firmly in control of the two types of men she needed to secure her power; those I have characterised in the contrast between the Cecils and

Essex. Being formidably learned, she could always compete with the
clerkly skills of men like the Cecils – she could produce a long Latin
speech extempore at the drop of a hat – and since they were
themselves men of modest origins she was able to retain the powerful
position of royal patron. Armoured in the myth of Tilbury, she
showed herself able to compete successfully against those warlike
aristocrats whose nobility and military skills were also needed to
secure her prestige and power, but whose 'unruly spirits' could just as
easily threaten it.

The lineaments of this complex king/queen synthesis are clearly
visible in the two portraits with which I began. In the 'Ermine Portrait'
they are overtly expressed by the sword, the armour-like jewelled
costume, Henry VIII's collar. But even in the mild and feminine
'Rainbow' portrait can be seen, depicted on the Queen's gown, the
eyes and ears of her secret service, watching and listening. And
the jewel in the serpent's mouth can be read as the heart of a conspir-
ator, ripped out by the executioner and shown bleeding to the people.

VI

Elizabeth had only a short time to live after the death of Essex, and
the old woman of those last years is a melancholy spectacle. Still
afraid of assassination and plots, she slept with an old sword by her
bed. Sir John Harington describes her 'walking much in her privy
chamber, stamping her feet at ill news, and thrusting her old rusty
sword into the arras in great rage' (quoted in Neale, 1934, 1960; 385).
From this space of history, in which surviving statesmen like Robert
Cecil were biding their time and preparing for the Queen's death and
the succession, springs another great myth of the age, eloquently
articulated by J. E. Neale:

> Robert Cecil . . . ruled; the civil servant in unprecedented suprem-
> acy: ability, but ability in how unexhilarating a personality! Faction
> of the old heroic pattern died with its superb, its insupportable
> exponent; and it almost seemed as if the soul of Elizabethan
> England also departed.   (Neale, 1934, 1960: 385)

A historical myth, perhaps: but certainly a mood of the age, expressed
nowhere so vividly as in Shakespeare. In some of the tragedies –
notably *Macbeth* and *Antony and Cleopatra* – we witness the fall of

that 'old heroic pattern', the death of the hero and his replacement by
the civil servant: the suspicious and canny Malcolm replaces Duncan
and Macbeth; Octavius Caesar supersedes the heroic Antony. Cleopatra's lines on Antony's death could be an elegy for the death of the
Elizabethan hero:

> O, wither'd is the garland of the war,
> The soldier's pole is fall'n! Young boys and girls
> Are level now with men. The odds is gone,
> And there is nothing left remarkable
> Beneath the visiting moon.   (*Antony and Cleopatra*, 4.15.64—8)

Spoken, around 1608, on stage by a boy who looked like a girl,
pretending to be an empress who had been as a ruler, very obviously,
'level with men'. The sentiment was clearly, even then, acknowledged
as an elegy for odds thankfully much shortened, for a world well lost.
Our democratic present, in which (at least in theory) 'the odds is
gone', and boys and girls ostensibly level with one another, is another
safe vantage-point from which to 'dream' an Antony, or an Essex.

Elizabeth certainly 'dreamed' her heroes, Leicester and Essex and
Ralcigh, just as Cleopatra dreamed her Antony. She created them:
they were the flowers of her court, and the stars of her age. But she
also had to destroy, imprison or execute those who tried to escape
from the form with which her dream invested them. Shakespeare's
history plays, as the following pages will show, were also dreams of
past heroism: nostalgic visions of lost plenitude, circumscribed by the
sober and chastening resignation of a self-consciously modern world
that had only a limited use for such vestigial survivals of its own
increasingly remote and distant past.

VII

Thus a female monarch and her sober-suited civil servants presided
over this civilised and peaceful culture that produced, in the 1590s, a
great cycle of historical dramas dealing entirely with war, and
dominated by figures of masculine heroism and military enterprise.
These plays construct images of an earlier England that is immediately recognisable as 'man's estate' (see Kahn, 1981); a violent world
ruled by men on the basis of feudal and chivalric values; a bygone

age, in which political power was equated with man, and with man's military prowess. The few women who claim or wield power in the plays do so by adopting the ways of men, like Queen Elinor in *King John*, who describes herself as 'a soldier and now bound to France' (*KJ*, 1.1.150). Queen Margaret in *Henry VI, Part Three* is described as an 'Amazonian trull' (*HVI3*, 1.4.114), leads an army into battle and participates in the capture and torture of her enemy. Most noticeable of all is Shakespeare's portrayal of Joan of Arc, 'La Pucelle' who in *Henry VI, Part One* crosses the gender divide by appropriating the armour and fighting skills of the aristocratic warrior, physically competing with man in single combat.

These reconstructions of that predominantly masculine and military past of the fourteenth and fifteenth centuries clearly mark themselves out in terms of historical difference from the late Elizabethan context in which the plays containing them emerged. Thomas Nash, in a passage discussed more extensively below, praised the historical drama precisely for its capacity to measure the extent of historical decline from the fifteenth century, and to rebuke, from that achieved historical distance, the 'effeminate' present day (Nash, 1592, 1969: 1592, 1969: 26). England could even seem, from the perspective of a foreign visitor and by comparison with other European countries, something of a 'woman's paradise', in which 'the women-folk ... have far more liberty than in other lands' (Platter, 1599, 1995: 45–6). Certainly in the 1590s a woman had successfully governed England for more than 40 years – a period by contemporary standards of longevity a literal lifetime, so that most English men and women of the age would have known no alternative to female rule. Far from being 'man's estate', the kingship of England remained an exclusively female property, since the virgin queen chose never to marry and share *her* 'estate' with a man. Her position of power was in sixteenth-century Europe by no means unique: in fact the period saw an unprecedented ascendance of female rulers and heads of state, such as Mary Tudor, Mary Stuart and the dowager Queen Catherine de'Medici in France, who all held the reins of political power at a time when, paradoxically, the dominant ideology endorsed male supremacy. Competitors promoted and supported to usurp or inherit Elizabeth's place were also mainly women: Mary Stuart, Arabella Stuart, the Infanta of Spain. As Anne Laurence points out, 'men's dominance is not synonymous with the oppression of women' (Laurence, 1994: 4). The history plays, which with the single exception of La Pucelle depict women as deriving their social positions and historical importance – as wives, widows and mothers – from men, thus reflect the dominant ideology, rather than any historical actuality, of late Tudor society.

Unlike the male monarchs of the history plays, men who tend to seize and maintain power by military force, Elizabeth, like her predecessor Tudor monarchs, gained and held her position of supremacy by law and diplomacy. The private armies that had constituted the currency of power throughout the 'Wars of the Roses' had been dismantled by the Tudors, and the aristocracy, in Rosalie Colie's term, 'gentled' (Colie, 1974: 186) – tamed and made civil – precisely in order to secure a robust and lasting domestic peace. Describing the character of Elizabeth's power in 1579, Stephen Gosson drew a clear distinction between military and civil rule:

> God hath now blessed England with a Queene, in vertue excellent, in power mightie, in glorye renowned, in gouernmente politike, in possession rich, breaking her foes with the bent of her brow, ruling her subjects with shaking her hand, remouing debate by diligent foresight, filling her chests with the fruites of peace, ministring justice by order of law ...   (Gosson, 1579, 1973: C5v)

However, even those male writers who celebrated the political virtues of civil rule were not free from that pervasive sense of regret at the lost glories of manly enterprise which represents a largely male, patrician anxiety at the loss of aristocratic independence. Stephen Gosson also prefigures Shakespeare's Richard III when he laments the disappearance of laddish physical pursuits such as wrestling, running and archery, in favour of more effeminate peacetime pleasures:

> the exercise that is nowe amongst us, is banqueting, playing, pipyng, and dauncing, and all suche delightes as may win us to pleasure, or rock us to sleepe ... Our wreastling at armes, is turned to wallowing in a Ladies laps, our courage, to cowardice, our running to ryot, our Bowes to Bolles, and our Dartes to Dishes.
> (Gosson, 1579, 1973: B8v–C)

In 1595 Sir John Smithe noted a distinct decline in military prowess, claiming that: 'the discipline Militarie of our auncestors ... is so forgotten and neglected amongst us' (Smithe, 1595, 1966: 431–2).

In the England of the 1590s military skills had become as much a sport as a necessity, increasingly celebrated at home as games, or as the arts, rather than the craft, of warfare. The Elizabethan descendant of Hotspur – 'brave Percy', that 'great heart' who stands in *Henry Fourth, Part One* as the apotheosis of antique chivalry – provides an example of this change between past and present. Unlike his warlike ancestor, Henry Percy the 9th Earl of Northumberland (nicknamed the 'Wizard Earl' for his interests in science and the occult) declined to take part in repressing border warfare on his Northumbrian estate (*DNB*, XLIV, 1895: 411–13). Instead he collected books on militaria, and himself wrote on the arts of war. He even invented an elaborate board-game which he called 'art militaire', played on an inlaid table with 460 toy soldiers (Batho, 1983: 16).

The most elaborate of these Elizabethan military games were of course the 'Accession Day Tilts', performances in the Queen's honour, pageants which were themselves staged spectacles recreating images, not of real battles, but of idealised military power and glory. Detailed portraits of the Elizabethan champions of the tilts present these glamorous young men in staged settings, wearing colourful, star-spangled costumes and brightly polished armour, their plumed helmets removed to display loose flowing and curled locks. According to one spectator, some even wore their hair 'hanging down to the girdle like women' (Strong, 1984: 95). It was these 'buckram giants' that Thomas Nash satirised as 'Peacocks', fireflies hovering colourfully around their Queen, 'glittring Attendaunts on the true Diana' (Nash, 1592, 1969: 39v). These 'paste sparklers who imitated the real star' (Banks, 1998) were no longer of course seeking advancement by acts of courage against the enemy, but vying for the attention, and currying the favour, of a woman.

VIII

Thus far I have sketched the social and cultural context in which these 'historical' plays of chivalric antiquity, epic heroism and masculine virtue were produced. I am suggesting that we need to understand these plays primarily in terms of historical, cultural and sexual difference, and as the celebration and exploration of values that were relatively marginal to central priorities of the late Tudor state. The plays depict a history clearly and sharply differentiated from their own contemporary present, and therefore understandably remote and alien. They trace a historical line in which supreme power remains unassailably masculine, from the perspective of a familiarity with female rule and some measure of female cultural power. They represent a male-dominated aristocracy preoccupied with war and military violence — both as key political methods, and as defining cultural characteristics of their class — from within a social context in which the residual traces of that armigerous nobility had been largely marginalised and emasculated. They paint images of civil war in a time committed to domestic peace; they analyse masculine power in a context of female authority; they recreate a lost aristocratic glory with a complex consciousness of genuine regret and relieved resignation. In a historical vision simultaneously influenced by aristocratic nostalgia and plebeian irony, they lament antique chivalric prowess, and glance critically, from a modern, civil and plebeian perspective, at antiquity's destructive self-contradictions, its legacy of glamour and glory, absurdity and arrogance.

2

History

The hand of the Lord was upon me, and carried me out in the spirit of the Lord, and set me down in the midst of the valley, which was full of bones,
And caused me to pass by them round about: and, behold, there were very many in the open valley; and lo, they were very dry.
And he said unto me, Son of man, can these bones live? And I answered, O Lord God, thou knowest.

Thus saith the Lord God unto these bones; Behold, I will cause breath to enter into you, and ye shall live:
And I will lay sinews upon you, and cover you with skin, and put breath in you, and ye shall live; and ye shall know that I am the Lord.

Ezekiel, XXXVII.1–3, 5–6

I

What did 'history' mean in the period that saw the production of Shakespeare's history plays? To some extent the question was readily answered by those great classical models, the Greek and Roman histories, which formed the basis for all Elizabethan historical theory and practice. Cicero's famous definition was enormously influential in establishing the functions of history as those of preserving memory, averting loss, and rescuing the past from oblivion:

> *Historia vero testis temporum, lux veritatis, vita memoriae, magistra vitae, nuntia vetustatis, qua voce alia, nisi oratoris, immortalitati commendatur?*

(as History, which bears witness to the passing of the ages, sheds light upon reality, gives life to recollection and guidance to human existence, and brings tidings of ancient days, whose voice, but the orator's, can entrust her to immortality?)   (Cicero, 1962: 224)

On these definitions 'history' meant a recovery of the past; a revival of things lost and forgotten; and a renarration of recuperated oblivion.

These rational functions of history became, however, in the early modern period, interwoven with ideas and images both more primitive and, from our retrospective vision, more prospectively modern or even 'postmodern'. When contemplating the capability of history to revive the past, and meditating on the disconcerting results sometimes gained when past and present intersect, early modern thinkers seem to have conceived of history, certainly metaphorically and even at some level literally, as a power of resurrection, a means of raising the dead. In the emblematic illustration prefacing Sir Walter Raleigh's *History of the World*, Death and Oblivion are depicted as counterparts. The expository poem this figure illustrates, attributed to Ben Jonson, translates Cicero's definitions:

From Death, and darke Obliuion (neere the same)
The Mistresse of Mans life, graue Historie,
Raising the World to good, or euill Fame,
Doth uindicate it to Eternitie.   (Raleigh, 1614: frontispiece)

Such analogies gradually became commonplace, linking together the remembering or commemoration of a historical personage or event; the artistic representation or imitation of such a subject in prose, poetry or visual art; and the literal raising of a spirit from the grave by miracle or necromancy.

These connections between the aesthetic and the occult, seemingly remote from Cicero's utilitarian prose, had been made very explicitly in the classical epics, where the hero journeys to the underworld in order to find a dead soul conversant with past and future. Odysseus has to dig a gravelike plot to summon the spirits of the dead, including the seer Tiresias, who reveals the future to him (Homer, 1946: 171–88); Aeneas enters the underworld, and is presented by the ghost of his father Anchises with an extrapolation of his own destiny that merges into the history of Virgil's own civilisation (Virgil, 1956: 147–74). Shakespeare was handling exactly such material when writing of Macbeth's meeting with the weyward sisters (who in their previous appearance had agreed to reconvene at 'the pit of Acheron' [*Macbeth*, 3.5.15]), a meeting in which Scotland's future history is revealed to him (*Macbeth*, 4.1).

It is hardly surprising that such preoccupations would pervade an intellectual period later labelled as the 'Renaissance', since the pervasive metaphors of exhumation, revivification, miraculous rebirth, that abound in historical writing, lie at the very heart of the periodisation (Lowenthal, 1985: 84–6; Greene, 1982: 32–3). Often such conceptions prefigure a key tool of modern historical research, archaeology, as in Vasari's fascinating description of Brunelleschi and Donatello digging among the foundations of Rome to exhume the secrets of its past (Vasari, 1550, 1965: 140–1). And inevitably again, there is also a strong religious dimension to this preoccupation with the living past, clearly exemplified in the symbolism of the Eucharist, in which, literally or metaphorically, a memorial ritual brings both body and blood to life: 'Doe this in remembraunce of me' (Common Prayer, 1552).

Thomas Nash drew on these various conceptions of history in his famous celebration of historical drama, which happens also to cite as its example Shakespeare's *Henry VI, Part One*:

> Nay, what if I prooue Playes to be no extreame, but a rare exercise of vertue? First, for the subiect of them (for the most part) it is borrowed out of our English Chronicles, wherein our fore-fathers valiant actes (that haue lyne long buried in rustie brasse and worme-eaten bookes) are reuiued, and they them selues raysed from the Grave of Obliuion, and brought to pleade their aged Honours in open presence: than which, what can bee a sharper reproofe, to these degenerate, effeminate dayes of ours?
>
> How would it haue ioyd braue Talbot (the terror of the French) to thinke that after he had lyne two hundred yeare in his Tomb, he should triumph againe on the Stage, and haue his bones new embalmed with the teares of ten thousand spectators at least, (at severall times) who in the Tragedian that represents his person, imagine they behold him fresh bleeding.   (Nash, 1592, 1969: 26)

While the hero Talbot has lain for centuries in his tomb, so his 'valiant actes' have lain similarly buried in defaced monuments and decomposing books. The contemporary stage not only recalls a heroic legend, but literally resurrects the hero from his 'worm-eaten' oblivion to 'represent his person' in the 'open presence' of the public theatre. The language of 'revival' and 'presence' claims for historical drama a power of concrete embodiment, as if the spirit of the past is literally in such exhibitions 'raysed from the Grave', and by the quasi-magical potency of the stage (not the neglected and 'worm-eaten' literary record) incarnated into the 'open presence' of public knowledge and direct, immediate contemporary perception.

At the same time, Nash contextualises this claim to embody 'presence' with a contrary language of 'representation' that focuses rather on the stage, on the 'Tragedian', on the spectators, and on the process of performance: the theatre enacts history in the concrete, bringing the dead to life, only by the power of the actor and the pleasure of the audience. Where the language of 'presence' metaphorically elides the distinctions between present and past, living and dead: the language of 'representation' acknowledges that this curious 'presence' is enabled only by absolute absence. The dead appear to live again, only in the *coup d'oeil* of theatrical artifice. Talbot is brought back (a point often missed in discussions of this passage [Kastan, 1982: 19; Rackin, 1990: 113–16]) but only to bleed afresh; not to live, but to die, again; or, as some sixteenth-century tragedian, playing Brutus, anachronistically imagined his historical counterpart to have prophetically foreseen, to 'bleed in sport' (*Julius Caesar*, 3.1.115) where his historical original bled in earnest. What gives history permanence is thus more than a rational process of patient reconstruction: it is rather a continually repeated sacrificial ritual, the rebirth and death of the hero. Present historical truth must contain, as Stephen Greenblatt argues, the awareness of permanent loss:

> It is paradoxical, of course, to seek the living will of the dead in fictions, in places where there was no live bodily being to begin with. But those who love literature tend to find more intensity in simulations − in the formal, self-conscious miming of life − than in any of the other textual traces left by the dead, for simulations are undertaken in full awareness of the absence of the life they contrive to represent, and hence they may skilfully anticipate and compensate for the vanishing of the actual life that has empowered them. (Greenblatt, 1988: 1)

In historical representation the dead, revivified, must die again; and history can escape 'the Grave of Oblivion' only by immediately reconsigning its souvenirs back again to the obscurity (and security) of the past. The condition of temporary presence is perpetual absence; 'that which is only living, / Can only die' (Eliot, 1963: 194).

II

Historiographical theory of the early modern period, firmly based on classical models, invoked as its cardinal principles, conveniently embodied in the quoted passage from Cicero that became a cornerstone of sixteenth century historical thinking, terms that have become for history in our own day intensively problematised: truth, memory, and instruction. First, sixteenth century historians and theorists of historiography were preoccupied with the problems of 'truth', in senses still considered proper to modern historiography: truth to historical record and historical recollection; the avoidance of false and forged versions, or what we would now call ideological appropriations, of the past. Historians should, according to Thomas Blundeville, 'tell things as they were done, without either augmenting or diminishing them, or swarving one jote from the truth' (Blundeville, 1574); or in Roger Ascham's words, 'write nothyng false' and 'be bold to say any truth' (Ascham, 1970: 126–7). The emphasis of course goes back to antiquity, where Aristotle distinguished between history ('what has happened') and poetry ('the kinds of things that might happen') (Aristotle, 1965: 43); Thucydides doubted the veracity of Homer's historical evidence ('It is questionable whether we can have complete confidence in Homer's figures' [Thucydides, 1954: 18]); and Lucian of Samosata defined the historian's method as simply 'laying out the matter as it is' (Lucian in Hobbes, 1629, 1723). The development in the early modern period of a positivist, factually based and objective conception of history (see Holderness, 1985; Rackin, 1990; Pugliatti, 1996) drew on a growing confidence in the power of evidence, in the capacity of historical records, both physical and verbal, to capture and reveal the truth of events; on a gradually developing awareness of the strong element of ideological inflection visible in much historical writing; and on the need to preserve a stance of neutrality and objectivity when confronted with the diversity of historical representations; as Holinshed put it:

> I haue in things doubtfull rather chosen to shew the diuersitie of their writings, than them to agree to my liking: leauing it neuerthelesse to each mans iudgement, to controll them as he seeth cause.   (Holinshed, 1587, 1965: II, Preface to the Reader)

But 'truth' as disinterested and value-free objectivity was not at this point, as later in a more positivistic environment it became,

clearly separable from 'truth' as revealed wisdom and moral instruction. In so far as history was considered to be a moral, didactic and
ideological medium, its 'truthfulness' could be thought of in three-
fold: either as accuracy or fidelity to record; as verisimilitude, a convincing plausibility; or as the revealed truth of moral instruction and
providential wisdom. History's positivist aspiration to provide 'an
orderly register of notable things said, done or happened in time
past.' was easily subordinated to larger moral and didactic missions:
to 'serve for the instruction of them to come' (Amiot, 1928: xiv); to
serve 'for a warnyng and monycion unto princes and gouernours
thereby to rule and order themselfe: and a comen wele' (Barclay,
1520: Preface); and to 'teach the subiects obedience to their King'
(Heywood, 1612, 1973: III, F3v). The slippage between 'truth' as
'fidelity to documentary record and primary evidence' and 'truth'
as 'trawthe', political loyalty to crown and state, was therefore no
difficult transition.

   Theorists of history were particularly well aware that the principle
of 'truth' becomes complicated when the medium of representation is
drama or poetry. But they were equally conscious of the complexities
of truth-telling even through the ostensibly transparent medium of
the classically trained historian's rhetorical prose. Poets such as Sir
Philip Sidney provocatively declared the fictional element in historiography to be its chief value ('The best of the historian is subject to the
poet', [Sidney, 1595, 1966: 37]). But even historians such as Bacon
openly advocated a poetic 'Feigned Historie', able to 'give some
shadow of satisfaction to the mind of Man in those points, wherein
the nature of things doth deny it, the world being in proportion
inferior to the soul' (Bacon, 1605, 1973: 82). We have seen Nash
expressing an accurate consciousness of the way in which historical
drama both 'presents' and 'represents' history. But the idea of a concrete historical presence that could literally be secured by historical
drama was expressed at its strongest and most uncompromising
by Thomas Heywood, who described the history-making powers of
the theatre as productive of a special kind of truth, setting before the
immediate senses of the spectator living and speaking incarnations of
historical characters:

> what English blood seeing the person of any bold English man
> presented and doth not hugge his fame, and hunnye at his valor,
> pursuing him in his enterprise with his best wishes, and as beeing
> wrapt in contemplation, offers to him in his hart all prosperous

performance, as if the Personator were the man Personated, so bewitching a thing is liuely and well spirited action, that it hath power to new mold the harts of the spectators and fashion them to the shape of any noble and notable attempt. What coward to see his contryman valiant would not bee ashamed of his owne cowardise? What English Prince should hee behold the true portrature of that [f]amous King *Edward* the third, foraging France, taking so great a King captiue in his owne country, quartering the English Lyons with the French Flower-delyce, and would not bee suddenly Inflam'd with so royall a spectacle, being made apt and fit for the like atchieuement. So of *Henry* the fift.   (Heywood, 1612, 1973: I, B4r)

Like Nash, Heywood attributes to historical drama the power of raising the dead; but unlike Nash, he recognises no discrepancy between presence and representation. Effective acting, convincing performance, 'Lively and spirited action', possess that necromantic, 'bewitching' potency of eliminating the distance between actor and character, 'Personator' and 'Personated'. The skilful performance elides the differences between present and past, living and dead, substance and shadow. Thus incarnated and concretised, history is free to accomplish its uplifting patriotic work of 'inflaming' contemporary spirits to emulate the heroic military achievements of the past. The spectator, 'wrapt in contemplation' of the actor, is 'bewitched' by an aesthetic rapture into surrendering a wholehearted loyalty, an irresistible emotional solidarity with those potent images of the past.

Heywood's passage usefully indicates the close interdependence of quite separate conceptions of 'truth'. Historical drama has firstly proved a means of bringing the 'truth' of national history, as knowledge, directly to the educationally disadvantaged:

playes haue made the ignorant more apprehensiue, taught the vnlearned the knowledge of many famous histories, instructed such as cannot reade in the discovery of all our *English* Chronicles. (Heywood, 1612, 1973: III, F3r)

Here Heywood agrees with Herodotus, who wrote in the hope of 'preserving from decay the remembrance of what men have done, and of preventing the great and wonderful actions of Greeks and Barbarians from losing their due meed of glory' (Herodotus, 1910: 1). Secondly, historical drama offers a verisimilitude, a 'true-to-life' representation that carries historical truth home to the spectator with unrivalled immediacy and force. Thirdly, this educational process, its presented examples being so unavoidably persuasive, secures a 'true' moral instruction, quickening the patriotic spirit with admiration for the past, emulation for the future, and obedience to the authority of the present:

> Playes are writ with this ayme, and carryed with this methode, to teach the subiects obedience to their King, to shew the people the vntimely ends of such as haue moued tumults, commotions and insurrections, to present them with the flourishing estate of such as liue in obedience, exhorting them to allegeance, dehorting them from all trayterous and fellonious stratagems.
>
> (Heywood, 1612, 1973: III, F3v)

III

In the historical plays themselves we can find examples of drama both claiming a truth-function, and admitting its own insubstantiality. The 'Prologue' to Shakespeare's *Henry VIII* (originally titled *All is True*) employs the same concatenation of truth-values as Heywood. The spectator is exhorted to forget the discrepancy between personator and personated, to imagine the dead revived in contemporary presence:

> Think ye see
> The very persons of our noble story
> As they were living ... (*Henry VIII*, Prologue, 25–7)

The Prologue dismisses mere theatrical spectacle, 'a show or two' as unworthy objects of attention:

> for, gentle hearers, know,
> To rank our chosen truth with such a show
> As fool, and fight is, beside forfeiting
> Our own brains, and the opinion that we bring
> To make that only true we now intend,
> Will leave us never an understanding friend. (*HVIII*, 17–22)

The ideal spectators of this truthful historical drama are 'Such as give / Their money out of hope they may believe', and who 'May here find truth too' (7–9).

But in the most elaborate articulation of historical drama as embodiment, incarnation, the word made flesh, the Choruses in *Henry V*, we find precisely the opposite effect. The Chorus continually exhorts the audience to supply, by a sustained imaginative participation, the topographical colour and realistic detail necessary to provide the drama with a concrete historical location:

> Think, when we talk of horses, that you see them
> Printing their proud hoofs i' th' receiving earth;
> For 'tis your thoughts that now must deck our kings.
>
> (*Henry V*, Prologue, 26–8)

That conviction of imaginative possibility, however, co-exists with a contrary exhortation to cancel such embodiment:

> But pardon, gentles all,
> The flat unraised spirits that hath dar'd
> On this unworthy scaffold, to bring forth
> So great an object.   (8–10)

Though the actors may, as in Nash's account, be the vehicles via which the great spirits of the past can be revived, in themselves they are nonentities, 'unraised' spirits, flat, unworthy, apologetically incapable of emulating the 'Object' they merely imitate. The tightly woven organic unity between personator and personated is here just as carefully disentangled: shadow and substance divide, actor and hero part company. The spectators find themselves expelled from the promised virtual reality of participation, and demitted to the banality of 'a show or two' in the unhistorical present.

Thus the dead hero resurrected in the 'open presence' of historical drama exemplifies the paradox of verisimilitude and vacancy, incarnate presence and disembodied absence. The dead hero bleeds afresh, but bleeds 'in sport'; the modern tragedian now triumphs on the stage, where the ancient warrior triumphed in the field. The historical drama enjoined on its spectators a full awareness of this paradox, self-reflexively holding together re-enactment and simulation, revival and fabrication, truth and pretence, history and theatre.

IV

In the early modern period, generally to the human race and specifically to a nation, history was thought of as equivalent to the individual
memory: as solemn memory retains or revives the past, so 'grave'
history recalls and revivifies antiquity. Personal memory, a restricted
and fragmentary record of particularised experience, could thus be
supplemented by the larger collective memory of times past, history,
the great commemoration of former civilisations, the register of
significant human actions and achievements.

> historie is accounted a verie necessarie and profitable thing, for
> that in recalling to mind the truth of things past, which other-
> wise would be buried in silence, it setteth before vs such effects
> (as warnings and admonitions touching good and euill) and layeth
> vertue and vice so naked before our eyes, with the punishments or
> rewards inflicted or bestowed vpon the followers of each of them,
> that it may rightly be called an easie and profitable apprentiseship
> or schoole for euerie man to learne to get wisedome at another
> mans cost.   (Beard, 1597, 1612: Preface)

It was of course as this racial and national memory-bank that history
claimed to provide such a rich source of knowledge, wisdom and
understanding. As the world's memory, history held the recollection
of events and their causes, and of historical characters good and bad.
History could show how one civilisation thrived with good government, while another collapsed under tyranny; how a vicious man was
justly punished, and a virtuous providentially rewarded.

> by reading of histories ... men may see the groundes and
> beginnings of Common-wealths, the causes of theyr encrease, of
> theyr prosperous maintenance, and good preseruation: and againe
> by what means they decreased, decayed, and came to ruine. There
> the vertues and vices of men do appeare, how by theyr good
> doinges they florished, and by their euill actes they decayed.
> (Brende, 1602: Preface)

Just as memory stores particular experiences and situations, so history
is composed of 'examples', which are both exemplifying instances,
and instructive models for current and future government and
conduct. This view can be seen expressed by Amiot:

> For it is a certaine rule or instruction, which by examples past,
> teacheth us to judge of things present, and to foresee things to
> come: so as we may know what to like of, and what to follow, what
> to mislike and what to eschew.   (Amiot, 1579, 1928: I, xv)

– or by Sir Thomas Elyot:

> Acts committed or done by other men, where of profit or damage
> succedynge, we may, (in knowing or beholdinge is), be therby
> instructed to apprehend the thing which to the publicke weale, or
> to our own persones, may be commodious; and to exchue that
> thing, which either in the begynnyng or in the conclusion, appear-
> eth noisome and vicious.   (Elyot, 1531, 1907: 280).

Thomas Puttenham's well-known explication of this theory shows
the argument at its most rational and elegant:

> There is nothing in man of all the potential parts of his mind
> (reason and will except) more noble or more necessary to the
> actiue life then memory; because it maketh most to a sound
> iudgement and perfect worldly wisedome, examining and com-
> paring the times past with the present, and, by them both consid-
> ering the time to come, concludeth with a stedfast resolution what
> is the best course to be taken in all his actions and aduices in this
> world.   (Puttenham, 1589, 1904: 40–1)

Puttenham thus elevates 'memory' to a very high ethical and
intellectual level, identifying it as a key moral function and a central
philosophical category. 'Experience', a constitutive term in philosophy and science, is after all only 'a mass of memories'; rhetorical and
historical 'examples', however persuasive or instructive, are nothing
more than 'the representation of old memories'. At the heart of the
argument is the decisive way in which 'memory' is declared conducive
to 'sound iudgement and perfect worldly wisedome'. In both the
moral microcosm of the individual and the grand political drama
of the state, the true apotheosis of memory (and history) is to
produce that 'stedfast resolution' determining ethical conduct and
national policy.

But this way of perceiving the analogy between history and memory is clearly a simplified, even sanitised comparison. Some sixteenth-
century writers in one way or another reluctantly admitted that

history does not always so readily disclose morally instructive patterns of providential justice; as Matthew H. Wikander puts it, 'Renaissance historians invoked and revoked providential explanations at will' (Wikander, 1986: 28); or as Bacon argued, since 'true history propoundeth the successes and issues of actions not so agreeable to the merits of virtue and vice', there was some merit in the capacity of poetry to 'feign them more just in retribution, and more according to revealed providence' (Bacon, 1605, 1973: II.iv, 2). In the same way memory was not regarded simply as a storehouse of useful examples, a database of instructive instances, an aide-mémoire to moral judgement and decision. Memory can also be a haunting, in which the present consciousness is overwhelmed by images of the past; disabled by nostalgia or the sense of loss, unnerved by the unbearable burden of recollection. Memory can bring with it not only an unappeasable dissatisfaction with the past's resistance to redemption, but also an intolerable pressure of instruction, setting unattainable standards or imposing impossible demands. In Puttenham's model, historical memory is an intellectual elegy of quiet reflection in which present piety can admire past virtue:

> For these regards the Poesie historicall is of all other next the diuine most honorable and ·worthy, as well for the common benefit as for the speciall comfort euery man receiueth by it: no one thing in the world with more delectation reuiuing our spirits then to behold as it were in a glasse the liuely image of oure deare forefathers, their noble and vertuous maner of life, with other things autentike, which because we are not able otherwise to attaine to the knowledge of by any of our sences, we apprehend them by memory.
>
> (Puttenham, 1589, 1904: 41)

Elsewhere, however, writers hinted at something of the more disturbing and intractable possibilities of memory, its capacity to 'weigh' in Marx's description of the past, 'like a nightmare on the brains of the living' (Marx, 1852: 15). In Nash, the 'deare forefathers' of Puttenham's gentle elegy return from the grave to shock and challenge the 'effeminate' complacency of their much degenerated descendants. A poet commenting on the 1632 Folio edition of Shakespeare's works figured historical drama as the regurgitation, for perverse purposes of pleasure, of what time has previously swallowed: 'in an ugly sort / Disgorging up his ravine for our sport' (I.M.S. in Wells and Taylor, 1987: xvi). Writers had recourse to ambiguous metaphors to articulate the character of an influence at once strengthening, encouraging, supportive; and at the same time also shaming, unnerving, filling the present with impossible emulation, terrifying fear of failure. It is at this juncture that history as *'vita memoriae'*, a symptomatic record of times past, consolidates into *'magistra vitae'*, an authority demanding an obedient response:

> therefore all menne, for the most parte, calle [Historie] the Mistresse of life ... bycause that with the examples of many things, shee dothe partly enflame most excellent menne, for the immortal glorie of praise and renowme, to all woorthy interprises: partly, bycause for feare of perpetuall infamie, shee letteth all wicked and naughty men from misdoing.   (Agrippa, 1575: Eiv)

Encouragement and anxiety, 'inflammation' and 'fear', are clearly two sides of the same coin. Even Puttenham, in his account of memory's effects, links the fostering of achievement to the anxiety of emulation, and the strenuous competitive effort to deserve the past, to a haunting fear of historical oblivion:

> Now because the actions of meane & base personages tend in very few cases to any great good example; for who passeth to follow the steps and maner of life of a craftes man, shepheard or sailer, though he were his father or dearest frend? yea how almost is it possible that such maner of men should be of any vertue other then their profession requireth? therefore was nothing committed to historie but matters of great and excellent persons & things, that the same by irritation of good courages (such as emulation causeth) might worke more effectually.
>
> (Puttenham, 1589, 1904: 43)

V

Cicero's term *'magistra vitae'* defines history as a teacher, and historical study as an education.

> An Historie is a declaration of thynges done with prayse or dispraise, whiche, as it were in a certayne liuely picture, doth set before our eies y Counsailes, Deedes and Endes of great things, y^e

Enterprises of Princes and Noble menne, with the order and description of times and places: and therefore all menne, for the moste parte, call it the Mistresse of life. (Agrippa, 1575: Eiv)

In one sense, the female gender of the adjective merely follows the Latin 'Historia', and is normally translated in editions of the classics as 'guide' or 'teacher'. But the early modern historical writers seized on that grammatical gendering to represent history as 'the Mistresse of life', a female governor with both authority to educate and power to instruct. A 'mistress' could be not only a domestic authority, in charge of a household of servants, but a female head of state, with power over many subjects. The image of 'history' as 'Mistresse' no doubt also drew on the figure of Clio, the Muse of history, and was strongly coloured by practical examples of feminine power, such as those provided by Mary Tudor and by Elizabeth herself. Certainly many contemporary formulations of this figure call to mind Elizabeth's iconography of power: wisdom combined with authority; a knowledge to instruct, with a power to enforce; and above all, that charismatic potency to incite her courtiers and subjects, by an orchestrated cult of adoration, to loyalty, admiration and enterprise.

The educational mission of history is not merely to teach and persuade by example of heroic achievements to emulate, and vicious behaviours to eschew. Together with its force of persuasion, history also has a power of command. Education is 'instruction' in a double sense, both example and order; it is demonstration and proof, but also duress and imposition. Vanished history was, in Eliot's words, 'not lost, but requiring' (Eliot, 1963: 201), insistently demanding present and future action. Since history, despite its Latin gender, was thought to speak so clearly of masculine achievement, there was a certain attractiveness in a wholly male educational model, where teacher, pupil and educational example shared a commonality of gender:

In the first of the *Olimpiads*, amongst many other actiue exercises in which *Hercules* euer triumph'd as victor, there was in his nonage presented vnto him by his Tutor in the fashion of a History, acted by the choyse of the nobility of Greece, the worthy and memorable acts of his father *Iupiter*. Which being personated with liuely and well-spirited action, wrought such impression in his noble thoughts, that in meere emulation of his fathers valor (not at the behest of his Stepdame *Iuno*) he perform'd his twelue labours ... Aristotle that Prince of Philosophers ... hee hauing the tuition of young *Alexander*, caused the destruction of Troy to be acted before his pupill, in which the valor of *Achilles* was so naturally exprest, that it imprest the hart of *Alexander*, in so much that all his succeeding actions were meerly shaped after that patterne, and it may be imagined had *Achilles* neuer liued, *Alexander* had neuer conquered the whole world.   (Heywood, 1612, 1973: I, B3)

Aristotle, Alexander, Achilles: in this alliterative fraternity the male tutor presents the male pupil with images of heroic masculinity, inflaming him to a spirit of emulation sufficient to encompass an ambition of global conquest. 'Historia' may have a feminine ending, but it has a male beginning, treating only of masculine endeavours. The Labours of Hercules were exercises in paternal imitation; no such valiant spirit accrued to Hercules, Heywood parenthetically notes, from the influence of his stepmother Juno. Heywood's heroic lineage consists of a succession of historical and legendary characters who by imitation and emulation of their paternal or quasi-paternal predecessors, demonstrate their worthiness to succeed to a place in the heroic pantheon. Caesar emulated Alexander, Alexander imitated Achilles, Achilles strove to resemble Theseus, Theseus sought comparison with Hercules, who in turn had to copy his father before 'hee held himselfe worthy to be called the son of *Iupiter*'. The function of historical instruction and historical example is conceived as the inculcation in young men, by precedent patriarchal example, of strength, virtue and heroic resolve.

One of the most original and sustained meditations on these problems of history and historiography is to be found in a play not conventionally designated as a 'history play' at all, but whose historical character is self-evident and exemplary: *Hamlet*. This 'Tragicall Historie' will be a useful starting-point for an exploration of that heroic tradition on which the historical drama of the 1590s drew, and from which it differentiated itself, in ways peculiarly interesting to modern historiography.

3

Hamlet

Why should it be thought a thing incredible with you, that
God should raise the dead?

Acts, XXVI.8

I

If history is a means of raising the dead, then Francis Barker is correct
to identify the Ghost in *Hamlet* as history itself, 'the sign ... of
historicity' (Barker, 1991b: 65), a spirit who is also 'raysed from the
Grave of Oblivion' (Nash, 1592: 26), to 'pleade' his 'ancient honours'
in open presence, and to provide a sharp reproof to 'degenerate,
effeminate dayes':

> *Ham.*   O, answer me! ... tell
> Why thy canoniz'd bones, hearsed in death,
> Have burst their cerements; why the sepulchre
> Wherein we saw thee quietly enurn'd
> Hath op'd his ponderous and marble jaws,
> To cast thee up again.   (*Hamlet*, 1.4.45–51)

As 'history', the Ghost reconciles the word's famous *double entendre*: it
is both the object and its referent, the signified ('history' as life lived
in the past), and the signifier ('history' as a story told in the present).
Saussure identifies two such meanings of history:

> history as the complex of social and material forces which modify
> the individual and the community in a succession of experienced
> presents, and history as a supra-individual, supra-communal, trans-
> temporal continuum, genetically or teleologically oriented.
> (Attridge, Bennington and Young, 1987: 191)

Or as Phyllis Rackin puts it, more simply: 'The word "history" is ambiguous, referring equally to the signifying text and what the text signifies' (Rackin, 1990: 33). That doubleness in the word also existed in the sixteenth century, where 'history' could be both 'notable things said, done or happened in time past'; and more generically a 'story', possibly but not exclusively an affective and illuminating narrative of such sayings, actions and events from 'times past'.

The Ghost is the return of the past, the dead resurrected in contemporary presence; a narrator *from* the past who recounts the history *of* the past. But the Ghost's 'presence' is of course, as Barker emphasises, in actuality highly unstable and indeterminate. The Ghost operates both to confirm, and to undermine, Cicero's famous aphorisms on the functions of history: he bears witness to the past, and carries messages from antiquity; he casts light on hidden truth, and reinstates the forgotten to memory; he provides clear instructions for the guidance of the living. But both his 'presence' and his impact on the present remain, in Hamlet's own word, 'questionable': his 'witness' proves confusing and disorientating; his 'light' baffles and blinds; he visits memory as a haunting, and his instructions prove impossible to obey. 'There is something disappeared, departed', as Derrida puts it, 'in the apparition itself as reapparition of the departed' (Derrida, 1994: 6). If the Ghost is 'history', then those historiographical theories that underpin his project of revisiting and revenge, together with the dramatic context in which they are mobilised, need themselves to be revisited.

II

Testis Temporum

The Ghost in *Hamlet* testifies as a 'third party and witness' (Derrida, 1994: 6). to a crime, his own murder. He is of course the key witness, the one whose testimony would disrupt, if produced in open court, the whole courtroom drama. The Ghost holds the kind of knowledge which, although from a positivist perspective a simple matter of 'fact' (he describes his own assassination from an observer's point of view, as a witnessed event, just as later it is brought in evidence as a spectacle for another 'court audience'), has become an arcane and secret knowledge, since the historical record has been rewritten to deface and obscure the truth:

Ghost.   the whole ear of Denmark
Is by a forged process of my death
Rankly abus'd ...   (1.5.36–8)

Where historical record can thus be falsified, 'witness' becomes a difficult and dangerous exercise. Hence the Ghost ensures that his secret history is silenced in the dumbstruck mouths of gagged observers, by swearing in his 'witnesses' not to testify, but to keep silent (1.5.143–61).

King Claudius's official *History of Denmark*, had it been written, would have been a narrative that tells of natural causes, legal succession, constitutional adoption of power and relationship. Thus history is exposed as a 'forged process', communicated to the attentive ear of Denmark, as a deadly poison was poured into the ear of the King:

Ghost.   And in the porches of my ear did pour
The leperous distilment; whose effect
Holds such an enmity with blood of man ...   (1.5.63–5)

In a very similar way in the 'Induction' to *Henry IV, Part Two*, Rumour (another name for a certain kind of history) requires his audience to 'Open your ears' so they may be stuffed 'with false reports' (1. 11; and see below, pp. 168–9). In *Hamlet*, just as that toxic infiltration visited such deadly changes on the royal blood, so a distorting and effacing historical narrative modifies the national consciousness of the Danish people, whose ears become resistant to the truth, strongly 'fortified' (as the soldiers say of Horatio's ears) 'against our story' (1.1.32).

In *Hamlet*, each subsequent death testifies to the universality of this 'forged process'. Claudius's first concern after the murder of Polonius is to construct an acceptable public justification:

King.   this vile deed
We must with all our majesty and skill
Both countenance and excuse.   (4.1.30–2)

In the official history, Polonius's death exemplifies a story of royal lunacy, parental indulgence, excess of trust and a venial lack of caution. In the unofficial but more 'truthful' history enacted by the play, it is evidence of fratricide and usurpation, corruption and conspiracy. Similarly Ophelia's interment in consecrated ground

falsifies the historical record, which has already been articulated in the
Queen's strange, second-hand, eye-witness account of what could
well be construed as a suspected suicide. In both cases 'great
command o'ersways the order' (5.1.222) which would otherwise
testify to the disturbing, even subversive, historical 'truth'. The play
simultaneously unearths the historical record, dragging and excavating the past, raising the drowned and murdered dead to tell their own
story, and demonstrates that 'forged process' of historiography
by which an entirely different narrative of historical process is
retrospectively constructed. The mortally wounded Laertes tries to
set the record straight, disclosing history as poetic justice. But
Hamlet's dying concern is with the likely future of that record, as his
personal 'history' is handed over to the historian, his witness placed
in the custody of a narrator:

> *Ham.*   what a wounded name,
> Things standing thus unknown, shall live behind me!   (5.2.336–7)

'report me and my cause aright' (5.2.331), he urges Horatio: 'tell my
story' (5.2.341). The responsibility initially conferred on Hamlet by
his father's Ghost was that of redirecting history into conformity with
truth, putting the record straight, setting right a 'disjoint' time: the
murdered father avenged, the fratricide 'justly served', an avenging
son restoring to true succession the broken dynastic line. But has
Hamlet himself proved adequate, either as director or narrator of
history? And can Horatio in turn be relied upon to narrate the
particular version of events requested, representing objectively, as
history, that history's subject and his proffered subjectivity, 'me' and
'my Story'? The historical actor's witness becomes a testament,
entrusted by will to an executor. Living history becomes narrative,
history becomes 'history'; can the will of a living friend be curbed by
the will of a dead prince? What safeguard can there be, in historical
reconstruction, against 'forged process'?

   The Ghost functions also more generally as 'time's witness', a
historical testament, come back from the dead like Lazarus 'to tell you
all, I shall tell you all' (Eliot, 1963: 16). Even the actors who
subsequently merely mimic King Hamlet and his tragedy share that
radical indiscretion: they 'cannot keep counsel; they'll tell all'
(3.2.137). As a Ghost, King Hamlet demonstrates the paradox of
historical testimony, since only the dead can verify their experience,
and the dead, inhabitants of 'The undiscover'd country, from whose

bourn / No traveller returns' (3.1.79—80) have (normally) no capability of speech. The play of course continually falsifies both that norm and Hamlet's aphorism, since it dramatises a world in which the borders between life and death are notoriously permeable, the traffic of returning 'travellers' continuous. The Ghost is a particularly voluble visitor, the revenant as raconteur; but later in the play a taciturn corpse 'cast ... up' from the grave exemplifies the customary silence of the departed: 'That skull had a tongue in it, and could sing once' (5.1.75). The skull of course, however vividly Hamlet may recall its occupant, remains 'dumb to us' (1.1.171), silently witnessing only to the inscrutability of the past.

Hamlet can, famously, put words into dead Yorick's mouth, even intimately recall the touch of his living body. The Ghost of King Hamlet, however, no mere theatrical prop or ventriloquist's dummy, has both a voice to utter, and a presence to authenticate, his narrative. But what constitutes the 'presence' of a dead king? What the soldiers see is an 'illusion', an astonishing 'likeness', a simulacrum, an amazingly accurate portrayal of their former sovereign, replete with 'the furtive and ungraspable visibility of the invisible' (Derrida, 1994: 7).

> *Ber.*   In the same figure, like the King that's dead ...
> Looks 'a not like the King?   (1.1.41—3)

The 'Apparition' is only an appearance, only *resembles* its living original; it is a simile, a shade, the shadow of a substance, an 'image' of the royal body. Within the dramatic narrative, there is of course a literal uncertainty about the Ghost's status: its 'questionable shape' (provoking as well as inviting question) eludes definition. On stage it is in every sense a shadow, since it is represented by a player who merely assumes the 'form' of departed majesty, an actor who is a shadow of the shade of the vanished presence of a long-dead king. As '*testis temporum*', an exhumed historical source, the Ghost's status is equally questionable, its meaning as indeterminate 'as the air'. 'A spectral asymmetry interrupts here all specularity' (Derrida, 1994: 6). Again, the classical epics provide some telling antecedents. We inevitably recall Homer:

> As my mother spoke, there came to me out of the confusion in my heart the one desire, to embrace her spirit, dead though she was. Thrice, in my eagerness to clasp her to me, I started forward with

my hand outstretched. Thrice, like a shadow or a dream, she slipped through my arms and left me harrowed by an even sharper pain.   (Homer, 1946: 176)

Or Virgil:

Three times he tried to cast his arms about his father's neck; but three times the clasp was vain and the wraith escaped his hands, like airy winds or the melting of a dream.   (Virgil, 1956: 168)

And again, Macbeth, perplexed by the witches' inexplicable vanishing:

Whither are they vanish'd? ... Into the air ...   (*Macbeth*, 1.3 80–1)

History's effort to grasp and possess a stable and enduring knowledge of the past proves elusive and self-dispersing:

Ber.   'Tis here!
Hor.   'Tis here!
Mar.   'Tis gone!   (1.1.141–2)

III

Lux Veritatis

As a witness, in the drama at least domesticated to the protocols of the English judicial system, we would expect the Ghost to tell 'the truth, the whole truth, and nothing but the truth'. But does the Ghost bear true witness to the past? It is Hamlet's question, obsessively recurring, alternately posed and resolved, affirmed and doubted again:

Ham.   It is an honest ghost ...   (1.5.138)

               The Spirit that I have seen
May be the devil ...   (2.2.594–5)

I'll take the ghost's word for a thousand pound ...   (3.2.281)

Although those who observe the Ghost in *Hamlet* naturally speak of it as a divided thing, an 'image' or 'illusion' that appears '*Together with*

that fair and warlike form' (my italics) of the old King, they nonetheless implicitly believe that what they are witnessing is in some
sense 'true':

Hor.   I might not this believe
Without the sensible and true avouch
Of mine own eyes. (1.1.56–8)

Hor.   Season your admiration for a while
With an attent ear, till I may deliver,
Upon the witness of these gentlemen,
This marvel to you. (1.2.192–5)

Ham.   'Tis very strange.
Hor.   As I do live, my honour'd lord, 'tis true … (1.2.220–1)

However 'strange' and unintelligible their observations, their testimony is asseverated on oath: 'As I do live … Upon the witness …
'tis true'.

What sort of 'light', however, does the Ghost shed over past,
present and future? 'Veritas', on the title page of Raleigh's *History
of the World*, holds aloft a sun, an originator of light, a bright
illuminating source; and in the corresponding poem Historia's vision
is 'lighted by the beamie hand / Of truth'. The Ghost travels only in
darkness, through the 'dead waste and middle of the night' (1.2.198),
between dusk and dawn, drawn back to his prison-house by the scent
of morning air. His is a light that 'breaks' (in Dylan Thomas's words)
'where no sun shines' (Thomas, 1952, 1966: 23). A creature of the
night, he revisits 'the glimpses of the moon' clad either in glimmering
steel, or (in the 'First Quarto' text) domestically dressed for interior
locations '*in his night-gown*' (Holderness and Loughrey, 1992: 81).
In Latin terms he is a 'lumen', light fitfully reflected, rather than a 'lux',
light irrefutably emitted. As Ralph Waldo Emerson said, in a phrase
apropos of history: 'Time dissipates to shining ether the solid
angularity of facts' (Emerson, 1907: 24). The Ghost is an 'uneffectual
fire', a transient apparition momentarily 'glimpsed' (in an optical
metaphor that links light with vision) in the flickering 'glimpses' of
the moon.

In the Ghost we see history 'through a glass, darkly', rather than
directly, 'face to face' (1 Corinthians, XIII.12). The Light of Truth
comes obliquely reflected from a shimmering spectral presence, not
blindingly emitted from an indisputable source. 'Truth' appears not as

the solid evidence of a cast-iron legal case, but as mere fitful glimpses, dim reflections in a cloudy mirror. The Ghost's ambiguous luminosity is paralleled by the indeterminacy of his bodily presence, 'here' then 'gone', and by the fragmentary character of the knowledge he imparts. He declines for example to impart one very significant 'whole history' (3.2.291), nothing less than the revealed mystery of the after-life, the 'secrets of [his] prison-house' (1.5.14). Tantalisingly proffered and frustratingly withheld, that story remains an 'eternal blason', never fully disclosed or interpreted, only teasingly adumbrated, fleetingly made visible in 'gleams' (Wordsworth's phrase) 'like the flashings of a shield' (Wordsworth, 1805, 1971: Book 1, l.614).

IV

Vita Memoriae

As we have seen, 'memory' can be thought of, whether in the sixteenth century or today, as blessing or curse, welcome visitation or terrifying nightmare, liberation or intolerable burden. Terms such as 'inflammation' and 'irritation', though probably less ambiguous in the Latinate chastity of early modern prose than in modern English, nonetheless suggest a painful mingling of emulative excitement and unworthy despair. Puttenham describes historical memory as a tranquil family reunion of past and present. But in *Hamlet*, memory is closely linked with various anxious and ambivalent strategies the living employ in order to come to terms with the dead.

Claudius, for instance, uses memory as a mechanism for reordering the past, writing its history as natural progression:

> *King.* Though yet of Hamlet our dear brother's death
> The memory be green ... (1.2.1–2)

This judicious balancing of an attenuated ritual of public mourning (funeral), with simultaneous rituals of continuity and succession (coronation and marriage) maps precisely the undivided continuum of dynastic history, in which the perishable individual monarch is subsumed into the permanence of the genealogical line, the sad 'memory' of a dead monarch weighed against a prudent 'remembrance' of his successor. The king is dead; long live the king.

Claudius insists that the state is in no way weakened or 'disjoint' by Old Hamlet's death. But it *is* threatened by young Hamlet's obsessive and inconsolable sense of bereavement. 'Mourning duties' are to Claudius an integral element – 'obsequious sorrow' – of dynastic succession and political continuity. Hamlet's persistence in an 'impious' and 'obstinate condolement' introduces an unwelcome discontinuity, as he continues to 'seek for [his] noble father in the dust' (1.2.71), staring downwards at the earth, not upwards towards the king; looking to death, not life, the past, not the future.

In clinging to an unappeasable and inconsolably wounded 'memory', Hamlet nurtures a destabilising and oppositional historical consciousness. Francis Barker (Barker, 1991b: 50) has argued that in the play memory is 'displaced' from history onto 'mourning', figured as individual bereavement and haunting, rather than collective loss and recuperation. Why hypostatise history as individual grief? Barker asks of the play; almost the same question as that demanded of Hamlet: 'Why seems it so particular with thee?' (1.2.75). In fact the painful individualised memory of lost plenitude is inseparable from a larger sense of historical absence, perhaps nowhere more strikingly than in Hamlet's implicit identification of the lost father with an estranged and irrecoverable past of which King Hamlet was an integral and unquestionable part:

> *Ham.* 'A was a man, take him for all in all,
> I shall not look upon his like again. (1.2.187–8)

The existential simplicity of that designation 'man' presupposes a world in which, not only can it be assumed, men *are* men, but such a statement can in itself (an impossibility in Hamlet's world as in ours) go unquestioned. To have been a man as was Hamlet *père* is to be incapable of even imagining the question insistently posed in the 1604/5 version by Hamlet *fils*: 'What is a man?' (Shakespeare, 1605, 1969: K3v). Clearly Hamlet cannot, by 'holding the mirror up' to his own face, see the father's 'like' in the image of the son. If Claudius is 'no more like my father / Than I to Hercules' (1.2.152–3), then Hamlet can scarcely resemble his own father, who, swelled into legend by the historical imagination, certainly *is* like 'to Hercules'. If such men are no longer in evidence, that innocent nominalistic world shaped by their masculinity has disappeared, and the survivors find themselves occupying an empty, unhistorical universe with no expectation of attaining any comparable greatness – knowing, perhaps, what Derrida called 'the doubtful contemporaneity of the present to itself' (Derrida, 1994: 39). Hamlet remembers history from a point at which he cannot see or feel himself as historical. He envisages, in other words, what recent theoreticians have called 'an end of history' (Fukayama, 1992; Barker, 1993). And, 'after the end of history', Derrida reminds us, 'the spirit comes' (Derrida, 1994: 10).

In *Julius Caesar* Cassius represents Caesar as arrogating to his own personal aggrandisement the entire history of Rome. Those eliminated from history thus become subjected to *unhistoricity*, as unmarked and unremembered as Puttenham's craftsmen and shepherds:

> *Cas.*   he doth bestride the narrow world
> Like a Colossus, and we petty men
> Walk under his huge legs, and peep about
> To find ourselves dishonourable graves.
>
> (*Julius Caesar*, 1.2.135–8)

Both the successful life, and the tragic death, of such a hero however reduce the surviving world to a flat desert of mediocrity, as Cleopatra in another 'Roman play' describes life after Antony:

> *Cleo.*   young boys and girls
> Are level now with men. The odds is gone,
> And there is nothing left remarkable
> Beneath the visiting moon.   (*Antony and Cleopatra*, 4.15.65–8)

– or as Hamlet describes a world voided of another soldier, a Denmark whose 'majesty' is 'buried' (1.1.48):

> *Ham.*   How weary, stale, flat and unprofitable,
> Seem to me all the uses of this world!   (1.2.133–4)

Although this transition from plenitude to vacancy is always represented chronologically, as historical cause and effect, it is present memory that, by generating visions of historical otherness, produces these waste landscapes of contemporary despair. The process itself is disclosed wonderfully in *Antony and Cleopatra*, where Cleopatra 'dreams' to the Roman ambassador Dolabella, a legendary Antony on the same gigantic scale:

> *Cleo.*   His legs bestrid the ocean; his rear'd arm
> Crested the world ...

Think you there was or might be such a man
As this I dreamt of?
Dol.   Gentle madam, no.
Cleo.   You lie, up to the hearing of the gods.
But if there be, or ever were, one such,
It's past the size of dreaming. Nature wants stuff
To vie strange forms with fancy; yet t'imagine
An Antony were nature's piece 'gainst fancy,
Condemning shadows quite.

(*Antony and Cleopatra*, 5.2.82–3; 93–9)

Here the process of remembering is explicitly defined as 'dreaming' or 'imagining' the hero in an exercise of nostalgic fantasy. If the historic Antony could be thought of as coterminous with Cleopatra's dream of him, he would have been a work of art too perfect for art to produce, a masterpiece of nature. Such a conception is, however, unimaginable, 'past the size of dreaming', therefore a mere 'fancy' or 'shadow'. If, as Hamlet argues, a dream itself is 'but a shadow' (2.2.259), then Dolabella is right to reprove Cleopatra's ambitious fantasy.

But Cleopatra, acting in this context as if she were a postmodern historian, affirms that history is composed wholly of shadows; that historiography is the work of 'fancy'; and that dreaming is the only realisation of memory. Further, she also 'knows' that she herself has no existence: that the 'I' with which she speaks is also an insubstantial 'shadow', realised only by that actor who will in some theatre of the future scurrilously 'boy [her] greatness'; by those 'quick comedians' who 'Extemporally will stage' her as 'Some squeaking Cleopatra' (5.2.215–19). The historical character Cleopatra has no existence, 'nor ever were one such'; s/he speaks only by virtue of an unhistorical, low-life comedian who re-enacts her tragic history a second time (Marx's phrase) as farce (Marx, 1852: 10).

V

Magistra Vitae

The Ghost in *Hamlet* is a tutor whose own life is the stuff of such heroic example, the appropriate object of such emulation. 'Our valiant Hamlet', hero of that great chivalric showdown with Fortinbras senior, exemplifies the virtues of the past, and teaches the lesson of its vices, using powerful examples of past events to inflame his son with a corrosive knowledge and a passion of emulation.

> *Gho.*   Mark me ... lend thy serious hearing
> To what I shall unfold ...   (1.5.2, 5–6)

A dutiful pupil, Hamlet gives the Ghost his full attention: 'Speak; I am bound to hear' (1.5.7). But education here requires action, not attention – 'So art thou to revenge, when thou shalt hear' (1.5.8). Knowledge imparted entails automatic compliance, immediate and decisive response. What Hamlet subsequently describes, as a process within himself, is a radical education in which the accumulated repository of personal experience is utterly annihilated by a recollection, a remembering of the past: personal memory is completely surrendered to the commemoration and command of history:

> *Ham.*   Yea, from the table of my memory
> I'll wipe away all trivial fond records,
> All saws of books, all forms, all pressures past,
> That youth and observation copied there.   (1.5.98–101)

Education is a recurrent preoccupation in *Hamlet.* The first appearance of the Polonius family is in a comically inflected scene of pedagogic reversion, in which the educator, Laertes, must himself be educated:

> *Oph.*   I shall the effect of this good lesson keep
> As watchman to my heart. But, good my brother,
> Do not, as some ungracious pastors do ...   (1.3.45–7)

Polonius's addresses to his children also foreground a teacherly emphasis: to his son, urbane counsel –

> *Pol.*   these few precepts in thy memory
> Look thou character.   (1.3.58–9)

– to his daughter, an exercise in education as oppression:

> *Pol.*   Marry, I will teach you: think your self a baby ...   (1.3.105)

Education is, in this context, a committal to memory of wise counsel. Polonius as tutor is clearly a humanist educator, advocating moral conduct and courtly manners. In his irresistible similarity to William Cecil, he speaks for educational principles that sit uneasily beside the laddish heroism glorified by Heywood. Burghley's unmistakably Polonial letter to his son explicitly disavows militarism in its recommendations for the education of children:

> Neither, by my consent, shall thou train them up in wars; for he that sets up his rest to live by that profession, can hardly be an honest man or a good Christian ... Besides it is a science no longer in request than use; for soldiers in peace, are like chimneys in summer. (Cecil, 1973: 80–1)

The educational context that characterises Hamlet and his peer group is rather, however, that humanist ideology that sought to balance the arts of war with the arts of peace. These anachronistic, Latin-speaking and courtly Dark Age Danes are students of Castiglione and Sir Thomas Elyot, rather than either warriors of an armigerous Viking clan, or sober-suited civil servants of a renaissance sovereign. In Ophelia's famous elegy for Hamlet's sanity, the prince appears as an apotheosis, 'our Sidney and our perfect man' (Yeats, 1933: 150) of that courtly and humanistic culture:

> *Oph.*   O, what a noble mind is here o'er-thrown!
> The courtier's, soldier's, scholar's, eye, tongue, sword ...
>
> (3.1.150–1)

The swordsmanship of such a man is of course courtly exercise rather than military exploit (see Elias, 1982: 235). It is this culture that Hamlet claims is erased from his memory. Yet he is so far from abandoning the educational principles of that culture that he can resist no opportunity of becoming himself a teacher: offering Polonius a commentary on a satire; discussing philosophy with Rosencrantz and Guildenstern; lecturing in drama to a company of players. Presented by the arrival of the actors with an opportunity to assume a pedagogic role, his first recourse is directly to '*magistra vitae*' – to classical legend, historical narrative and a memorably instructive example of ruthless tyranny:

> *1 Play*   'Anon he finds him
> Striking too short at Greeks; his antique sword,
> Rebellious to his arm, lies where it falls
> Repugnant to command ...   (2.2.462–5)

A roused vengeance sets him new a-work;
And never did the Cyclops' hammers fall
On Mars's armour, forg'd for proof eterne,
With less remorse than Pyrrhus' bleeding sword
Now falls on Priam.   (2.2.482–6)

Here, though, historical instruction, addressed to himself as well as
others, becomes ambivalent. Pyrrhus' butchery of Priam is a re-
enactment of Claudius's assassination of King Hamlet; but in addition
the 'roused vengeance' of Pyrrhus' hideous assault represents the
bloody resolution Hamlet seeks, and cannot find, in himself. For him
there is no simple object-lesson, as there was for Alexander studying
the deeds of Achilles, in the story of Troy.

The player presents a historical image of brutality and violation
(akin to the murder of Hamlet's father) rather than an image of
virtuous heroism (such as the open and public vengeance the Ghost
wishes Hamlet to execute on Claudius). That violent image should,
according to the programme of historical education urged by Nash
and Heywood, operate to inflame proper vengeance, and irritate the
exasperated spirit to noble enterprise, as the image of a murdered
father operates on Laertes. But on the more fastidious disposition of a
fully fledged Renaissance humanist like Hamlet, the example might
surely be expected to act otherwise. The image of Priam's sword
'repugnant to command', falling from a nerveless hand, chimes so
closely with Hamlet's own metaphoric confessions of weakness, his
desire to 'melt' and 'resolve' (1.2.129–30), his guilty awareness of
having 'laps'd in time and passion' (3.4.107), as to render the
historical example deeply ambivalent.

In his encounters with 'Historia', Hamlet thus finds himself, as
many critics have seen him, positioned uneasily between competing
and incompatible imperatives: here between the ambitious educational mission of humanist history as an ethical programme, and the
brutal tyranny and simplicity of '*res gestae*'. This view of Hamlet goes
right back of course to very early critical positions such as those of
Goethe ('A beautiful, pure, noble and most moral nature, without the
strength of nerve which makes the hero, sinks beneath a burden
which it can neither bear nor throw off'); Schlegel ('Hamlet has no firm
belief in himself or in anything else'), and Bradley (see Edwards, 1985:
33–6). Trying to teach the present from the past, trying to derive
wisdom from historical example, Hamlet finds himself reliving and
transmitting a nightmare. This is nowhere so clearly apparent as in

the 'closet scene' where he presents the two contrasting portraits to Gertrude:

> *Ham.*   Look here upon this picture and on this,
> The counterfeit presentment of two brothers.
> See what a grace was seated on this brow;
> Hyperion's curls; the front of Jove himself;
> An eye like Mars, to threaten and command ...
>
> This was your husband. Look you now, what follows:
> Here is your husband, like a mildew'd ear,
> Blasting his wholesome brother.   (3.4.53–7; 63–5)

Hamlet's use of the two portraits as an ethical object-lesson, designed to provoke self-examination in his mother, is also a deployment of the educational function delegated to history. He formally compares past with present examples – 'examining and comparing the times past with the present' (Puttenham, 1589, in Smith, 1904: 40) and derives from them instructive images of good and evil, as did the art of historical comparison, setting 'vertue and vice so naked before our eyes ... that it may rightly be called, an easie and profitable apprenticeship or schoole' (Beard, 1597, 1612: 'Preface'). Hamlet's attempt to teach his mother is not therefore simply a moral exhortation, but a history lesson, very much along the lines indicated by theorists like Amiot:

> [History] is a certaine rule or instruction, which by examples past, teacheth us to judge of things present, and to foresee things to come: so as we may know what to like of, and what to follow, what to mislike, and what to eschew.   (Amiot, 1579, 1928: I.xv)

Present and future conduct can thus be derived from the contemplation of comparative historical examples: 'Repent what's past', Hamlet concludes his lesson to Gertrude; 'avoid what is to come' (3.4.150).

   In the context of Hamlet's salutary history lesson, the portraits are mere teaching resources, visual aids to illustrate the points to be learned: the past seems securely captured and contained in that elegant neo-classical depiction of King Hamlet as 'Hyperion' or 'the herald Mercury'. But just as in dramatic realisation, the shadow of the absent dead, reunited by the charisma of representation with its original substance, commands disturbing, unnerving, de-stabilising powers; so the portrait was thought capable, by virtue of its strange veri-similitude, not merely of simulating, but of raising, the dead.

It was particularly the specular arts that were thought to have this necromantic power of imitation, as Alberti claimed in his *Della Pittura*:

> Painting contains a divine force which not only makes absent men present ... but moreover makes the dead seem almost alive ... Plutarch says that Cassander, one of the captains of Alexander, trembled through all his body because he saw a portrait of his King.   (Alberti, 1966: 63)

– which is echoed in Horatio's reaction to the 'form' of his former sovereign, when Bernardo make the obvious comparison: 'Looks it not like the King?'

> *Hor.*   It harrows me with fear and wonder.   (1.1.43–4)

Here in the closet-scene, out of the portrait of King Hamlet in baroque costume, steps the ghost of the old king in person, *'in his night-gown'*. The instruction he brings is quite at odds with the lesson his son has been attempting to teach:

> *Ham.*   Do you not come your tardy son to chide,
> That, laps'd in time and passion, lets go by
> Th'important acting of your dread command?   (3.4.106–8)

Despite his chivalrous concern for Gertrude, the Ghost has no interest in history as a curriculum for moral development; his concern is only with *res gestae*, or rather with *res non gestae*, deeds not performed, commandments unfulfilled, as he observes the traditional mission of masculine heroism apparently marginalised by the humanist educational programme of the Renaissance (see Ferguson, 1979: ch. 1).

For the Ghost has not succeeded, as Hamlet is the first to admit, in 'inflaming' and 'irritating' his son to deeds of manly courage. Instead the ambition to fulfil revenge has been displaced onto other activities, tangential to his fundamental purpose, though manifestly closer in spirit to that humanistic culture which produced the new historiography. 'History may be servitude, / History may be freedom' wrote T. S. Eliot (Eliot, 1963: 219). Or as Mark Leone puts it, 'A crucial aspect of the individual's sense of free will is a knowledge of his own history that does not dominate, overburden or destroy him' (Leone, 1981: xxiv, 341). All Hamlet's attempts to use 'history' for liberation find him wound all the more securely in the toils of history as an enslavement to the past. 'The future', Derrida remarks, 'can only be for ghosts' (Derrida, 1994: 37).

VI

Nuntia Vetustatis

'*Nuntia vetustatis*' was clearly understood, as a term, to carry an emphasis different from '*testis temporum*', an inflection signalled by the use of colourful translations such as 'Antiquity' (rather than simply 'old times'), and 'Herald' (rather than simply, as for instance Sir Thomas Elyot (Elyot, 1538) rendered it in his *Dictionary*, 'messenger'. Thus Richard Stanyhurst and the author of the prefatory poem in Raleigh's *History* both prefer such terms:

> History is ... the register of antiquity, the trumpet of chivalry. (Stanyhurst in Holinshed, 1577, 1965: 'Epistle Dedicatory' to 'The Description of Ireland')

> Times Witnesse, Herald of Antiquitie,
> The Light of Truth, and Life of Memorie. (Raleigh, 1614: frontispiece)

The deployment of such overtly 'antique' language clearly implied an awareness of historical anachronism. '*Testis temporum*' could suggest continuity and ease of communication between past and present: the witness is one who both saw the event in the past, and testifies to it in the present, so the verbal report or written record is tied to the event by a bond of experience. '*Nuntia vetustatis*' by contrast invokes a double discontinuity. 'Antiquity' is not just time past, it is also time different; an old time, a time radically dissimilar to the present. In these historiographical metaphors, past culture and past values are transmitted to the present by that curious antiquarian figure the herald, custodian of ancient symbols, curator of antique records, orator of archaic tongues.

Hamlet takes its audience immediately and directly back to such an 'antiquity', the time of old King Hamlet (who is depicted, we may remember, as 'the herald Mercury / New-lighted on a heaven-kissing hill' [3.4.58–9]):

> *Hor.*   Our last king,
> Whose image even but now appear'd to us,
> Was, as you know, by Fortinbras of Norway,
> Thereto prick'd on by a most emulate pride,
> Dar'd to the combat.   (1.1.80–4)

The linguistic effect of the archaic and specialised vocabulary Horatio deploys to describe this combat 'Well ratified by law, and heraldry' (1.1.87), is to isolate this historic action, and to differentiate it from the common language of the play's historical present, projecting the 'combat' back into a distinctively alien culture of the past. The two dead kings occupy an ancient chivalric society where a passage of arms has great symbolic and judicial significance. The present of the play is by such devices clearly marked off from the past: those Renaissance kings and courtiers who fight out their disputes by summit negotiation or a game of fencing, rather than by chivalric ordeal or wager of battle, look back, not across years, but across a fault-line of historical change, to that heroic and chivalric antiquity.

The old Scandinavian legend of Amled is adapted to locate the play's present, as John Turner puts it, 'somewhere in that transitional period within European feudalism where strong centralising monarchies were bringing the great aristocratic houses under control' (Holderness, Potter and Turner, 1990: 58). That historical transition produced, as Mervyn James defines it, 'a multi-cultural situation' (James, 1978: 28–32) where ethical imperatives give way to baffling moral choices. Thus in *Hamlet*, the trumpet of chivalry initiates not a decorous and ceremonial re-enactment of feudal grandeur, but a crisis of communication, precipitated by a larger crisis of signification, that finds its ultimate derivation in a crisis of cultural authority; or as Barker phrases it, 'a crisis in politically effective, symbolically sanctioned discourse, and in the possibility of the representation of sovereignty' (Barker, 1991b: 33). It was clearly possible in the early seventeenth century to regard the antique language and iconography of heraldry – although still of great importance to the early modern nobility, extensively used in court ceremonial, and its signs coveted by the rising bourgeoisie – as in large part a manifest anachronism (but see Peck, 1995). Here the present is decisively haunted, not rationally counselled, by the past. The clarion call to heroic action sounds in a vacuum, since the values and imperatives that previously underpinned such chivalric virtues have shifted, attenuated, or died away.

How then could antiquity inform and advise the present, if antiquity comprised so radically dissimilar and incommensurable a world? What could the old heroes of the past teach the new men of the Renaissance? What possibilities were there in practice, other than perilously to 'revive old factions', for such men to 'follow an antique drum'? (Eliot, 1963: 220) What, after all, *were* the lessons of history?

Recent commentators on Shakespeare's historical drama have suggested that the trumpet of chivalry, which in the middle ages called imperatively to battle, in the early seventeenth century could summon the imagination only to nostalgia:

> Driven by nostalgia, humanist historians struggled to recuperate a lost feudal past to validate a bewildering, unstable present.
> (Rackin, 1990: 104)

But as we have seen, certainly in *Hamlet*, bewildering instability is not a condition of the present to be remedied by such recuperation of the past; rather one of the effects such recuperation can have on the present. In so far as history continued to teach those same lessons of heroic example and military achievement, then its instruction would inevitably have 'bewildered' a dominant culture which had already relegated such virtues, except professionally and ceremonially, to a relatively specialised civil role. Certainly in those instances where men did seek to emulate the greatness of the past on these terms, in episodes such as the Essex rebellion, their armigerous machismo could be guaranteed to produce, if only temporarily, some measure of 'instability'.

VII

In *Hamlet* we see history setting up encounters between past and present that are as likely to produce anxiety and despair as to inflame excellent men to deeds of courage. The history of *res gestae* was at an end: the 'renaissance' sought a new historiography. It is now generally acknowledged that such a historiography was in process of development. A materialist approach to physical evidence, and a secular conception of historical causes, were ushering in new perspectives on the past. Written records were subjected by philology to increasingly searching critical inquiry. Physical remains were examined for the story they had to tell about the past. Providential manipulation ceased to provide a convincing explanation of the causes of events. Some historians began to perceive the history of nations as historical geography rather than dynastic succession. Legal historians began to understand the nature of feudalism.

Together these new approaches precipitated that critical awareness of anachronism, of the past as a foreign country, that partially helped to provide the early modern period with its contradictory 'modern' consciousness of enlightenment and fear, liberation and disorientation, 'confidence and anxiety' (Lowenthal, 1985: 82) – birth was felt as pain of separation as well as *'vita nuova'*; or as Perry Anderson puts it, 'the Renaissance discovered itself with a new, intense consciousness of rupture and loss' (Anderson, 1974: 148). 'Renaissance', Derrida pertinently asks, 'or *revenance*?' (Derrida, 1994: 36). For if the past was not a nightmare burden, then the present could grow beyond it to a progressive future. But by corollary the present must from certain perspectives have seemed historically adrift, loose from its moorings, unable to emulate or recapture the past:

> Each inheritance demands to be revered and rejected ... Any effort to balance the past's benefits and burdens implies some awareness that we need to cherish the past and also need to get rid of it ... If we follow admired exemplars we can never hope to resemble them; if we deny our precursors' greatness we cannot match their accomplishments.   (Lowenthal, 1985: 74)

Or in Hamlet's own words:

> What a piece of work is a man! ... And yet to me, what is this quintessence of dust?   (2.2.304–6)

Shakespeare's 'historical' drama stands at a critical point of transition in that long and complex process that problematised and alienated the past (Holderness, Potter and Turner, 1987: 16–19). These plays enact a process during which a sense of the past as close and familiar – immediately legible from a continuous record, reliably and reassuringly intelligible as the unfolding of providence – mutated into a consciousness of the past as distant, remote, alien; as ambiguous evidence requiring critical examination, as a tunnel to be explored, a burial site to be excavated — or a corpse to be exhumed (see Lowenthal, 1985: 84–5; Greene, 1982: 92).

VIII

If *Hamlet* begins with a risen Ghost who powerfully reaffirms the sovereignty of dynastic history, and seeks to initiate a continuation or revival of *res gestae*, its penultimate action focuses on history as archaeology, a literal unearthing of the past. The gravedigger's irreverent exhumations historicise the unhistorical, and subject to satirical examination the pretensions of those who dominate history:

> There is no ancient gentlemen but gard'ners, ditchers and grave-makers; they hold up Adam's profession.   (5.1.30–1)

Adam appears here in double guise, as the first gentleman 'that ever bore arms' (5.1.33), grand parent of the escutcheoned and armigerous nobility; but also as that 'Goodman Delver' (5.1.14) later to be celebrated by the Levellers and Diggers, the natural man whose 'arms' were only instruments for holding a spade. Dynastic and demotic historical traditions are thus thrown into conflict.

In this process of excavation, death is the great leveller, reducing cultural privilege and social priority to a common denominator of disintegration. The 'fine revolution' (5.1.88) which brings all human beings to the same end, all property to the same 'quintessence of dust', is linked in Hamlet's earthy satire to a process of levelling in society as a whole: 'the age is grown so picked that the toe of the peasant comes so near the heel of the courtier' (5.1.135–6). Hamlet glimpses a dehistoricised modern landscape in which social mobility has produced a flattening of distinctions that imitates the remorseless and indiscriminate homogenising of death itself.

The standard great heroes of history are also present in this discourse; not glorified as they are in Nash and Heywood, but reduced to the lowest common denominator of mortality. The servant Yorick lies in the same earth as his royal master King Hamlet. In the grave kings and clowns are mingled physically, as they were, to Sir Philip Sidney's aristocratic distaste ('Their plays be neither right tragedies nor right comedies, mingling kings and clowns' — [Sidney, 1595, 1966: 67]) mingled dramatically on the Elizabethan popular stage. Alexander the Great and Julius Caesar come to the same 'base uses' as the craftsman, the shepherd, the sailor.

Thus, in an imaginative rather than an intellectual way, in metaphor rather than theory, the historical consciousness of the renaissance instinctively sought a connection between that forward-looking historical method – in a broad sense, archaeology – that operates by unearthing relics, excavating the past to discover its physical evidence; and the tantalising possibility of a history that is no longer structured by aristocratic genealogy, but rather shaped by the lives of those forgotten men and women, hitherto dropped into the oubliettes of history, whose lives, closer to the soil, humble or humiliated, prepare them better for inhumation. The vertical lines of mediaeval historiography, structured by divine will and aristocratic genealogy, are seen giving way to the horizontal lines of a recog-nisably modern historiography, where all are levelled into a common destiny. The secrets of the past were to be sought, not by looking upwards towards gods or kings, but downwards towards the earth that held so many of history's secrets.

Hamlet, soon to participate in that democracy of death, is closely linked with this philosophy of history not only in terms of his facility for mingling with clowns and adapting their language and perspec-tive. For he too is doomed, as they are, to unhistoricity. He represents a hiatus in the continuum of dynastic succession. He was 'likely', Fortinbras affirms, had he been 'put on', to have 'prov'd most royal'. But he is not 'put on' (5.2.389–90). He remains a mere subject of King Claudius, with no place of his own in the annals of sovereignty. His story is, at the end of the play, although dramatised to completion, in some profound sense yet to be narrated, yet to become 'history'.

4

Richard III

And there went out another horse that was red: and power
was given to him that sat thereon to take peace from the
earth, and that they should kill one another: and there was
given unto him a great sword.

Revelation, VI.4

I

In *Henry VI, Part Three*, after the Battle of Wakefield in which the
Duke of York is killed, Edward and Richard Plantagenet share
the vision of a trinity of suns:

Rich.   See how the morning opes her golden gates
And takes her farewell of the glorious sun.
How well resembles it the prime of youth,
Trimm'd like a younker prancing to his love!
Edw.   Dazzle mine eyes, or do I see three suns?
Rich.   Three glorious suns, each one a perfect sun;
Not separated with the racking clouds,
But sever'd in a pale clear-shining sky.
See, see! they join, embrace, and seem to kiss,
As if they vow'd some league inviolable.
Now are they but one lamp, one light, one sun.
In this the heaven figures some event.
Edw.   'Tis wondrous strange, the like yet never heard of.
I think it cites us, brother, to the field,
That we, the sons of brave Plantagenet,
Each one already blazing by our meeds,
Should notwithstanding join our lights together
And overshine the earth, as this the world.   (*HVI3*, 2.1.21–38)

After the killing, or martyrdom, of York, with its echoes of the
Crucifixion (he is crowned with a paper crown, and given a napkin to

wipe his face — *HVI3*, 1.4) the Plantagenet destiny falls naturally to York's three sons, Edward, George and Richard. They of course are the three 'suns' who appear and unify in a vision of political ascendancy which, by its theological suggestion of some new indivisible Trinity, naturalises and endorses the prospect of Plantagenet league and power. In this metaphoric context the sun is both a symbol of majesty as a goal, the supreme power by which the Plantagenets aspire to 'overshine the earth'; and an emblem (historically borne as a chivalric badge on Edward's shield) of their own natural force and warlike energy, already well attested by their fearsome military reputation ('blazing by our meeds'). Thus when Edward sets his target as the recovery of his father's dukedom, Richard quickly corrects his insufficiently ambitious brother, the only appropriate objective of their heroic destiny being the crown itself, an unbearable brightness that none but the the irrepressibly ambitious are brave enough to look upon:

> *Rich.*   Nay, if thou be that princely eagle's bird,
> Show thy descent by gazing 'gainst the sun:
> For chair and dukedom, throne and kingdom, say ...
> (*HVI3*, 2.1.91–3)

By the end of that play Edward is on the throne, as Edward IV: but Richard is already dissociating himself from his brother's triumph, muttering in witty and malevolent asides his sense of ambition frustrated and personal destiny unachieved, already in anticipation of a subsequent historical opportunity (perhaps even of an expected dramatic revival) beginning to devise and delineate an alternative political agenda (*HVI3*, 5.7).

At the beginning of *Richard III*, the 'sun of York' is firmly established as the royal solar power that now manifestly 'overshines the earth':

> *Glo.*   Now is the winter of our discontent
> Made glorious summer by this sun of York;
> And all the clouds that lour'd upon our house
> In the deep bosom of the ocean buried.   (*RIII*, 1.1.1–4)

The bright sunlight of historical success shines over a scene of peace, but it is a peace constituted and defined by the war out of which it has been established:

Now are our brows bound with victorious wreaths;
Our bruised arms hung up for monuments;
Our stern alarums changed to merry meetings,
Our dreadful marches to delightful measures.
Grim-visag'd war hath smooth'd his wrinkled front,
And now, instead of mounting barbed steeds
To fright the souls of fearful adversaries,
He capers nimbly in a lady's chamber
To the lascivious pleasing of a lute.   (1.1.4–13)

Thus it is the 'monuments' of battles won, and of heroic feats accomplished (as summarised by Edward – 'What valiant foemen, like to autumn's corn / Have we mow'd down' – at the end of *Henry VI, Part Three* [5.7.3–4]) that both facilitate and stabilise an essentially relative and temporary peace.

Richard's famous opening soliloquy is an elegy for the loss of a heroic past, a warrior nostalgia that laments the passing of war, and expresses a witty and scathing contempt for the boredom and triviality of peace. But war and peace are, in Richard's perception, actually much more closely, even dialectically interrelated, the one definable only in terms of the other's momentary absence. Power is achieved, and maintained, by military strength and success: hence the characteristic activities of peace, dancing ('capers nimbly') and music ('pleasing of a lute'), directly echo their martial counterparts of riding 'barbed steeds', and the military rhythms of the 'dreadful march'. In defining his own relation to his time, Richard is not simply expressing distaste for, or lack of sympathy with, peacetime pursuits ('I in this weak piping time of peace / Have no delight'), but rather positively preferring to occupy that hinterland of war which is always peace's counterpart and shadow.

Richard sees himself, and roots his self-consciousness, in the externalised image of his own shadow, sharply adumbrated by the pervasive sunlight of Plantagenet ascendancy:

But I – that am not shap'd for sportive tricks,
Nor made to court an amorous looking-glass ...

Why, I, in this weak piping time of peace,
Have no delight to pass away the time,
Unless to spy my shadow in the sun
And descant on mine own deformity.   (1.1.14–15, 24–7)

On the face of it, Richard identifies his being in entirely negative terms, shadow being the opposite of substance, and his deformed shape as alien to the pleasures of the court, as it is at home on the field of battle. But in the distinction between the 'amorous looking-glass' and the 'shadow in the sun' we find a contrast of two modes of reflection: on the one hand the 'flattering glass' of a narcissistic gaze, that endorses peacetime vanity and complacency; and on the other the shadow, produced by interposing a body between the source of light and the silhouetted image. The one image presupposes a self-absorbed compliance with superficial representation (the glass is 'amorous' because it flatters the appearance, seeming to love it, as well as inviting the glance of the 'amorous' onlooker's vanity); the other is achieved by the force of a will prepared to block the light, to stand out against and resist the otherwise universal mood of demilitarised celebration. The image in the looking-glass improves on the original, tells each viewer that he or she is the fairest in the land; while the silhouette enhances deformity, adding a further dimension of grotesqueness to an already idiosyncratically twisted physical and psychological shape.

Prevented therefore, by the fundamental pathological alienation adumbrated in this shadow-image, from participation in the sunlit world of courtly pleasures, Richard describes his range of options for the future as limited to two categories of being — civilian or warrior, courtier or soldier, lover or villain:

> And therefore, since I cannot prove a lover
> To entertain these fair well-spoken days,
> I am determined to prove a villain
> And hate the idle pleasures of these days.   (1.1.26–9)

The word 'determined' captures perfectly the wilfully paradoxical nature of Richard's self-definition, which turns precisely on the relation between historical causation (the modern sense of 'determined', here of course derived from the early modern legal sense of 'limited', 'set by cause') and voluntaristic 'self-fashioning', personal resolution, the freedom to determine one's own destiny. Within a more simplistic commonsense semantics, Richard would be either 'determined to be a villain' by the inevitable influence of his historical destiny; or would be seen here in the act of 'determining' ('resolving', 'deciding') that such would be his adopted historical role. The paradox lies of course at the heart of historiographical controversy, as it lies at the heart of

Christian theology (as in Milton's conundrum, 'Fixt Fate, free will, foreknowledge absolute' [Milton, 1674, 1961, Bk. II, l. 560, p. 215]) but is also central to the theory of drama: How is a character 'built'? From what sources, psychological and social, cultural and dramatic, does action flow? How do we explain, from the complex mingling of personal motivation and environmental pressure, the meaning of 'character'? Is an actor a free agent, capable of guiding his own destiny, or a mere function of dramatic dénouement, trapped within the plot-lines of his constructed theatrical world?

II

A further dimension is added to these paradoxes by the pervasive contrast between imprisonment and liberty, bondage and freedom; which in turn delivers a further level of conflict in the opposition of loquacity and speechlessness, articulacy and silence. Richard refers to himself as 'curtail'd', inhibited by that luckless combination of heredity and environment that has stranded a deformed and violent soldier in an oppressive time of tranquil normality, and prevented from speaking openly, as when the guard Brakenbury forbids him 'private conference' (1.1.86) with his brother. But it is of course his brother Clarence who, ostensibly for his own 'safety' (1.1.44), is committed to imprisonment in the Tower, just as Lord Hastings, by an equally arbitrary cause, is from the same prison temporarily 'delivered' (1.1.69). Richard promises to 'deliver', to 'enfranchise' (1.1.110) Clarence from the 'imprisonment' he himself has engineered; and welcomes the 'new-delivered Hastings' (1.1.121) (whom he is later to have executed) to the 'open air' (1.1.124) of 'liberty' (1.1.77). Yet he speaks of his own condition as one of virtual imprisonment or subjugation, never 'safe', one of Queen Elizabeth's 'abjects' (1.1.106); and accepts Hastings' representation of him as a royal eagle 'mew'd' (1.1.132), while common 'kites and buzzards' (1.1.133), the queen's kinsmen, 'prey at liberty'. Even more irksome than the ennoblement of such parvenus is the influence of the queen and the king's mistress, Jane Shore, who appear in Richard's fantasy as a potent matriarchy: 'Why, this it is', he tells Clarence, 'when men are rul'd by women' (1.1.62). Similarly, although one of the most loquacious of historical characters, Richard complains of an irksome restriction on freedom of speech: the king's wife and mistress, 'mighty gossips in our monarchy' (1.1.82), monopolise the power of open expression, while he, notwithstanding his rank and status, purports to be silenced by fear. It is only in soliloquy that this historical actor, exercising both the wide freedom of the stage, and the power of unimpeded eloquence, explains the connection between others' confinement and his liberty, his own verbosity and the secrecy of his motives:

> God take King Edward to his mercy,
> And leave the world for me to bustle in!   (1.1.151–2)

He will marry Anne:

> not all so much for love
> As for another secret close intent ...   (1.1.157–8)

His silence is not enforced, but voluntary and deliberate; his free expression works to obscure, not clarify, meaning. Similarly his claim to be confined is designed to enable and facilitate a supreme liberty of action ('the world ... to bustle in'), and his apparent offers to 'enfranchise' others are rather designed to imprison them in a web of his own devising ('another secret close intent'). The condition of his freedom is others' imprisonment; the secret of his eloquence, others' silence. It is only towards the play's close that both the voices he has sought to still, and the ghosts of those dead he has endeavoured to silence, return to fill his ears and haunt his dreams.

III

Richard of Gloucester seems, impossibly, well informed of all these theoretical debates, and well ahead of all the interpretative strategies by means of which we seek to define and explain him. His image of his own shadow defines him as an effect of historical causation, the shadow cast athwart his twisted body by the brilliant illumination of his brother's accession to the throne. But of course, in the historical drama, everything is made out of nothing; the actor himself is but a 'walking shadow' (*Macbeth*, 5.5.24); and shadow is the only basis of substance, the absence of real history that alone facilitates its theatrical representation, the presence of history in the artifice of dramatic realisation. As well as being the passive symptom of historical causation, Richard's shadow is also the dark ambiguous fertility of the role, a 'walking shadow', that open space in which the actor has substantial liberty to invent the historical character. Thus the decision to 'prove a villain' is as much a gesture of self-casting, the choice of a character, as it is a resigned submission to historical determinism; and an indication that Richard, the historical character, represented via the dramatic role, is presented as self-consciously aware of his own actorly status: he is an actor within the medium of a historical narrative, since he is conscious that his 'character' can be enacted only by the presence of such an actor in concrete theatrical realisation.

Aware then of these extra-textual conditions of his own possibility, Richard displays an acute consciousness of history's 'shadow', of that marginal space where history is made not only by deaths and accessions, battles and executions, but also by the potency of the shadow-world, the dimension of dreams and fantasies, self-fulfilling prophecies and enabling fictions:

> *Glo.*   Plots have I laid, inductions dangerous,
> By drunken prophecies, libels, and dreams ...   (1.1.32–3)

Such 'dreams' are the means by which history is guided and directed: in Richard's consciousness they are both ancillary to, and constitutive of, very precise plans of historical sequence and succession, formed on the basis of who exactly will die before and after whom:

> He [Edward] cannot live, I hope, and must not die
> Till George be pack'd with posthorse up to heaven   (1.1.145–6)

The plot against Clarence is accomplished with great simplicity: scathing of the king's fear and gullibility, revelling in his own superior cleverness and cunning, Richard explains that Clarence has been committed to the Tower because his name begins with G:

> This day should Clarence closely be mew'd up –
> About a prophecy which says that G
> Of Edward's heirs the murderer shall be.   (1.1.38–40)

Just as his rhyming jingle mimics the rhythms of 'drunken proph-ecies', so Richard jokes with Clarence about the absurdity of the charge he himself has fabricated:

> *Clar.*   His majesty ... hath appointed
> This conduct to convey me to th' Tower.

Glo.   Upon what cause?
Clar.   Because my name is George.
Glo.   Alack, my lord, that fault is none of yours:
He should, for that, commit your godfathers.   (1.1.43–8)

Richard's humour derives from his self-confident mastery of the situation, his sense of superiority to his foolish and trusting brothers; and from a kind of creative zest at his own capacity to initiate and manage change, using as his weapons and instruments the armoury of that shadow-world of dream and prophecy of which he himself, for the moment supreme in his power over life and death, has no apprehension.

In the account of Clarence's dream that precedes and foreshadows his murder, however, this shadowland becomes, as it later becomes for Richard, terrifyingly real.

Clar.   O Lord, methought what pain it was to drown,
What dreadful noise of waters in mine ears,
What sights of ugly death within mine eyes!
Methoughts I saw a thousand fearful wrecks,
A thousand men that fishes gnaw'd upon,
Wedges of gold, great anchors, heaps of pearl,
Inestimable stones, unvalued jewels,
All scatt'red in the bottom of the sea;
Some lay in dead men's skulls, and in those holes
Where eyes did once inhabit there were crept,
As 'twere in scorn of eyes, reflecting gems,
That woo'd the slimy bottom of the deep
And mock'd the dead bones that lay scatt'red by.   (1.4.21–33)

The dream is a premonition both of death, and of the manner of the dreamer's murder by violent immersion: but it is also a vision of history.

Richard had, in the play's opening scene, jestingly hinted at the king's intention as Clarence's rebaptism, thus removing his name, its unfortunate initial letter, and with it his apparent danger to the crown. If Richard had studied St Paul as frequently as he swears by his name, he would naturally be familiar with the theological paradox explicated in the Epistle to the Romans, that 'so many of us as were baptized into Jesus Christ were baptized into his death' (VI.3). Grotesquely, Clarence *is* baptised, but into death, not life; in wine, not water. Nonetheless the violent ceremony enacted by his killers, as anticipated in the dream, inducts him into a new dimension, within which his powers of envisioning both past and future become preternaturally intensified. In the dream, the occasion of his drowning is clearly set in a historical context: he and Richard are leaving England for France, looking back towards their native shore, and recalling incidents in the Wars of the Roses:

> thence we look'd toward England,
> And cited up a thousand heavy times,
> During the wars of York and Lancaster,
> That had befall'n us. (1.4.13–16)

It is from the shores of England, in memory reoccupied by scenes of civil war, that Clarence embarks on his last long voyage; and when knocked overboard by his brother, the protagonist who is determined to protract and perpetuate those wars, the sea he falls into is as much the past as it is the future. It is that same 'ooze and bottom of the sea' described by Canterbury in *Henry V* as littered with 'sunken wreck and sumless treasuries' (*HV*, 1.2.165); an underworld in which the drowned dead lie 'dumb and deep' (Thomas, 1952, 1966: 80), their scattered bones mingling with the lost magnificence of their foundered riches. There also Clarence sees graphic examples of simulated immortality, empty skulls from within which glowing jewels shed the 'uneffectual fire' (*Hamlet*, 1.5.190) of an unnatural and lifelike light.

This dream of drowning into history is merely preparatory to Clarence's subsequent vision of Hell, in which the individual nightmare is formalised into a classical visit to the underworld, clearly signalled by overt literary reference. Clarence dreams of crossing 'the melancholy flood' in the company of 'that sour ferryman *that poets write of*', and thereby reaching 'the kingdom of perpetual night' (1.4.45–7):

> The first that there did greet my stranger soul
> Was my great father-in-law, renowned Warwick,
> Who spake aloud 'What scourge for perjury
> Can this dark monarchy afford false Clarence?'
> And so he vanish'd. Then came wand'ring by
> A shadow like an angel, with bright hair
> Dabbled in blood, and he shriek'd out aloud

'Clarence is come — false, fleeting, perjur'd Clarence,
That stabb'd me in the field by Tewksbury.
Seize on him, Furies, take him to your torment!'
With that, methoughts, a legion of foul fiends
Environ'd me, and howled in mine ears
Such hideous cries that, with the very noise,
I trembling wak'd, and for a season after
Could not believe but that I was in hell,
Such terrible impression made my dream.   (1.4.48—64)

The characters of history — Warwick, and the young Prince of
Wales — here arise, as ghosts from the past, to reproach the living or
lament their own loss, as do the dead in Homer and Virgil, but also in
exactly the way that the ghosts of Richard's victims — including of
course Clarence's own shade — will rise to reproach and curse Richard
on the night before Bosworth. Reanimated shades from the past are
resurrected to play a shadowy role in a drama of the present. But that
drama of the present is also a drama of the past, and the 'living'
characters — such as poor Clarence, here stranded in a fearful present,
and wholly absorbed into the otherworlds of a grim past and a
terrifying future — are no less artificially animated 'shadows' than the
ghosts who, when embodied in living actors, 'appear' (in both
the supernatural and the theatrical senses) on stage before them.
In Richard's parallel dream at the end of the play, Clarence, the
shadow of a historical character, will appear on stage as a revenant,
no less embodied, and no more substantial, as a ghost, than he is as a
'poor player', the theatrical 'shadow' of a long-dead figure from a
remote history.

IV

The play's first ghost, one who is also to return at the close, that of
King Henry VI, appears as a corpse: but the lifeless remains of the
murdered king prove dramatically capable of renewing historical
meaning, shaping the conflicts of the present, and adumbrating the
destiny of the future:

Anne.   Set down, set down your honourable load —
If honour may be shrouded in a hearse;
Whilst I awhile obsequiously lament

Th'untimely fall of virtuous Lancaster.
Poor key-cold figure of a holy king!
Pale ashes of the house of Lancaster!
Thou bloodless remnant of that royal blood!   (I.2.1–7)

'Honour' is not a property of the dead, safely 'shrouded in a hearse', but lies in the gift of the living, and is retained by the dead only in so far as their successors continue to ascribe such reputation to them. Since Henry's body is being taken from St Paul's to the obscurity of Chertsey, and it is clear that the Yorkist victors are unlikely to preserve the honour of his memory, such honour as he possessed must be 'shrouded in a hearse', or lost to memory altogether. The images deployed in Anne's description certainly suggest absence, emptiness, vacancy: 'pale ashes' of a burnt-out fire, the flat metallic icon of a 'key-cold figure'. The corpse is a 'bloodless remnant' of its own 'royal blood', the symbolic blood of dynastic continuity unnaturally exhausted, with the political dispossession of the Lancastrian line, in the literal blood that physically sustains human vitality, and can be shed as easily from the arteries of a king as it can be spilt from common veins. When Anne seeks to raise Henry's ghost, it is ostensibly only that he may hear the crying of her own 'lamentations', and that her mourning tears may hope to heal, in a final extreme unction, the wounds of his martyrdom:

Be it lawful that I invocate thy ghost
To hear the lamentations of poor Anne,
Wife to thy Edward, to thy slaughtered son,
Stabb'd by the self-same hand that made these wounds.
Lo, in these windows that let forth thy life
I pour the helpless balm of my poor eyes.   (1.2.8–13)

But in fact the spirit that Anne brings to life in her speech is not that of her departed father-in-law, but rather the supernaturally potent apparition of his murderer, her husband-to-be, Richard of Gloucester:

Curs'd be the hand that made these fatal holes!
Cursed the heart that had the heart to do it!
Cursed the blood that let this blood from hence!
More direful hap betide that hated wretch
That makes us wretched by the death of thee
Than I can wish to adders, spiders, toads,
Or any creeping venom'd thing that lives!

If ever he have child, abortive be it,
Prodigious, and untimely brought to light,
Whose ugly and unnatural aspect
May fright the hopeful mother at the view,
And that be heir to his unhappiness!   (1.2.14–25)

At the opening of *Henry VI Part One*, the ghost of Henry V is invoked
to chasten and rebuke a degenerate present. Here the discarded
corpse of the dead king remains firmly constituted within the role of
victim, attention being focused on his wounds, and on the absent
blood that has emanated from them. The contemplation of his death
here represents an admission of weakness, not a release of power.
By contrast the image of his murderer, extrapolated from the
evidence of the butchered corpse, grows into something of
considerable potency and substance: Richard's hand, and heart, and
blood figure in the speech as concrete elements of a powerful physical
presence. Anne's curse on Richard's unborn child, though not to be
fulfilled as prophecy, serves only to strengthen the vision of his
power, since it replicates the conditions of his own 'untimely' birth
and his congenital deformity.

Even when the corpse does begin to show those signs of revived
or simulated vitality that we can now associate with historical
resurrection, even when his wounds, like 'brave Talbot's', are seen to
be 'fresh bleeding' (Nash, 1592, 1969: 26) in dramatic representation,
it remains questionable whether the source of that activity lies in
the risen dead, or in the theatrical energy that awakens it; just as the
sources of history lie somewhere between the innate and intrinsic
meanings of the past, and the constructed artifice of historiographical
reproduction:

> *Anne.*   Behold this pattern of thy butcheries.
> O, gentlemen, see, see! Dead Henry's wounds
> Open their congeal'd mouths and bleed afresh.
> Blush, blush, thou lump of foul deformity,
> For 'tis thy presence that exhales this blood
> From cold and empty veins where no blood dwells;
> Thy deeds, inhuman and unnatural
> Provokes this deluge most unnatural.   (1.2.54–61)

That figure of heroic revival, of an irrepressible masculine energy
capable of breaking the bonds of death, that we meet continually in

these pages – the ghost of Hamlet's father bursting his shroud, the imperial ghost of Henry V, still presiding over England in *Henry VI, Part One*, 'brave Talbot' treading the boards of the Rose to bleed again in the epic celebrations of heroic drama – is here echoed, but not exemplified. In death, as in life, Henry remains the passive spectator of his own injuries, uttering a voiceless complaint through the opening 'mouths' of his wounds, the newly circulating blood serving only to decoagulate his clotted scars, not to reanimate his 'bloodless' corpse. The true cause of the mystery lies therefore not in any miracle of historical resurrection, but in Richard's power to generate activity and facilitate change, his capacity to make things happen around him: "tis thy presence that exhales this blood' (1.2.58) (a line whose rhythm prefigures the Chorus in *Henry V* – 'For 'tis your thoughts that now must deck our kings' [*HV*, 'Prologue', 28]). In the old superstition, the physical 'presence' of the victim's assassin reawakens wounds which disclose the murderer's guilt, blood drawn again in a mystical repetition of the crime. On that level, it is the corpse that utters truth, brings meaning to light; but here also Richard's theatrical 'presence' is the power that provokes the action, as indicated clearly by the transitive verb 'exhales'. Finally the incident exemplifes the potency of the historical drama to secure, from its raw material of insubstantial shadows, a convincing 'presence' capable of renewing absent time, resurrecting lost ages, summoning up 'remembrance of things past'.

Indeed it is partly by recalling the past, resurrecting its vanished characters and representing their history, that Richard accomplishes his objective. Hitherto his masculinity has been so purely preserved that he has never before wept, he tells Anne; his eyes 'have never shed remorseful tear':

No, when my father York and Edward wept
To hear the piteous moan that Rutland made
When black-fac'd Clifford shook his sword at him . . .   (1.2.156–8)

To validate his own unassailable masculinity, he naturally cites examples from recent history, outstanding examples of heroic military greatness such as his own father, York, and Anne Neville's father, Warwick. Unusually, but appositely, the *exempla* they provide at this point are not ones of heroic masculinity, but rather ones of womanly pity and compassion. York is described as weeping for the death of a child, Richard's own younger brother the Earl of Rutland, who was killed by Clifford (see *HVI3*, 1.3 — York and Edward were not of course dramatically present at Rutland's killing, nor was Edward there with his father to 'hear' the story dramatised by Margaret — *HVI3*, 1.4). Given such motions of natural compassion in such legendary heroes, it is all the more remarkable that Richard remains unmoved, that his 'manly eyes did scorn an humble tear'.

Since Richard describes York's reaction to the death of Rutland, he is actually at this point himself acting as a historian, narrating the personal response of an important witness to a key incident of what has already become history; drawing from the past an instructive example to demonstrate some issue of the present, and to guide some direction of the future. The characteristically multilayered narrative of historiography then deepens even further, as Richard describes how Warwick narrated the story of an event he himself had only heard, the killing of York:

> Nor when thy warlike father, like a child,
> Told the sad story of my father's death,
> And twenty times made pause to sob and weep
> That all the standers-by had wet their cheeks
> Like trees bedash'd with rain ...   (1.2.159–63)

Again, the renarration does not match the dramatic representation of these events in *Henry VI, Part Three*, where Warwick is busily dismissive of 'news' he had heard some considerable time before it reaches York's sons — 'Ten days ago I drown'd these news in tears' (*HVI3*, 2.1.104). But those discrepancies, typical enough of historical report, serve only to emphasise the paradoxical effect in historical narrative of distancing and immediacy. This *is* history, a narrative that has reached the present from various different sources and through a process of incremental repetition. But it becomes 'History' by virtue of its vivid dramatisation, in compelling and effective language, of past events.

The persuasive force of this particular recuperation of history lies in its juxtaposition of polarised opposites — strength and weakness, violence and pity, male and female. The image of tough, resilient warriors succumbing to 'unmanly' grief, stained with weeping like the erect and noble trees 'bedash'd with rain', highlights and intensifies the miraculous accession of emotion in Richard himself, a man so hardened he could remain unmoved by the tale of his own little brother's murder. Finally Richard draws his dizzying dance of opposites to its logical conclusion, yielding his own power, through its symbol the sword, to the woman, while he himself strips his breast in a gesture of sexual surrender.

> If thy revengeful heart cannot forgive,
> Lo here I lend thee this sharp-pointed sword;
> Which if thou please to hide in this true breast
> And let the soul forth that adoreth thee,
> I lay it naked to the deadly stroke,
> And humbly beg the death upon my knee.   (1.2.173–8)

What he hands over to the woman is both heroic force and sexual charisma: he kneels in military surrender as well as erotic supplication. The whole sequence, with its overt references to the persuasive power of historical recuperation, identifies Richard's territory as an extreme form of 'postmodern' historiography, which seeks the past only to confirm and illuminate its own pre-selected contemporary meanings.

V

In keeping with this voluntaristic historiography, Richard's final soliloquy, after the successful seduction of Anne is completed, again lays bare the wholly theatrical nature of the reality he constructs around himself:

> Was ever woman in this humour woo'd?
> Was ever woman in this humour won?
> I'll have her; but I will not keep her long.
> What! I that kill'd her husband and his father –
> To take her in her heart's extremest hate,
> With curses in her mouth, tears in her eyes,
> The bleeding witness of her hatred by;
> Having God, her conscience, and these bars against me,
> And I no friends to back my suit at all
> But the plain devil and dissembling looks,
> And yet to win her, all the world to nothing!   (1.2.227–37)

The 'winning' of Anne is simultaneously a *coup-de-théâtre*, a triumph of 'dissembling', and an epic achievement of heroic masculinity, since

the traces of Richard's history of violent killing, far from being
concealed or denied, are manifestly foregrounded in the medium
of his courtship. The 'bleeding witness of her hatred' – time's
witness – the corpse of Henry VI, both testifies to Richard's mur-
derous criminality, and provides the evidential basis for Anne's hatred
of him. Nonetheless he has succeeded, using the weapons of his
violent masculinity, in accomplishing what reads more like a rape –
'to take her in her heart's extremest hate' – than a courtship or
seduction. On the basis of this victory, Richard finds his own
historical being transformed by the success with which he has both
appropriated the past, and manipulated the present:

> Hath she forgot already that brave prince,
> Edward, her lord, whom I, some three months since,
> Stabb'd in my angry mood at Tewksbury?
> A sweeter and a lovelier gentleman –
> Fram'd in the prodigality of nature,
> Young, valiant, wise, and, no doubt, right royal –
> The spacious world cannot again afford;
> And will she yet abase her eyes on me,
> That cropp'd the golden prime of this sweet prince
> And made her widow to a woeful bed?   (1.2.239–48)

The opposition between Richard (the 'plain devil', 1.2.236), and
Edward, the fruit of nature's bounty ('Fram'd in the prodigality of
nature' [1.2.243]) poses the question in conventional terms of good
and evil, angelic and satanic, heaven and hell. Having been favoured
with so 'sweet' and 'lovely' a husband, what could explain Anne's
persuasion to 'abase her eyes' on his unnatural counterpart, other than
some masterly feat of diabolical deception? But the process is more
complex: for as the grim reaper who has 'cropp'd the golden prime' of
her sweet prince, Richard has mysteriously absorbed the qualities
of his victim, become himself, to all intents and purposes, 'sweet' and
'lovely', 'valiant, wise, and, no doubt, right royal'. Violence has
turned to sweetness, pain to pleasure; the ugly, unnatural and degenerate to the 'golden prime' of nature's fertile prodigality. Thus having
transformed the perception of himself, established an alternative
being in the eyes of another, Richard, as actor, finds himself utterly
transformed:

> I do mistake my person all this while.
> Upon my life, she finds, although I cannot,

Myself to be a marv'llous proper man.
I'll be at charges for a looking-glass,
And entertain a score or two of tailors
To study fashions to adorn my body,
Since I am crept in favour with myself,
I will maintain it with some little cost.
But first I'll turn yon fellow in his grave,
And then return lamenting to my love.
Shine out, fair sun, till I have bought a glass,
That I may see my shadow as I pass.   (1.2.252–63)

Though Richard began his play by speaking of historical determinism, here he voices a theory of extreme voluntarism, a belief in the
absolute power of the will to fashion both itself and its historical
context. Richard has mistaken his person in believing it to be the product of heredity and environment, twisted to deformity by the past,
and relegated to marginality by the present. In fact, since he is, on
objective evidence, the 'marvellous proper man' he has planted in
Anne's perception, that must needs also constitute his historical
identity; and his casual and disrespectful attitude towards the historical past – 'I'll turn yon fellow in his grave' (1.2.260) – is of a piece
with that virtually postmodern sense of unanchored liberty. In a
fantasy that links the traditional power of the aristocracy both with
the new economic power of the Elizabethan bourgeoisie, and with the
conspicuous consumption and ostentatious luxury of those flashily
attired 'upstart crow[s]' (Greene [1592], in Greenblatt, 1997: 3321),
the actors of the theatre, Richard will acquire, by purchase, the
properties that will, in turn, authenticate his new-found role: personal
services, fashionable clothes, and particularly the flattering glass that
can be guaranteed to reflect back to him his transformed physical
shape. The bright sunlight now throws a different shadow, and
Richard can make that shadow assume the reality of substance. What
do we see in the 'glass' of history, after all, but a 'shadow'?

VI

Discussion of the play's dramatic texture has demonstrated that issues
of historiography are in continual play, colouring both surface
narrative and deeper structural levels. These issues – which centre
around the paradox of history as a real finite past, and a constructed

contemporary narrative – are in this play linked with moral and psychological questions about freedom of the will against the pressures of the past; with theatrical problems concerning the place of character and motive within a relatively fixed dramatic framework; and finally with philosophical, even religious paradoxes about reality and representation, which interrogate the 'substance' of history, of drama, of the human world, in the dark light of the 'shadows' – language, the actor, transient mortality – through which the various manifestations of 'substance' – history, the theatre, human life – are always perceived and apprehended.

What we would probably consider such 'theoretical' issues are also openly and self-consciously rehearsed at many points in the play. Consider for instance the way in which an anonymous 'scrivener' (scribe) is introduced onto the stage purely for the purpose of demonstrating the Orwellian capacity of power, ruthlessly held and deployed, to manipulate the past.

> *Scriv.* Here is the indictment of the good Lord Hastings;
> Which in a set hand fairly is engross'd,
> That it may be to-day read o'er in Paul's.
> And mark how well the sequel hangs together:
> Eleven hours I have spent to write it over,
> For yesternight by Catesby was it sent me;
> The precedent was full as long a-doing;
> And yet within these five hours Hastings liv'd,
> Untainted, unexamin'd, free, at liberty.
> Here's a good world the while! Why who is so gross
> That cannot see this palpable device?
> Yet who so bold but says he sees it not?
> Bad is the world; and all will come to naught,
> When such ill dealing must be seen in thought. (3.6. 1–14)

The manipulation and fixing of legal documentation is manifestly an attempt to rig the verdict of history, to put in place a phoney record from which a particular interpretation of the past can then be drawn. The role of the scrivener, the writer and record-keeper, in this process is obviously critical, since it is his laborious application that composes the record into a certain predetermined shape. The trick, he admits, is a 'palpable device', easily detectable by anyone who is not utterly stupid. But what holds the imposture in place is fear, a conspiracy of silence among those who, though fully aware of the deception, rightly fear reprisal from the historical document's powerful 'authors'. Here then the play takes time to reveal the processes and instruments by means of which history is fashioned by the historical agent's free-wheeling and voluntaristic, ruthlessly unscrupulous manipulation of the past.

In an earlier scene a digressive discussion of key theoretical issues in historiography is focused on the pervasive symbolic mass of the Tower of London. Throughout this play and others the Tower retains its repertory of significations – antiquity, defensive security, arbitrary imprisonment, and clandestine murder. In an exchange between the young Edward, Prince of Wales and heir to the throne, and the governing magnates Gloucester and Buckingham, the initial symbolic value of the Tower is not simply endorsed or restated, but theoretically interrogated:

> *Prince.*   I do not like the Tower, of any place.
> Did Julius Caesar build that place, my lord?
> *Glos.*   He did, my gracious lord, begin that place,
> Which, since, succeeding ages have re-edified.
> *Prince.*   Is it upon record, or else reported
> Successively from age to age, he built it?
> *Buck.*   Upon record, my gracious lord.
> *Prince.*   But say, my lord, it were not regist'red,
> Methinks the truth should live from age to age,
> As 'twere retail'd to all posterity,
> Even to the general all-ending day ...
>
> That Julius Caesar was a famous man;
> With what his valour did enrich his wit,
> His wit set down to make his valour live.
> Death makes no conquest of this conqueror;
> For now he lives in fame, though not in life.   (3.1.68–78, 84–8)

The young prince is sufficiently expert in historical study to be able to differentiate between oral and documentary history, between historical interpretations grounded in physical record, and those perpetuated by tradition. The Prince's argument is that historical knowledge ought to be, literally, transhistorical, declared as manifest and open truth, like religious revelation; surviving unaltered through the ages, and communicated consistently to successive generations; as incontrovertible during its passage through history as it will be when all human truth comes under judgement at the 'general all-ending day'.

This theory of history is of course quite unacceptable to Richard, who depends precisely on 'History's' attachment to those documentary and physical records he can adjust and manipulate for his own ends, such as the indictment of Lord Hastings. Ironically the figure chosen to exemplify this transhistorical history is a key representative of the classical heroic tradition from which Richard also claims descent, Julius Caesar. Caesar's greatness is not tied to physical existence, any more than his reputation for heroism and intelligence ('valour' and 'wit') depends upon reliable historical records. 'Death makes no conquest of this conqueror' in a double sense: Caesar is still, as a historical character, very much alive, continually resurrected he 'yet lives'; but he 'lives in fame' — the incontrovertible purity of his honour survives the detraction and manipulation of historical reconstruction.

Richard comments on this exposition with a dismissive aside, that is then corrected to an expression of apparent agreement. The two juxtaposed statements, the covert and the deceptive, together link the polarised terms of this controversy:

> Glo. [*Aside*] So wise so young, they say, do never live long.
> Prince. What say you, uncle?
> Glo. I say, without characters, fame lives long.
> [*Aside*] Thus, like the formal vice, Iniquity,
> I moralize two meanings in one word.   (3.1.79–83)

The 'one' word in question is of course 'long', the adjective of duration, the fundamental dimension of history. 'Fame', Richard agrees, can live long 'without characters': historical reputation is not dependent on documentary inscription or physical record. But the initial semi-humorous aside poses the opposite view: being too smart for his own good, the young prince's life must be terminated, if only to confound his own theory. At the same time Richard voices a supreme confidence in his capacity to protect his own actions from exposure to the searchlight of 'History': in the secretive ambiguity of the aside, he reiterates his faith in dissimulation, in the indeterminacy made possible by semantic fertility, in his ability to 'moralize two meanings in one word'.

Richard is confident, then, that he will easily be able to nip in the bud the young prince's heroic aspiration, in which he foresees himself

restoring national pride, situating himself within the heroic line that
runs from Julius Caesar to his grandfather Henry V:

> *Prince.*   An if I live until I be a man,
> I'll win our ancient right in France again,
> Or die a soldier as I liv'd a king.
> *Glo.*   [*Aside*] Short summers lightly have a forward spring.
>
> (3.1.91–4)

The aspiration remains a mere possibility, an example of 'what might
have been', one of the passages 'we did not take', one of the doors
history chooses to have 'never opened' (Eliot, 1963: 189); but the
effect of its exemplification is to interrogate, in the light of the heroic
tradition itself, Richard's opportunistic manipulation of its language
and its code. The possibility of a conquering Edward V lies there,
unused, in one of 'virtual history's' empty corridors; but as Richard
leads the kingdom deeper into defeat and national disgrace, it
comments eloquently on such perversions of chivalry and heroism as
the slaughter of a child, still in the 'forward spring' of his innocence
and youth. And although Richard believes that he can hide the truth
implicit in that potentiality behind his own crooked record, the
murder of the two princes will become a potent accusation in the
play's pervasive choric deployments of elegy and lament; and of
course, in the final dénouement, the massacred innocents will
themselves rise from the dead to reproach their murderer, and to help
seal Richard's final military defeat. 'For there is nothing hid, which
shall not be manifested; neither was anything kept secret, but that it
should come abroad' (Mark, 4.21).

The substance of history, then, will be seen to lie not in physical
remains and documentary characters, but rather in myth and legend,
oral tradition and story. The point is made precisely by the other
young prince, Edward Plantagenet's son, Richard of York:

> *Yor.*   Marry, they say my uncle grew so fast
> That he could gnaw a crust at two hours old.
> 'Twas full two years ere I could get a tooth ...
>
> *Duch.*   I prithee, pretty York, who told thee this?
> *York.*   Grandam, his nurse.
> *Duch.*   His nurse! Why she was dead ere thou wast born.
> *York.*   If 'twere not she, I cannot tell who told me.
>
> (2.4.27–9, 31–4)

Pressed to identify the source of this biographical detail, the boy first invents a witness, one who could be imagined as both professionally qualified, and in a position to observe the infant Gloucester's premature teething; then, when the reliability of his source is questioned, the validity of the story is authenticated by reference to those most generalised of sources, popular memory and oral tradition. The point is, that the truth the story contains is in no way dependent on its historical accuracy. The myth of Richard's monstrosity is continually reattested and confirmed by his own monstrous actions; the present constructs a myth of origin commensurate with its own terrifying contemporary experience.

VII

Prior to, and parallel with, the young Prince of Wales's aspiration towards a never-to-be-achieved heroic future, a conversation between three anonymous 'citizens' registers a similar hope for the future of the kingdom, in turn undermined by forebodings of calamity and intimations of a tragic outcome:

> *3 Cit.*   Woe to that land that's govern'd by a child.
> *2 Cit.*   In him there is a hope of government,
> Which, in his nonage, council under him,
> And, in his full and ripen'd years, himself,
> No doubt, shall then, and till then, govern well.   (2.3.11–15)

Despite this vision of political hope, a discouraging parallel is also drawn between Edward's minority and that of Henry VI; and it is the pessimistic Third Citizen who has the final word:

> *3 Cit.*   By a divine instinct men's minds mistrust
> Ensuing danger ...   (2.3.42)

This 'divine instinct', expressed here by a popular voice, is clearly more closely in touch with that dark substratum of reality within which the future is being shaped, than is the sceptical and machievellian consciousness shared alike by Richard and Buckingham, and by their aristocratic enemies and allies. The citizens' instinctive premonition of tragedy contrasts with Hastings' confident dismissal of such admonitory signs. When Lord Stanley's dream that 'the boar

had razed off his helm' (3.2.11) foreshadows danger from Richard,
Hastings waves both his fears and his dreams aside:

Tell him his fears are shallow, without instance;
And for his dreams, I wonder he's so simple
To trust the mock'ry of unquiet slumbers.   (3.2.25–7)

Hearing of the imminent executions of Rivers, Grey and Vaughan,
Hastings expresses a complacent satisfaction at the spectacle of
another's tragedy:

But I shall laugh at this a twelve month hence,
That they who brought me in my master's hate,
I live to look upon their tragedy.   (3.2.57–9)

'Tragedy' here is a misfortune that happens to others, a drama at
which Hastings believes he can sit a comfortable spectator. 'Tragedy'
is also of course a particular literary and theatrical genre, a set of
codes and conventions that are used to artificially simulate such
scenes and actions of disaster. This is exactly how Richard defines the
term, in the marvellously ironic and metadramatic scene where he and
Buckingham act out a parody of the conventional tragic genre:

Glo.   Come, cousin, canst thou quake and change thy colour,
Murder thy breath in middle of a word,
And then again begin, and stop again,
As if thou were distraught and mad with terror?
Buck.   Tut, I can counterfeit the deep tragedian;
Speak and look back, and pry on every side,
Tremble and start at wagging of a straw,
Intending deep suspicion. Ghastly looks
Are at my service, like enforced smiles;
And both are ready in their offices
At any time, to grace my stratagems.   (3.5.1–11)

Here tragedy is seen purely as a superficial patina of emotion that can
be 'counterfeited': it seems to have no depth or rootedness in reality
or in the human mind. Richard and Buckingham, actors pretending
to be historical characters pretending to be actors, perform a grotesque shadow-dance of death, strut and fret upon the stage as if
'shadow' existed independently, unanchored to any substantial

reality, unrooted in any deeper dimension. And yet their philo-sophical perspective is a crude materialism that attributes no reality or meaning to the world of shadows. They enter and occupy it only as a vantage-point from which to control and manipulate what they see as true reality — the political world of the naïve, the gullible, the weak, those who are easily deceived, duped, and eliminated. 'Tragedy' is simply a pretence, a 'counterfeit', a good joke that can be practised on others.

'Tragedy' becomes real to Hastings, as eventually it becomes real to Richard and Buckingham, only when the arbitrary sentence is pronounced of his own present death. Too late he realises the signif-icance of those signs he chose, in his confidence and complacency, to ignore:

> *Hast.* Woe, woe, for England! not a whit for me;
> For I, too fond, might have prevented this.
> Stanley did dream the boar did raze his helms,
> And I did scorn it and disdain to fly.   (3.4.82–5)

Hastings simplistically attributes his tragedy to Queen Margaret's 'heavy curse':

> O Margaret, Margaret, now thy heavy curse
> Is lighted on poor Hastings' wretched head!   (3.4.94–5)

The idea of a divinely sanctioned scourge or curse, placed upon England by the murder of Richard II, is of course fundamental to the early providential interpretation of the history plays (Tillyard, 1944; Campbell, 1947). But here the curse is symptom, not cause, of the time's condition.

VIII

It is Margaret herself who offers one of the most eloquent descriptions of the shadow-world, in a scene (4.4) where the clamorous voices of three mothers bear witness to the reality of Richard's tyranny, and through lament and mourning insistently bring back the memories of the dead. Margaret sets the scene by assuming her choric role of vengeful witness, and defining herself as

spectator at a theatrical performance, the prelude ('induction') to a
'tragical' dramatic representation:

> A dire induction am I witness to,
> And will to France, hoping the consequence
> Will prove as bitter, black, and tragical.   (4.4.5–8)

The Duchess of York declares her sorrows in an aphoristic speech
which links the figure of the living ghost, the metaphor of the theatre,
and the construction of historiography:

> Dead life, blind sight, *poor mortal living ghost,*
> *Woe's scene,* world's shame, grave's due by life usurp'd,
> *Brief abstract and record* of tedious days ...   (my italics, 4.4.26–8)

Her being abnegated by the deaths of all her sons but Richard, she
perceives herself already as one of history's thin ghosts, vacant
remnant of a present already becoming past. As such she is also aware
of herself as a character in a drama, acting out 'woe's scene',
occupying in the present a simulated past, doomed to fulfil her tragic
role as one of the dispossessed, widowed by history. Lastly she is
herself, in microcosm, a chronicle of the times: the 'record' of her own
sad story, and in turn a 'brief abstract' of the history through which
she has lived.

Margaret's parallel definition of historical truth is focused on
Queen Elizabeth, but reaches out towards wider implications.
Ostensibly defining Queen Elizabeth as a usurping substitute for
herself, Margaret in the process identifies all power and authority, in a
compelling and comprehensive set of figures, as empty and
insubstantial. Recalling the choric admonitions of Act 1, scene 3,
Margaret reminds Elizabeth that:

> I call'd thee then vain flourish of my fortune;
> I call'd thee then poor shadow, painted queen,
> The presentation of but what I was,
> The flattering index of a direful pageant ...
> A dream of what thou wast; a garish flag
> To be the aim of every dangerous shot,
> A sign of dignity, a breath, a bubble,
> A queen in jest, only to fill the scene.   (4.4.82–91)

All the historical actors in this tragic spectacle, this 'direful pageant', are of course 'poor shadows': to be historical is to be dead, and to be an actor is to be but a shadow. As a character, Elizabeth is a mere image, a 'painted queen'; as an actor *she* is a boy 'painted' to resemble that which *he* is not. She is 'dream' not reality; 'sign' not signified; 'shadow', not substance. It is the female experience of loss, dispossession, rejection, that provides the women with such penetrating insight into the vacancy of historical being, the emptiness of mortality. Later in the same speech Margaret uses phrases which, though aimed at Elizabeth, clearly relate to Richard:

> For she being *fear'd of all*, now *fearing one*;
> For she *commanding all, obey'd of none*.   (my italics, 4.4.103–4)

The tragic example points directly towards the Richard who finds himself, on the night before Bosworth, both afraid of himself ('fearing one') , and eavesdropping by his followers' tents ('obey'd of none') to hear evidence for his own mistrust (5.3.221–2).

It is not for nothing, then, that Richard tries to stifle these voices of truth in the noise of war, to silence female eloquence by the bullying noises of masculine militarism:

> Strike alarum, drums!
> Let not the heavens hear these tell-tale women
> Rail on the Lord's anointed. Strike, I say!
>   *[Flourish. Alarums.*
> Either be patient and entreat me fair,
> Or with the clamorous report of war
> Thus will I drown your exclamations.   (4.4.148–53)

The curse with which Richard's mother leaves him anticipates his final nightmare:

> Therefore take with thee my most grievous curse,
> Which in the day of battle, tire thee more
> Than all the complete armour that thou wear'st!
> My prayers on the adverse party fight;
> And there the little souls of Edward's children
> Whisper the spirits of thine enemies
> And promise them success and victory.   (4.4.187–93)

On the night before the battle the Duchess's prophecy is fulfilled to the letter, when the ghosts of the murdered dead – Prince Edward, Henry VI, Clarence, Rivers, Grey and Vaughan, Hastings, the two young princes, Lady Anne, and Buckingham – rise to lay their own curses on Richard, wishing on him weakness and fear, success and victory to his enemies. Here the past is resurrected as a haunting, and the voices of the dead cry out against their murderer from beneath the ground. The same actors who have throughout the play counterfeited history's dead, brought them living in simulated vitality into the arena of the drama, now reappear, though living themselves, to represent these same historical characters dead.

To Richard, the world of shadows thereby becomes substantially real:

> By the apostle Paul, shadows to-night
> Have struck more terror to the soul of Richard
> Than can the substance of ten thousand soldiers ... (5.3.216–18)

But in the theatre, where 'ten thousand soldiers' would invariably be represented by a few 'poor players', and where there is no 'substance' save that of 'shadow', Richard's realisation of the nature of history seems long overdue. The return of the actors in what is almost a grotesque 'curtain-call' testifies more to the power of the theatre to bind and loose both living and dead, than to the self-evident absence of substance, and the undeniable emptiness of shadow.

IX

Hitherto Richard has sought to dominate the shadow-world by the force of his own individual will, deploying its alien language and iconography to terrify others, drawing on its dark powers to eliminate all rivals and contenders. At last he awakes into nightmare to find himself surrounded by a host of fellow-shadows, and obliged to acknowledge the relationships which bind him indissolubly to them. Light and darkness, sleep and waking, present and past, are not after all separate worlds, safely cordoned off from one another: the barriers between them have collapsed, allowing the free passage of living and dead, across the borders, 'Between two worlds become much like each other' (Eliot, 1963: 218).

The fear that Richard has fostered in others, and denied in himself (revealing it only by his unacknowledged 'timorous dreams' [4.1.85]), here invades his waking consciousness, transgressing the boundary between dream and reality. Though he tries to restore it by a dismissive phrase – 'I *did but* dream' – his subsequent soliloquy demonstrates that the dream has been thoroughly internalised, as where his 'sins' flock to reproach him, just as the ghosts gathered to deliver their damning testimony:

All several sins, all us'd in each degree,
Throng to the bar, crying all 'Guilty! guilty!'   (5.3.198–9)

The substance of the dream is a resurrection of the past; but as Richard emerges from it, it is the future he is seeing, the Battle of Bosworth, the image of his own imminent death:

Give me another horse. Bind up my wounds.
Have mercy, Jesu!   (5.3.177–8)

Already, in other words, he partakes of the same substance as the dead who have haunted him, and is beginning to perceive himself as part of, rather than separate from, that world of ghosts.

The tightly preserved insularity Richard has always used to define himself, right from the sharply etched shadow of the opening soliloquy, has also collapsed. Richard no longer knows himself as a subject, as an integrated self. The cohesive and individual 'I' of that earlier self-revelation has here broken into a disaggregated third-person address: 'Richard loves Richard'; and all attempts to restore its unity only further intensify the effect of alienation:

Richard loves Richard; that is, I am I.
Is there a murderer here? No – yes, I am.   (5.3.183–4)

The multiple roles Richard has deployed and performed with such mastery and skill now press upon him as symptoms of a disintegrating personality – the figure of the 'villain' he initially adopted as a convenient persona now haunts him as an aspect of personality he is forced, paradoxically, to both acknowledge and deny.

I am a villain; yet I lie, I am not.   (5.3.191)

As a historical character he has been a man of many faces; as an actor he has played many roles; as a historical construction he represents the convergence of multiple historical records and reports. All these diversified pressures, hitherto turned inwards and closely protected, here explode outwards and disclose the truly multiple, variously constructed nature of historical being.

The 'thousand several tongues' that Richard now hears as an inner clamour are of course the voices of those past and present shadows, against which he has consistently sought to define himself. The delusively untrammelled ego is obliged to acknowledge the network of human and social relations within which its apparently isolated existence is shaped and formed. The voice, loud and eloquent, that has sought to silence all others in absolute domination, now articulates the truly collective and collaborative nature of language. The will that sought to impose its unchallenged hegemony, proves uncertain even of its own integrity of being. The body that has sought to block light and dominate space, can be seen visibly disintegrating into spirit, sucked urgently towards the black hole that leads towards the shadow-world. The star-actor who has happily hogged the stage, allowing his fellow-players to find such light as they can, now finds himself both assimilated to the general body of the cast, and, finally, inextricably trapped within the lines of a conventional tragic dénouement.

X

Throughout the drama Richard has believed himself to be fully in control of his environment in all its temporal dimensions: present, past and future. He has ruthlessly forced the present to conform to the exigencies of his will; renarrated the past to establish his own preferred interpretations; and manipulated historical records so as to pre-empt future historical understanding. But he has done so by assuming unreal distinctions between past and present, shadow and substance, dream and reality. As the little prince predicted, historical testimony can transcend the records that seek to fix its form and limit its survival; historical truth can, paradoxically, be transhistorical: 'Foul deeds will rise, / Though all the world o'erwhelm them, to mens' eyes' (*Hamlet*, 1.2.256). The historic dead do not lie quiet and silent, but rise in historical resurrection to witness to the truth, and to cry out against the malefactor. In the historical drama, an actor falls only in counterfeit death, and readily rises again at the dramatist-sorcerer's invocation, at the call of the action, or at the summons of the finale, that temporary curtailment of the shadow-play world. Nor do we observe here anything so definite as a 'Tudor myth' of providential retribution and potent, determining curse. We can see all there is to see, merely by watching the 'puppets dallying' (*Hamlet*, 3.2.240): men both make, and mistake, their own history. And though the phrase I have adapted there was coined by Marx (Marx, 1852: 10), we need a touch of the Third Citizen's 'divine instinct' fully to perceive that truth.

5

Henry VI, Part One

Why abodest thou among the sheep-folds, to hear the
bleatings of the flocks?
'The Song of Deborah', Judges, V.16

I

It is customary to regard the plays of the so-called 'First Tetralogy' —
the *Henry VI* plays and *Richard III* — as more direct and straightforward expressions of the 'Tudor Myth' than the later plays of the
second 'cycle' (*Richard II*, the two parts of *Henry IV*, and *Henry V*).
If one begins with *Henry VI, Part One*, it is at first glance entirely
natural to think of this play's concern with 'history' as deeply embedded in the continuous and integrated narrative of the chronicles,
focused therefore on the crown and on the dynastic struggles over
its possession; on aristocratic rebellion and internecine warfare; on
succession and usurpation, regicide and revenge. Whether we are
looking at the play, as did earlier critics like Tillyard (1944), as a seg-
ment of a large epic of England, enacting parables of order and
disorder, or from a more modern historicist view of the plays as
dramatising sophisticated and theorised representations of history,
the main outlines of its historical shape are self-evident. The play
begins with the auspicious funeral of Henry V, and ends with the fatal
marriage of his son to Margaret of Anjou — both stages in the
descent of England from a proud imperial conqueror to a nation
internally torn by civil war. Henry VI succeeds as an infant king to
a Protectorate, destabilised by aristocratic rivalry and competition.
The latter are exemplified as contests for public influence, as in the
factional fighting between Gloucester and Winchester (1.3); more
dangerously, as the quarrel between Somerset and Richard
Plantagenet in the Temple garden (2.4), where the floral insignia of
the subsequent civil wars is chosen; and the irresponsible squabbling
between York and Somerset (4.3, 44) which undermines the English

war effort. The dynastic framework of these struggles is elaborately unfolded and extrapolated into past narrative and future projection, in the scene where Mortimer delivers to Richard the narrative of his father's execution and his own disinheritance (2.5). From this background arises Richard's claim to the throne, and the eventual temporary ascendancy of the house of York. A sequence of choric commentaries from the Duke of Exeter (e.g. 4.2.183ff.) enforces the play's preoccupation with issues of authority and resistance, sovereignty and disloyalty, unity and dissension.

Elizabethans (at least from the tiny scrap of evidence that remains to us of this play's reputation, Thomas Nash's description of the play as the revival of 'brave Talbot'), seem to have thought of it as a play about a figure who doesn't even appear in the above summary of its historical narrative and political themes. Although Talbot was clearly thought of by Nash as central to the play's historical project, his centrality has often been marginalised in interpretations that focus on an overall historical design – *Henry VI, Part One* has even been produced without him. The play's other central figure, Joan of Arc, or as she is more commonly known in the play, simply 'La Pucelle', is also in some senses more or less irrelevant to the narrative traced above.

So although prima facie the play is concerned with the broad outlines of a royal and aristocratic masculine dynastic history, its central figures are a soldier, a woman, and a child; and its central themes are not so much history as providential narrative, or history as process and theory (though such conceptualisations are certainly implicit), but rather 'the process of historical representation' (Rackin, 1990: 29) – history as a manifestly contemporary exercise of lament and resurrection, nostalgic longing and sober reflection, vivid re-enactment and saddened resignation.

II

In the chronological sequence of historical events within which these plays were formulated, and into which they were editorially ordered by the First Folio, the conclusion to *Henry V* and the opening of *Henry VI, Part One* are inextricably joined together by content, theme and textual contingency (although in theatrical history *Henry VI, Part One* opened to a world as yet innocent of that subsequent dramatisation). *Henry V*, a 'prequel' to the historically subsequent but theatrically precedent *Henry VI, Part One*, ends with a coda that is both prospective and retrospective, recalling the earlier dramatisation of a posterior historical narrative:

> Small time, but, in that small, most greatly lived
> This star of England. Fortune made his sword;
> By which the world's best garden he achieved,
> And of it left his son imperial lord.
> Henry the Sixth, in infant bands crown'd king
> Of France and England, did this king succeed;
> Whose state so many had the managing
> That they lost France and made his England bleed;
> Which oft our stage hath shown.   (*Henry V*, 'Epilogue', 5–13)

A moment of historical achievement, captured in a moment of theatrical triumph, is contextualised by sobering retrospect and chastening prophecy: since the future destruction of Henry V's epic success, the loss of his French conquests, has already been amply demonstrated on this same 'stage'.

When *Henry VI, Part One* begins, with Henry V's funeral, that editorially constituted textual contingency secures an intimate connection between the two plays, as if the coda to the later play were a retrospective 'trailer' for the earlier. The historical narrative seems to pass naturally from Henry V's glory, to his death and the subsequent erosion of his national achievements. But there is another chronology at work, in which the revival of Henry V's heroic memory, with which *Henry VI, Part One* begins, is a rehearsal for the subsequent production of the play *Henry V*, a theatrical ritual which can be conjectured to have performed, at least in the view of witnesses such as Nash and Heywood, a double function very similar to the funeral rites celebrated in Westminster Abbey – that of furnishing an illustrious historical example for emulation and imitation; and that of providing a sharp reproof to the present's degenerate, effeminate days.

Certainly the spirit of the dead 'star of England' – 'King Henry the Fifth, too famous to live long!' (*HVI1*, 1.1.6) – appears in his successor's court at Humphrey Duke of Gloucester's conjuration – 'Henry the Fifth, thy ghost I invocate' (1.1.52) – with an effect not unlike the apparition of old King Hamlet to his disinherited son. The dead hero-king is already here conjured as the historical myth previously/subsequently celebrated in the coda to *Henry V*, the warrior monarch who occupied such 'small time, but in that small,

most greatly lived' ('Epilogue', 5); 'Henry the Fifth, too famous to live
long' (*HVI1*, 1.1.6) – a figure of such epic plenitude that mundane
history could hardly hold him. Here permanent fame seems to stand
in inverse ratio to longevity, a paradox hinted at by Edward Halle's
account of a king 'whose fame by his death as liuely florysheth as hys
actes in hys lyfe were sene and remembred' (Halle, 1548, 1809: 113).
An intensive concentration of historical achievement raises and
constellates the legendary king, already a 'star', infinitely high above
the short and petty scene of his earthly victories.

> His brandish'd sword did blind men with his beams;
> His arms spread wider than a dragon's wings;
> His sparkling eyes, replete with wrathful fire,
> More dazzled and drove back his enemies
> Than mid-day sun fierce bent against their faces.
> What should I say? His deeds exceed all speech:
> He ne'er lift up his hand but conquered.   (*HVI1*, 1.1.10–16)

Henry's spirit is invoked by Gloucester in terms that combine an epic
figure of military force with a symbolism of divine and superhuman
power, somewhere between Achilles and the Archangel Michael. 'His
deeds exceed all speech': rhetoric slides off into hyperbole without
truly capturing the hero's immense achievement – 'He ne'er lift up
his hand but conquered.'

Gloucester's eulogy, however, also opens up a discrepancy
between the size of the dead king's awesome reputation, and the
scale of the worldly achievement in which it is based. Was Henry V's
objective (as imagined by Shakespeare, conjectured by the historians
Halle and Holinshed, and reportedly admitted in the king's own
deathbed confession) the conquest of France as an end in itself, or
rather the expansion and consolidation of a unified English nation-
state by recovery of an allegedly expropriated inheritance? And
although posterity cannot strip away the guerdon of conquest, it can
certainly reverse national fortunes. What remains of the political
achievement, if it proves to have been invested solely in the king's
charismatic person, and to be inseparable from the sustained *force
majeur* of military success?

The Duke of Exeter broaches this more pessimistic possibility
by figuring death as a defeat – this is one battle, after all, in which
Henry V failed to conquer. If the king's body is the incarnation of
royal power, then its absence renders the quasi-religious ceremony

of royal glorification a vacant ritual, and aristocratic power finds itself worshipping an empty box, a shameful symbol of national humiliation:

> Henry is dead and never shall revive.
> Upon a wooden coffin we attend;
> And death's dishonourable victory
> We with our stately presence glorify.   (1.1.18–21)

Although Exeter here establishes a critical point about authority and succession, his error is to confuse the literal with the symbolic in historical narrative and memorial ritual. Henry is in fact already in process of revival, as historical memory simultaneously recalls his military successes, and creates his legendary reputation. The effect is made explicit by use of the familiar imagery of History as resurrection and exhumation, with its dual potency of liberation and haunting. The hero's spirit is implored to function as an epic patriarchal protector, guarding England's destiny in a divine chivalry; but simultaneously it is acknowledged that such a historical example of legendary potency can equally operate to humiliate and shame the unhistorical present:

> *Bed.*   Henry the Fifth, thy ghost I invoke:
> Prosper this realm, keep it from civil broils,
> Combat with adverse planets in the heavens.
> A far more glorious star thy soul will make
> Than Julius Caesar or bright − (1.1.52–6)

Bedford's panegyric is interrupted by news, direct from the front line, of France's national revival, a message likely to raise the dead king in wrath from his tomb:

> the loss of those great towns
> Will make him burst his lead and rise from death.   (63–4)

The quarrel between the mourners, over their dead king's body, opens up that central theme broached in the coda to *Henry V*, of the realm left without a strong monarchical authority, destabilised by aristocratic conflict and treachery − what later Sir William Lucy will call the 'vulture of sedition' (4.3.47), feeding in the bosom of the English high command, and betraying to loss:

The conquest of our scarce-cold conqueror,
That ever-living man of memory,
Henry the Fifth.   (4.3.50–2)

In the course of voicing the violence of their differences, the nobles draw attention to their own dependence on the unifying power of the armigerous monarch (and implicitly to the dependence of national unity on successful foreign conquest), by describing the unkinged realm as a habitation of weakness, a kingdom of puny children and wailing women. The king is 'an effeminate prince ... like a schoolboy' (1.1.35–6); England is left by Henry V's death 'a nourish of salt tears, / And none but women left to wail the dead' (1.1.50–1).

III

The play, then, begins with an elegiac vision, looking back to a better world inhabited by such ideal figures of chivalry as Henry V, a world sustained by the explicitly masculine values of physical heroism and military achievement: a fifteenth-century illustration shows the figure of the Earl of Warwick, fully armed, supporting in one hand the Church, in the other the baby king (*Rous Roll*, Plate 3). However, the model for present heroism is always to be found, as it was found in Thomas Heywood's heroic lineage, in past exemplars. The tradition of English heroism is formally acknowledged by the temporarily discomfited French, in a remarkable multinational merging of history and fiction, framed by an explicit literary reference:

Froissart, a countryman of ours, records
England all Olivers and Rowlands bred
During the time Edward the Third did reign.
More truly now may this be verified;
For none but Samsons and Goliases
It sendeth forth to skirmish.   (1.2.29–34)

The fourteenth-century French chronicler Froissart, whose narrative forms one of the bases for the earlier history subsequently to be dramatised, is cited as defining English heroism by reference to French chivalric literature, as well as to the legendary epic heroes of the Old Testament. The obvious sentiment of national chauvinism (even their French enemies admit that the English are invincible)

Plate 3   Richard Beauchamp, Earl of Warwick, holding the infant Henry VI, from Add. 48976 in the British Library. Reproduced by kind permission of the British Library

needs to be read in a context which brackets such assumptions within a retrospective, elegaic tradition, more effective in idealising past glories than in celebrating present achievements. For the truth of the matter is, as the play goes on to show, that such antecedent glories are permanently in the past, and the present has no hope of emulating them. Deeper anxieties are couched within Alençon's comparison, if one thinks of the subsequent histories of Talbot and Salisbury as modelled on the careers of Samson (defeated by a woman, Judges, XVI), and Goliath (killed by a boy, 1 Samuel, XVII).

This will seem at first sight unconvincing, if only because the great example of Henry V, and the great (and relatively recent) victory of Agincourt occupy such a commanding position in the play's frame of reference. The brothers of Henry V, also heroes of Agincourt, Exeter and Bedford, lead the new French campaign together with other venerable survivors of that heroic tradition such as Salisbury; and are explicitly recognised as sustaining both the chivalric tradition of noble exploit, and the historical memory of national achievement:

> The noble Duke of Bedford ...
> A braver soldier never couched lance ... (3.2.132–4)

> In thirteen battles Salisbury o'ercame;
> Henry the Fifth he first trained to the wars ... (1.4.78–9)

Both these warriors are, however, old men, heroes of a former day. The dying Bedford, raised like Uther Pendragon from his sickbed, merely observes the siege of Rouen (though he dies in contentment, echoing the Biblical Simeon [Luke.II.30], having seen his salvation in his 'enemies' overthrow'); and Salisbury is ignominiously slaughtered by a sniper, the audacious and insubordinate gunner's boy.

The present inheritor of their courage and chivalric devotion, however, Lord John Talbot, stands formidably at the centre of the play's heroic ethic; and indeed defines it, standing before the walls of Rouen, explicitly by reference both to historical precedent of such warrior kings as Henry V and Richard I –

> as sure as English Henry lives
> And as his father here was conqueror,
> As sure as in this late-betrayed town
> Great Coeur-de-lion's heart was buried –
> So sure I swear to get the town or die. (3.2.80–4)

– and to the chivalric order of the Garter Knights:

> When first this order was ordain'd, my lords,
> Knights of the Garter were of noble birth,
> Valiant and virtuous, full of haughty courage,
> Such as were grown to credit by the wars;
> Not fearing death nor shrinking for distress,
> But always resolute in most extremes.
> He then that is not furnish'd in this sort
> Doth but usurp the sacred name of knight,
> Profaning this most honourable order. (4.1.33–41)

The occasion of this speech is Talbot's stripping of the Garter insignia from Sir John Fastolfe for an act of cowardice at the battle of Patay (repeated within the play at the siege of Rouen). Chivalric heroism defines itself primarily in opposition to cowardice; but it is also acutely class-conscious, distinguishing itself as nobly born from base, degenerate and contaminated blood. It is a matter of disgrace, far exceeding the pain of wounds or the humiliation of capture, that Talbot is stabbed in the back by 'A base Walloon' (1.1.137). Talbot scrupulously declines liberty from capture, when the condition is an exchange of prisoners in which he is matched with 'a baser man of arms' (1.4.30). The French having recaptured Rouen, Talbot regards their refusal to submit themselves to open combat (a strategic absurdity) as a degrading badge of demeaning social status:

> Like peasant foot boys do they keep the walls,
> And dare not take up arms like gentlemen.   (3.2.69–70)

These two key aspects of the armigerous nobility's chivalric code – individual courage in action supporting the enduring reputation for honour of family and class – are invoked in the play by metaphors of memorial and monument. Talbot will establish a monument to Salisbury, which promises implicitly to credit him with the sack of Orleans (in which of course he took no part), mourn his former glories ('What a terror he had been to France'), and protest against 'the treacherous manner of his mournful death' (2.2.15–17).

IV

But it is not only against cowardice and baseness that this heroic code distinguishes and identifies itself. Chivalry and feudal militarism are masculine domains, the one a cultural statement of the other. Just as, in more primitive social formations, one of the primary functions of communally organised armed force was to protect women and children (along with other communal property); so in the chivalric tradition the obligations of the noble knight prominently include the defence of those weaker members of society. But in the world of Henry VI, women and children are not safely enclosed within that protective ring of steel. The fact that the king is a child is of no consequence for Talbot, who loyally and consistently acknowledges his duty to defend the crown. The military champion draws power, on behalf of his sovereign, from preceding warrior kings, and thereby strengthens the authority of the present 'English Henry'. His heroic ethic is an idealised feudalism, in which aristocratic and military values are inseparable from notions of crown and commonwealth. On the other hand, Talbot has serious problems with women who refuse their allotted role in traditional society, particularly in the case of Joan, La Pucelle, figure of gender transgression, 'a woman clad in armour' (1.5.3). Talbot has no means of explaining the unnatural strength of Joan, who overcomes him in combat, except by recourse to a language of witchcraft.

> Here, here she comes. I'll have a bout with thee.
> Devil or devil's dam, I'll conjure thee;
> Blood will I draw on thee — thou art a witch ...
> Heavens, can you suffer hell so to prevail?   (1.5.4–9)

From the outset Talbot, like all the English and their Burgundian allies, mocks Joan's pretensions to virginity — 'A maid, *they say*' (2.1.21, my italics), and naturally links the vocabularies of sexual transgression, unfeminine behaviour and diabolical powers — 'I will chastise this high-minded strumpet' (1.5.12), 'that railing Hecate' (3.2.64), 'Foul fiend of France and hag of all despite' (3.2.52); 'Well, let them practise and converse with spirits' (2.1.25).

Although subject to military defeat by Joan, Talbot is thus able to preserve the dignity of his code by circumstantial explanations: a woman should not in any event be 'clad in armour' (1.5.3); a woman with masculine physical strength must needs derive it from unnatural sources such as witchcraft or diabolical power. In short, a woman who crosses the prescribed gender and sexual boundaries at any one point is automatically declared guilty of transgression on all possible grounds: it follows from Joan's assumption of masculine rather than feminine activities that she must needs be sexually dissolute rather than chaste, corrupt rather than morally respectable, unruly and 'railing' rather than obedient and submissive; even ugly rather than beautiful.

Talbot's other encounter with a woman shows him successfully negotiating a situation of difficult 'unruliness', and restoring an appropriate conventional balance between the sexes. Initially the traditional division of gender values appears to be firmly in place: Talbot is invited, as conqueror of Orleans, to join a 'virtuous lady' who 'with modesty admire[s his] name'. He appears to welcome the diversion as a proffered sexual encounter, an extension rather than an inversion of conquest, the defeated submitting sexually to the victor, as implied by Burgundy's observation:

> I see our wars
> Will turn unto a peaceful comic sport,
> When ladies crave to be encount'red with.   (2.2.44–6)

In practice Talbot clearly foresees a trap, and only *appears* to offer himself in personal 'encounter', meanwhile insuring by secret military preparation against a suspected conspiracy. In this way the hero precipitates a scene of apparent inversion, in which the woman of a conquered people (who can also be imagined, and is often played, as taller than he is!), seeks to reverse the military outcome, and to ridicule Talbot's pretensions to heroic lineage:

> I thought I should have seen some Hercules,
> A second Hector ...
> Alas, this is a child, a silly dwarf!
> It cannot be this weak and writhled shrimp
> Should strike such terror to his enemies.   (2.3.19–20, 22–4)

An attempt is then made to cancel Talbot's heroic credentials, subject him to female power, and attribute to him the stature and weakness of a child. The Countess identifies Talbot's person as a counterfeit reflection of his reputation, to which he manifestly, by physical appearance, fails to live up. This idea is then developed via the concepts of substance and shadow:

> Long time thy shadow hath been thrall to me,
> For in my gallery thy picture hangs;
> But now the substance shall endure the like
> And I will chain these legs and arms of thine.   (2.3.36–9)

The Countess already possesses in 'thrall' Talbot's legendary reputation, in the form of a portrait; now she will imprison that bodily substance which seems by contrast so inadequate a token. By calling in his men, Talbot redefines the relation between substance and shadow: the heroic legend does indeed have concrete reality, but it is a reality of masses rather than individuals, of armies not heroes, of a nation rather than a man. In himself, Talbot may constitute only a poor sign; but the heroic legend he points to is that of a national heroism, 'England' rather than simply 'Talbot':

> I am but shadow of myself.
> You are deceiv'd, my substance is not here;
> For what you see is but the smallest part
> And least proportion of humanity.   (2.3.50–3)

As the Countess wonderingly asks: 'How can these contrarieties agree?' (2.3.59). In this example of masculine military-erotic success, Talbot successfully unites these 'contraries' between private and public, individual and state, citizen and commonwealth, substance and shadow. In the moment of his final heroic testing, however, this apparently robust unity fragments and disintegrates.

V

Talbot's heroic end proves an ironic nemesis rather than the epic apotheosis it ought to have been. Embattled to relieve the siege of Bordeaux, he finds himself isolated and surrounded, cut off from supply by the irresponsible factiousness, the 'private discord' (4.4.21) and 'worthless emulation' (4.4.22) of the English commanders York and Somerset. Drawn up before Harfleur, Talbot historically echoes, dramatically anticipates Henry V's words before Harfleur (*HV*, 3.3), which in turn had echoed the speech of Henry's father Bolingbroke before the walls of Flint Castle (*RII*, 3.3):

> Open your city gates,
> Be humble to us, call our sovereign yours ...
> But if you frown upon this proffer'd peace,
> You tempt the fury of my three attendants,
> Lean famine, quartering steel, and climbing fire ...
>
>   (4.2.5–6, 9–11)

Surrounded and outnumbered by the enemy, Talbot re-enacts the hopeless odds of Agincourt, and responds with the same reckless courage, stoicism, and determination, the same submission to the concurrence of divine will and national interest, as his illustrious predecessor:

How are we park'd and bounded in a pale –
A little herd of England's timorous deer,
Maz'd with a yelping kennel of French curs!
If we be English deer, be then in blood ...
God and Saint George, Talbot and England's right.   (4.2.45–8, 55)

It is at this point of extremity, however, that the respective fates of
Talbot and Henry V part company. Though as always incapable
of cowardice, insensible to his own danger, when peril of premature
death threatens his own son he literally betrays every principle of his
chivalric and aristocratic code, gravitating towards the very cowardice and baseness he despises. Where Henry V before Agincourt casts
bitter shame on any soldier who has thoughts of flight, and insists
on the superiority of heroic death over prudent life, Talbot seeks
to persuade his son to save himself by fleeing from the battle, and to
preserve the Talbot name, not in heroic legend by courageous self-
sacrifice, but opportunistically by tactical withdrawal. The responses
to those exhortations of young John Talbot, within whom the paternal heroic ethic is thoroughly inculcated, clearly indicate the extent to
which Talbot is here deserting the standard of his own heroic values:

Tal.   dear boy, mount on my swiftest horse,
And I'll direct thee how thou shalt escape
By sudden flight. ...
John.   Is my name Talbot, and am I your son?
And shall I fly?   (4.5.9–13)

Tal.   Wilt thou yet leave the battle, boy, and fly,
Now thou art seal'd the son of chivalry?
Fly, to revenge my death when I am dead ...
In thee thy mother dies, our household's name,
My death's revenge, thy youth, and England's fame ...

John.   On that advantage, bought with such a shame,
To save a paltry life and slay bright fame,
Before young Talbot from old Talbot fly,
The coward horse that bears me fall and die!
And like me to the peasant boys of France,
To be shame's scorn and subject of mischance!
                              (4.6.28–30; 38–9; 44–9)

In this final exigency, the masculine hero and aristocrat becomes
everything he has always consistently patronised, despised or

contemned — woman, coward and plebeian. Talbot's chivalric values transgress normal gender and class demarcations. His masculine protectiveness, which ought to be inherited by the male heir, slides into an irresistible maternal impulse to protect by salvation the loved child. But in that chivalric ethic, the glory of the mother resides only in the heroism of the son, and to identify him with the mother ('in thee thy mother dies') is actually to deny him the proper and distinguishing masculinity that is the heritage of parturition. As the boy points out, since the honour of mother and family depends on the masculine achievements of husband and son, it is absurd to try to save family honour by custodial protectiveness of the male who exists only to protect and glorify, if necessary by his own heroic sacrifice, the family and its honourable name.

Similarly, in exhorting the boy to escape, Talbot risks creating an analogy with the play's symbolic coward, Sir John Fastolfe, who runs away precisely to 'save [him]self by flight' (3.2.105). Young John Talbot recognises that such conduct would invalidate both honourable lineage and aristocratic status, implying both illegitimacy and social exclusion, bastardy and baseness, and would make of the proud and legitimate son 'a bastard and a slave' (4.5.15). This complex of ideas is tied together in the rhyming analogy between 'womb' and 'tomb':

> *Tal.*   Shall all thy mother's hopes lie in one tomb?
> *John.*   Ay, rather than I'll shame my mother's womb.   (4.5.34–5).

Talbot's assertion is that if both son and father die, then the honourable 'womb' that served as a repository of the family's 'hopes' will become by analogy the 'tomb' of family annihilation. His son points out that it is shameful life, not glorious death, that converts a womb of hope into a tomb of despair. The lifegiving female receptacle of hope is reproduced in this symbolic exchange as a monument to heroic virtue, the tomb that swallows but also preserves the courageous actions of both husband and son. The mother is of course quite effaced, virtually obliterated as both person and female in this construction, assimilated into the masculine environment of dynastic chivalry; the womb is appropriated as a scene of manly death rather than of womanly procreation.

The idea of the father as sole progenitor is further extended in the course of the battle, where by defending his son Talbot is credited with giving him rebirth:

John.   O, twice, my father, twice am I thy son!
The life thou gav'st me first was lost and done
Till with thy warlike sword, despite of fate,
To my determin'd time thou gav'st new date.   (4.6.6–9)

Thus the father redeems the moment of weakness in which he resembled the false, female parent, by proving himself the true, male parent, his phallic blade the instrument of procreation. Legitimacy, in this ideological context always open to dispute on the basis of the unreliable female element, can be decisively proven by the assertion of patriarchal law (a curious reversal of biological reality, where the irrefutable emergence of an infant from the womb in terms of reliability compares – at least before DNA testing – favourably with the notorious ambiguity of paternity). In military action son and father become indivisible, part of one another (symbolised by a physical bonding actually possible only with the mother):

John.   No more can I be severed from your side
Than can yourself yourself in twain divide.
Stay, go, do what you will, the like do I;
For live I will not, if my father die.   (4.5.48–51)

It is of course the mother who 'divides' herself in twain to give birth, from whose side the son is severed, and upon whose life, during pregnancy, the foetus is absolutely dependent. Here all these conditions are located instead in the figure of the father. Finally, it is the father's arms, not the mother's womb, that become the boy's container, taking back the life they gave him: 'Now my old arms are young John Talbot's grave'. Talbot's final eulogy for his son is a miniature epic poem formulated in heroic couplets:

Where is my other life? Mine own is gone.
O, where's young Talbot? Where is valiant John? ...
Dizzy-ey'd fury and great rage of heart
Suddenly made him from my side to start
Into the clust'ring battle of the French;
And in that sea of blood my son did drench
His overmounting spirit; and there died,
My Icarus, my blossom, in his pride.   (4.7.1–2, 11–16)

Talbot's eulogy combines paternal admiration with maternal tenderness, figuring the boy as the overweening legendary Icarus, perishing gloriously in his pride; but also as 'my blossom', the child rendered fragile and vulnerable by an image at once symbol of natural growth and familiar term of endearment. While the language of the heroic tradition validates the blood-drenched sacrifice of an 'overmounting spirit', the vocabulary of parental affection creates, in that image of the blood-soaked and trampled flower, the unbearable anomaly of a child's death.

VI

One of the most remarkable features of this play is that Talbot's 'mighty opposite' is a woman who adopts as her *raison-d'être* this very destabilisation of gender and class boundaries that accompanies Talbot's heroic downfall. Joan is, of course, as a historical character the centre of an enormously complex and powerful body of historical and religious narrative and legend. Those aspects of her extraordinary career that have attracted fictional and dramatic attention (Shaw, 1924; Keneally, 1974) are: the romance convention of a low-born subject inexplicably achieving greatness and heroic success; the gender transgression affirmed by an armigerous woman; the religious and magical reverberations of innocence symbolised in virginity, and cruelly persecuted by martyrdom; and the historical oddity of a demonisation that was so swiftly reversed, by rehabilitation, at the demands of political expediency. Thus Joan's historical legend is based on a powerful armoury of contradictions: an exemplar of low-born greatness; a heroic woman; a martial maid; a victimised innocent; a heretic who became a national heroine, and a witch who eventually secured the status of sainthood.

Joan therefore by definition made herself available for contradictory readings and incompatible ideological appropriations. This capacity for iterability can be seen, at its simplest level, though differently inflected, in the historical accounts of Halle and Holinshed. Their narratives draw on the contradictory views of Joan necessarily embedded in the conflicting testimonies of warring nations. Halle makes no attempt to take the French perspective on Joan seriously, or to represent it at all fairly: instead he dismisses it out of hand as a manifest and palpable absurdity. From the outset, Halle affirms, Joan was clearly a perverted, vicious and low-class fanatic:

a mayd of the age of xx. yeres, and in mans apparell, named Ione
... which was a greate space a chamberleyn in a commen hostery,
and was a rampe of suche boldnesse, that she would course horses
and ride theim to water, and do thynges, that other yong maidens,
bothe abhorred & wer ashamed to do ... She (as a monster) was
sent to the Dolphin ... rehersyng to hym, visions, traunses, and
fables, full of blasphemy, supersticion and hypocrisy, that I maruell
much that wise men did beleue her, and lerned clarkes would write
suche phantasies.   (Halle, 1548: 148)

Halle's dismissal of Joan depends, therefore, on a rejection of any
authority in the narratives that formed his sources: his French fellow-
chroniclers were simply blinded by a persuasive zealot, or duped by
an adroit confidence trickster. Holinshed, characteristically, delivers a
more detached and even-handed reflection of these contradictory
national views:

a yoong wench of an eighteene yeeres old, called Ione Are ...
Of favour she was counted likesome, of person stronglie made and
manlie, of courage great, hardie and stout withall, an vnderstander of
counsels though she were not at them, great semblance of chastitie
both of bodie and behauiour, the name of Iesus in hir mouth about
all hir businesses ... A person (as their bookes make hir) raised vp by
power diuine, onelie for succour to the French estate then deepelie
in distresse ...   (Holinshed, 1587, 1965: III, 163)

Both writers on the other hand close their accounts of Joan with a
strict and unmitigated condemnation of her as a fraud; her counterfeit
virtue and fake inspiration beyond all doubt proven by her low-class
associations, military adventures and manlike dress and life-style:

where was her shamefastnes, when she daily and nightly, was
conuersant with comen souldiors ...? Where was her womanly
pitie, when she ... slewe, man, woman, and childe ...? Where was
her womanly behauor, when she cladde her self in a mannes
clothyng ...? Then these thynges, beyng thus plainly true, all men
must nedes confesse ... she was no good woman ... she was no
sainct.   (Halle, 1548: 159)

found though a virgin, yet first, shamefullie reiecting hir sex
abominablie in acts and apparell, to haue counterfeit mankind,

and then, all damnablie faithlesse, to be a pernicious instrument to hostilitie and bloudshed in diuelish witchcraft and sorcerie, sentence accordinglie was pronounced against hir.

(Holinshed, 1587, 1965: III, 170–1)

VII

The last judgement on Joan offered by *Henry VI, Part One* is similarly unconditional, delivered in a scene of brutal comedy in which the victorious English ridicule all her claims to sanctity and virtue, eliciting from her cowardly confessions designed to save her from the stake. Loosely and erroneously based on the historical Joan's recantation (she did deny her voices, but she didn't 'plead her belly'), this travesty is endorsed by the earlier scene (5.3) in which Joan is represented in conversation with evil spirits. These scenes belong to the same discursive domain as the harsh executive summaries of Halle and Holinshed, and in turn to the ideological context of a crudely chauvinistic English nationalism: Joan's claims to divine communication with Sts Margaret and Katherine are held in sufficient disrespect for the alleged saints to be unequivocally transformed into potent though unreliable 'Fiends', hitherto propitiated, in a satanic parody of the Eucharist, by Joan's own blood. Here both Joan's power, and whatever successes have accrued to the 'glory' of France, are unmistakably represented as dependent on the powers of darkness. Joan's subsequent assertion that her career was by contrast founded on the inspiration and power of divine grace, clearly in this context is made to ring unmistakably hollow.

Just as Halle flattened out Joan's history into a stridently bigoted and chauvinistic antihagiography, so some 'official' critical judgements have accepted the play's closure as its final judgement on Joan of Arc, and have reproduced her as a coherent and consistently presented villain: 'the final avowal of her condition is no more than the fulfilment of the earlier implications' [Cairncross, 1962: xl]). Before the play reaches this closure, however, the representation of Joan throughout the play participates fully in the unresolved contradictoriness of her historical legend. Where Halle presents a relentlessly English point of view, the play permits a dynamic interaction of the conflicting French, English (and even to some degree the Burgundian) perspectives that conspired to weave the complex tapestry of Joan's history. These multiple perspectives revolve around certain key metaphorical or narrative constructions of Joan as saint, prophetess, inspired shepherdess, female warrior; and alternatively as whore, witch, parvenu and coward.

Broadly speaking, these perspectives tend naturally to divide along the axes of the international military conflict, or more precisely along the national demarcations subsequently mapped onto it by a later historiography. To the French in the play, Joan is, from the outset, a 'holy maid' destined to be a national saviour:

> Which, by a vision sent to her from heaven,
> Ordained is to raise this tedious siege
> And drive the English forth the bounds of France.   (1.2.52–4)

The Christian imagery that collects around Joan (combined as it certainly is with classical and more exotic 'orientalist' references) is emphatically Roman Catholic, dwelling particularly on the iconography of the Virgin Mary. She refers to herself as a 'humble handmaid' (3.3.42) ('Behold the handmaid of the Lord', Luke, 1.38) and describes her encounter with an apparition of Our Lady which echoes various Biblical passages, including the Annunciation and Epiphany from the Gospel of Luke (I.26–38, II.8–14):

> Heaven and our Lady gracious hath it pleas'd
> To shine on my contemptible estate.
> Lo, whilst I waited on my tender lambs ...
> God's mother deigned to appear to me,
> And in a vision full of majesty
> Will'd me to leave my base vocation
> And free my country from calamity.   (1.2.74–6, 78–81)

Despite the consensus of the critical tradition, Joan's mission of divinely inspired national revival is offered in these scenes dramatically without any obvious contextualising irony. Her achievement in repelling the English invaders is fully acknowledged by the French, and is to be celebrated, in a foreshadowing of her subsequent canonisation, by the establishing of monuments which contrast interestingly with the warrior's tombs of her enemies:

> We'll set thy statue in some holy place,
> And have thee reverenc'd like a blessed saint ...   (3.3.14–15)

Joan is also compared to the mother of the first Christian Emperor Constantine, Helen, who was credited with the recovery of the true cross; under the banner of Christ, Joan will excavate and revive France's lost glory.

Of course there is an anchronistic subtext distinguishing the Roman Catholicism of the French, with its emphasis on the Virgin and the Communion of Saints, from a stout English Protestantism that sees the faith of the enemy as idolatry, heresy and diabolism:

> let them practise and converse with spirits:
> God is our fortress ... (2.1.25–6)

But it would surely be a grotesque oversimplification, and even a complicity with an archaic (though still of course very persistent) religious prejudice, to read this as a straightforward settling of the issues. On the contrary, as Gabrielle B. Jackson says, the play 'locates itself in areas of ideological discomfort', and 'uses culturally powerful images ambiguously, providing material from different members of a diverse audience to receive the drama in different ways' (Jackson, 1988: 65).

VIII

In addition to the construction of Joan as virgin saint and national heroine, she is attributed with magical powers of prophecy, both Christian – she is like one of the daughters, 'virgins and prophe-tesses', of the evangelist Philip – and like the Roman Sybil, a pagan seer readily adopted by the early Christians:

> The spirit of deep prophecy she hath,
> Exceeding the nine sibyls of old Rome:
> What's past and what's to come she can descry. (1.2.55–7)

Equipped with that capability of past and future vision, Joan appears almost as a *Zeitgeist*, a spirit of History, able to elucidate the prior subjugation, and to foretell the future victory, of France. She even offers a compelling and powerful theory of history as a series of cyclical epochs, governed by laws of development and decline:

> Glory is like a circle in the water,
> Which never ceaseth to enlarge itself

Till by broad spreading it disperse to nought.
With Henry's death the English circle ends;
Dispersed are the glories it included.   (1.2.133–7)

And it is as a new Astraea, the Golden Age goddess of Justice, that Joan promises to banish the Iron Age of English occupation and restore a 'golden day of victory' (1.6.31) to France.

There can be no doubting, either in the play or in the common historical record, the effectiveness of Joan's powers, whencesoever they derived. The dramatised La Pucelle remains until her capture (unlike the historical Joan) virtually undefeated; and her supremacy in battle remains unchallenged. All those heroic actions are performed, explicitly, by a woman. Despite the strong and pervasive emphasis of the historical record on her manliness and cross-dressing, which as we have seen figures largely in the charge-sheets of Halle and Holinshed, Shakespeare's play presents her unequivocally as a woman, and a beautiful one at that; a 'Fair maid' (1.2.64) , blessed with a manifest and undeniable beauty (Halle had suggested that her election of chastity had more to do with ugliness than with sanctity). Within a very short space Charles is acknowledging her sexual attractive- ness – 'Impatiently I burn with thy desire' (1.2.108) – and the observers of his drawn-out conference with Joan suggest that he 'shrives this woman to her smock' (1.2.119), perhaps merely a proverbial aphorism, but perhaps also an apparent indication that the boy actor would have been expected to wear female attire. Certainly Joan is always addressed by the French as 'woman', 'maid' or 'virgin'. When legendary parallels are sought, they invoke figures of strong women, such as Deborah, victor over the Canaanite kings (Judges, IV), or the Amazons, not of women who posed as men.

What the English see in Joan is in every respect precisely the opposite of this French perspective. They see not a saint, but a 'witch' (1.5.6), a 'fell banning hag' (5.3.42), an 'enchantress' (5.3.42), a 'railing Hecate' (3.2.64), the 'foul fiend of France, and hag of all despite' (3.2.52). They see not a virgin, but a 'strumpet'(1.5.12, 5.4.84), 'Encompass'd with . . . lustful paramours' (3.2.53). Even Joan's physical appearance is open to contradictory interpretations: where the French see beauty, they see ugliness: 'See how the ugly witch doth bend her brows' (5.3.34).

But the most remarkable feature of the play is less the oppositional confrontation of these mutually contradictory perspectives, than the possibilities of passage between them. Two characters in the play undergo a direct conversion from one ideology to the other – from 'French' to 'English', or vice versa – the Duke of Burgundy, and La Pucelle's father.

IX

The scene in which Burgundy is persuaded to break his alliance with England and to join the French (3.3) shows La Pucelle deploying powerful patriotic rhetoric that draws on the vocabularies of pacifism, chivalry, nationalism and religion. Burgundy is accused of betraying and wounding 'fertile France', the common mother of French and Burgundian alike. But he is also metaphorically placed in the position of a mother, helplessly watching her child dying.

> *Puc.*   Look on thy country, look on fertile France,
> And see the cities and the towns defac'd
> By wasting ruin of the cruel foe;
> As looks the mother on her lowly babe
> When death doth close his tender dying eyes,
> See, see the pining malady of France.   (3.3.44–9)

Burgundy is thus exhorted to feel a masculine shame at the unnatural violence he has inflicted on his own mother's 'breast'; and a maternal anguish at the fate of his country. A powerful appeal to the patriarchal family as synonymous with 'nature' initiates a reorientation of Burgundian violence from imputed matricide to chivalric protectiveness.

> Behold the wounds, the most unnatural wounds,
> Which thou thyself hast given her woeful breast.
> O, turn thy edged sword another way;
> Strike those that hurt, and hurt not those that help!   (3.3.50–3)

Within this ideological context 'English' blood demands to be copiously shed and casually wasted; while 'French' blood assumes a sacramental capability of redemption. Natural tears shed for Burgundy's betrayal then have the potency of Christ's redeeming blood, able to 'wash away' a country's guilt and pain.

One drop of blood drawn from thy country's bosom
Should grieve thee more than streams of foreign gore.
Return thee therefore with a flood of tears,
And wash away thy country's stained spots. (3.3.54–7)

The appeal closes with an allusion to the parable of the Prodigal Son (Luke, XV.11–32): the 'wasting ruin' of a misdirected life (as the Prodigal Son 'wasted his substance', Luke, XV.13) the anguish of parental injury, all freely forgiven, forgotten in a father's fond embrace:

Come, come, return; return, thou wandering lord;
Charles and the rest will take thee in their arms. (3.3.76–7)

Burgundy's submission and restoration to national community are figured in a similar range of metaphorical contexts. Initially he suspects the witchcraft attributed to La Pucelle by his allies; but he also acknowledges that some summons of 'nature', prompted by La Pucelle's invocations of family, country and faith, may be involved.

Either she hath bewitch'd me with her words,
Or nature makes me suddenly relent. (58–9)

His final acquiescence mingles the languages of chivalry, warfare, courtly love and religion:

Bur. I am vanquished; these haughty words of hers
Have batt'red me like roaring cannon-shot
And made me almost yield upon my knees.
Forgive me, country ... (78–81)

He is 'vanquished' like a soldier, but also like a courtly lover; subdued in chivalric quarrel, but felled by the ordnance of modern military technology; and he yields 'upon [his] knees' in a gesture that combines military defeat, knightly submission, romantic surrender, and religious supplication.

The whole exchange is, on the other hand, framed by a series of dramatic suggestions that imply quite different interpretations of Burgundy's reclamation than that suggested by the internal dialectic of the above exchange, and have been read as indicative of a corrosively ironic representation. La Pucelle, for example, announces her intention of persuading Burgundy to change sides in a language of politic expediency and opportunism:

> By fair persuasions, mix'd with sug'red words,
> We will entice the Duke of Burgundy
> To leave the Talbot and to follow us.   (3.3.18–20)

And Charles explicitly exhorts her to bewitch Burgundy with her suasive rhetoric: 'enchant him with thy words' (3.3.40). Most significant of all is Joan's final comment on Burgundy's transformation:

> Done like a Frenchman – *[Aside]* turn and turn again.   (3.3.85)

This line is invariably identified, as here in the Alexander text, as an ironic 'aside', addressed to the contemporary theatre audience, playing on a sixteenth-century nationalist sentiment anachronistic to the historical context, and inappropriate to the 'character' of Joan of Arc. Hence it has seemed reasonable in many critical accounts to infer that this reference wholly undermines both the significance of Burgundy's conversion (which becomes mere trickery and deception), and the power and beauty of Joan's language of domestic and political piety. Yet the line is not so marked in the Folio text, and can be read quite naturally as part of the address to Burgundy, extending the metaphors of circling and homecoming developed through the speech, and culminating as physical action in Burgundy's embracing of the French nobility. 'Done like a Frenchman' is therefore an admiring tribute to a new-found patriotism, and the action of 'turning' entirely in keeping with the rest of the speech.

Joan's father enacts a similar transmigration in the opposite direction. The Shepherd appears both as a 'natural' father, a simple man of common language, affection and piety; and a romance parent who has sought for his long-lost daughter through 'every country far and near' (5.4.3), for her sake shed 'many a tear' (19), and who requests that she kneel for his blessing in a potential gesture of reconciliation, forgiveness and benediction that would restore 'natural' relationship and heal community. La Pucelle's rejection of him, however, turns his language into the vindictive demonising discourse of the English: 'cursed drab ... burn her, burn her' (5.4.32–3).

York and Warwick see this exchange as symptomatic of La Pucelle's unnatural perversion of class and gender norms: Joan denies mother and father, family and social origin. But this must be understood not simply as a denial of truth and a betrayal of nature, but rather as a reaffirmation of the basic terms of Joan's political mission and historical legend. Were she to accept her father, she would be permitting herself to be contained within the restrictive parameters of patriarchal normality (as, momentarily, the historical Joan acquiesced in the patriarchal and episcopal authority of the Church in her recantation). Joan rather insists that her origin is royal, her mission divine; her blood sufficiently noble to justify armigerous status, her virginity sufficiently intact to symbolise a pious chastity.

This potent affirmation of Joan's virtue and sanctity seems then immediately contradicted by the subsequent confession of promis-. cuous correspondence, and an illegitimate pregnancy. Yet there is much more to this dénouement than misogynistic humour. Female critics have pointed out the absurdity of male readings that assume Joan's claims to have slept with the entire French nobility as literally true (Jackson, 1988: 42). But both parties to that quarrel confine their attention, oddly, to the question of sexual promiscuity, and miss the crucial symbolic idea of a child, fathered collectively by the French aristocracy, and born from the superhuman femininity of the French saint and national heroine.To the English, the threat of such patriarchal potency is sufficient to justify, even for mere suspicion in that kind, killing it in its mother's womb.

X

To employ her own metaphor of the circle in the water, that transient shape that forms and reforms, opens and disperses in an infinite sequence of self-renewing motions, Joan is the true centre of *Henry VI, Part One*, an empty and self-generating space of plenitude and vacancy, presence and absence. The figurative process contained in the metaphor again suggests the process of historical reconstruction and re-enactment: in history, names and legends are history ephemerally 'writ in water'; yet in 'History' they become clearly etched on the past's reflexive surface. The waters close together again into smooth and unblemished anonymity, as the gentle oceans close, at the end of Herman Melville's *Moby Dick*, over the sunken Pequod; or as the material world is figured in Cardinal Newman's simile, 'like an image on the waters, which is ever the same, though the waters ever flow' (Newman, 1857: 164). But another disturbance, another penetration, will always reactivate that process of perpetual motion.

Another variant of the same paradoxical figure pervades the plays in the image of the walled city, besieged, breached and occupied, alternately forced open to admit invaders, then repelling and closing against them. Joan's virginity seems similarly capable of breach and closure, possession that yet leaves the body intact. Thus the siege of Orleans is initially repelled, the city's perimeters sealed, by Joan's military force, leaving Talbot's mind spinning in an apprehension of fortunes reversed, glories 'dispersed':

> My thoughts are whirled like a potter's wheel;
> I know not where I am nor what I do.   (1.5.19–20)

Subsequently the English penetrate the citadel under cover of darkness (2.1), leaving the French describing, in their mutual recrimination, the paradoxical co-existence of openness and closure. Each commander protests the absolute security of his defensive position, but Charles, in a series of sexual innuendoes, reveals the exact point at which the body of the city was breached:

> And, for myself, most part of all this night,
> Within her quarter and mine own precinct
> I was employ'd in passing to and fro
> About relieving of the sentinels.   (2.1.67–70)

Even if 'quarter' and 'precinct' do not strongly enough convey carnal transaction, 'passing to and fro' and 'relieving' certainly do. We are not therefore surprised at Burgundy's glimpse of the couple fleeing 'arm in arm', 'like a pair of loving turtle-doves / That could not live asunder day or night'. But France's scattered strength can readily be recuperated, dispersal reintegrated into unity, the breached body resealed, as indicated in Joan's resolute order to regroup:

> Gather our soldiers, scatter'd and dispers'd ...   (2.1.76)

Similarly Joan's symbolic virginity, a key factor in her representation of power, seems capable of surviving the Dauphin's presumed penetration, and miraculously reforming, like the surface of water after ripples have dispersed. In Act 3, scene 2 the French, significantly disguised as peasants, in turn by stealth infiltrate Rouen. Joan discovers the city's point of 'weakness'; she disappears through that aperture, muffled in her peasant's smock, and then reappears on the city's battlements, thrusting forth as a beacon to her followers a flaring torch of liberty. It is not, therefore, a condition of unviolated chastity, but a miraculous power of self-renewal that enables Joan to be breached and healed, to disperse and reform; to vanish into darkness, clad in humble garments, and reappear in monumental magnificence as France's virgin saint and national heroine, holding aloft the torch of victory that is one of the illuminations (*lux veritatis*) of history itself.

The masculine hero, by contrast, in this play endures not just military defeat, but the decisive collapse of his feudal and chivalric ethic. Where Joan achieves her own version of Elizabeth's myth of Tilbury, by appropriation reconciling femininity with militarism, Talbot finds himself tangled and lost in a bewildering chaos of ideological and gender contradictions. Both hero and heroine leave behind a lingering testimony : Sir Thomas Lucy claims that the Talbot ashes will produce 'A phoenix that shall make all France afeard' (4.7.93); while La Pucelle leaves the English her 'curse' (5.4.86). But while the male heroic corpse is left visible on the battlefield, 'Stinking and fly-blown' (4.7.76), Joan's body is removed from the stage to be cremated into sainthood. Her legacy, curse or blessing, continues to haunt both the play and the culture in which it has been both appropriated and dispossessed.

6

Henry V

And I saw, and behold a white horse: and he that sat on him had a bow: and a crown was given unto him: and he went forth conquering, and to conquer.

Revelation, VI.2

I

The famous opening Chorus of *Henry V* provides a brilliant exposition of the complex relations between past and present, representation and presentation, history and theatre:

> pardon, gentles all,
> The flat unraised spirits that have dar'd
> On this unworthy scaffold to bring forth
> So great an object. Can this cockpit hold
> The vasty fields of France? Or may we cram
> Within this wooden O the very casques
> That did affright the air at Agincourt? ('Prologue', 8–14)

At one level a mere technical apology for the limitations of the contemporary theatre, the opening Chorus also expresses a defensive conviction of the present as immeasurably inferior to the past. Just as history seems to impose standards of heroism impossible to emulate, so are the actors conscious of themselves as unworthy representatives of the aristocratic subjects they are attempting to imitate. This 'diminution effect' is then applied generally to the contemporary world, in contradistinction to the past; particularly to the events and characters of history, as compared with the actors who merely simulate their vanished greatness; and specifically to the relative standings, within the social hierarchy, of modern plebeian actors and the antique aristocratic figures of historical legend.

The Globe theatre, that 'unworthy scaffold' with its flat and unadorned wooden stage, is the banal and unhistorical present, a 'wooden O' which in its very shape figures the perceived relative vacuity of the modern world. The theatre is a mere 'cockpit', a place of sport and trivial entertainment, where actors strut their feathers and fly at one another in raucous and petty squabbles. Those actors themselves are 'flat unraised spirits' in at least two senses. They are low-life, plebeian craftsmen who don't share in the lofty nobility possessed by the kings, queens and nobles whom they represent; they are rather mere supernumerary characters like Puttenham's shepherds and sailors who, though inhabitants of a historical drama, have no role to play in the drama of history. Equally they are compared to the spirits of the dead, 'flat', ineffective, without vitality; disembodied, they remain 'unraised', incapable of engaging with the vibrancy of corporeal existence, the concrete substantiality of real historical process.

Yet each of these disclaimers contains the potentiality for quite other levels of meaning. The wooden 'O' of the theatre can seem a lifeless vacuum, an emptiness, a mere nothing. But like the female womb, such an empty space can also be the source of all vitality, all existence. The players, though embedded in a medium of popular entertainment comparable to a bear-baiting or cock-fight, can nonetheless by the power of their 'invention' represent themselves as 'princes' who 'act', actors who can make a kingdom of their stage. The power of 'imaginary forces', like the necromantic potency of historical reconstruction, can indeed raise the dead, lift those 'flat' spirits into fully embodied, moving or terrifying, incarnate phantoms of theatrical representation.

The central paradox of history as revival is here therefore fully elaborated. All glory and greatness — the casques of Agincourt, the proud-hooved horses — are in the past, irrevocably lost in the dark backward and abysm of time. From its level platform of contemporaneity, the present can only glance over its shoulder in nostalgic recollection of a vanished magnitude. And yet the only means by which that transient glory can be apprehended is through the 'imaginary puissance' of theatrical representation, past splendour resurrected into full daylight, a brittle glory that nonetheless gleams brightly in the mirror of history.

The mechanisms by which this operation is conducted are openly and unashamedly declared in metaphors derived from the modern bourgeois world of financial accounting:

> since a crooked figure may
> Attest in little place a million . . .

>   let us, ciphers to this great accompt,
> On your imaginary forces work.   ('Prologue', 15–18)

Although the 'crooked figure', a circular 'O', may appear to be a vacant, hollow sign, it has the semiotic capability of vastly increasing the magnitude of its referent. Like the ostensibly empty 'O' of the theatre, the numerical zero can in practice signify plenitude and totality: just as the minuscule 'ciphers' of book-keeping can represent an infinitely larger sum of wealth, so the actors can stand in for the greatness of history. On the stage one man can signify a thousand, as in *Henry VI, Part One* the body of Talbot, the 'smallest part / And least proportion of humanity' (*HVI1*, 2.3.52–3), signifies the vast substance of an army, a nation, a kingdom.

So by emphasising the distance between history and the historicity of the theatre, the Chorus is claiming, rather than disclaiming, cultural power. Those modern technical and artisanal processes of acting, book-keeping, writing for the stage, seem from the aristocratic stand-point of the past to be trivial and hollow processes, mere gaps in the substance of a culture that ought to consist uniformly of great men and their deeds. But it is for precisely that reason that they are capable of opening up a space for active and positive intervention on the part of the historical drama. The theatre may be a wooden 'O', but it can still fill that empty space with grand narratives of English history. The book-keeper's tiny clerical inscription seems a mere squiggle, but it has the power to augment number and increase scale. The dramatic writer, granted at best an ambiguous status by the traditional codes of his society, can nonetheless, in this arena, 'make kings his subjects' ('I.M.S.', in Wells and Taylor, 1987: xli; see below, Conclusion). The popular audience, a collective of unhistorical characters constituted into the passivity of spectatorship, can by its 'thoughts' collaborate in the production of history.

Together these cultural forces conspire to create a collective historical imagination that has enormous and varied powers of freedom and control:

>   jumping o'er times,
> Turning th' accomplishment of many years
> Into an hour-glass ...   ('Prologue', 29–31)

The historical imagination, through the lively physical exertions of the actors, can exercise a virtually acrobatic liberty over chronology, 'jumping o'er times'; but at the same time condensing the passage of many years into a 'two hours' traffic' of the stage, confining the scope and scale of history into a strictly delimited space measurable by chronometer. Within the hour-glass the dust of vanished existence is contained, pent fast, shaped into a form both fixed and fluid, compact and evanescent; as in Hopkins' metaphor: 'soft sift / In an hour-glass — at the wall / Fast, but mined with a motion, a drift' (Hopkins, 1996: 99). Every grain of sand stands for a man, or an event, or a historical reality. In measured flow the dust is channelled into a tiny aperture (another 'O' or empty space) and thereby mimics the process of time, dust to dust, the present flowing imperceptibly but inevitably into past.

The hour-glass is of course a metaphor for the passage of time. But it is also a tool of measurement, an instrument of demonstration, a practical and utilitarian technology for controlling as well as acknowledging time. Time is measured by the empty space that appears after the sand that filled it has gone, so in one sense time is the absence of presence. But the sand has not disappeared, it has merely flowed into another space. By simple inversion of the hour-glass, the whole process can begin again, the dust of time recycled to initiate another passage: another hour, another play, another ritual enactment of that endless process of making and remaking, losing and finding; earth to earth, ashes to ashes, dust to dust.

Far from appearing here as a trite emblem of an abstraction 'Time', in the context of this Chorus the hour-glass is a packed and potent symbol of the way in which historical drama can simultaneously acknowledge the loss of the past, and yet by a simple trick of 'turning' formally re-enact and review its passage. A skilled craftsman's flick of the wrist, or a mountebank conjurer's sleight of hand, are the apparently trivial preconditions for a re-enactment of history. Just as the Chorus is as much concerned with the material conditions of production as with what is produced, the emphasis of this meta-phor is only partly on the process signified by the hour-glass's operation. It is also on the hour-glass as a tool, and on the bold artisanal skill that can 'turn' a history of aristocratic achievement into a modern and popular cultural process.

II

The image of history as reawakening is first broached by Henry him-self in the Council that determines the legitimacy of war with France:

take heed ...
How you awake our sleeping sword of war.   (1.2.21–2)

The tenor of the speech is throughout cautious and responsible. The
hero is also a king, who must take full responsibility for the death and
destruction entailed in the prosecution of an unjust war, in which
every shed drop of 'guiltless blood' constitutes a 'sore complaint':

'Gainst him whose wrongs gives edge unto the swords
That makes such waste in brief mortality.   (1.2.27–8)

Though concerned here primarily with analysing the justice of his
cause, Henry's language at this point opens up to provide a glimpse
of history seen from the democratic perspective. In the *longue durée* of
history, the individual life seems to occupy precious little space and
time; 'brief mortality' supervenes only temporarily on the 'waste
sad time' (Eliot, 1963: 195) of history's expanse. But paradoxically,
those actions likely to prove historical and fill past time with enduring
memory, are those that reduce that brevity even further, making of
human life within history a lost emptiness, a 'waste'.

Nonetheless it is at his 'charge' and 'conjuration' (where 'conjuration' can be either 'solemn adjuration' or 'necromantic incantation')
that the sleepy ghosts of the past are disturbed:

Cant.   Gracious lord,
Stand for your own, unwind your bloody flag,
Look back into your mighty ancestors.
Go, my dread lord, to your great-grandsire's tomb,
From whom you claim; invoke his warlike spirit ...   (1.2.100–4)

The process of historical resurrection that the Chorus has disclosed as
the means by which the play *Henry V* comes into being, is here shown
in operation within the imagined time and space of the represented
historical action. Ostensibly, Canterbury's exhortation simply con-
firms legitimacy by reference back to historic authority: Henry claims
the throne of France from his great-grandfather Edward III. But in this
heroic poetry, more is involved than the establishing of a genealogical precedent. We have considered Nash's account of 'brave
Talbot' being disinterred to re-enact his heroic life on the modern
stage; and the ghost of Henry V himself, at the opening of *Henry VI,
Part One*, escaping his tomb to shame and terrify his unworthy
successors. Now in order to propose and vindicate the heroic

historical sense that needs an Agincourt for its fulfilment, the Archbishop conjures the ghosts of Edward III and his son the Black Prince.
Anachronistically the heroes of the fourteenth century are credited
with 'play[ing] a tragedy' (1.1.106): if the present can dramatise the
past, why shouldn't the intermediate past of the fifteenth century
represent its own history prospectively as historical drama? Henry is
advised to 'go to' his grandfather's tomb, undertake a chivalric
pilgrimage to a site sanctified by heroic legend, in order to discover,
in his own ancestry, the meaning of his kingship. The present, in other
words, can read in the inscriptions of such monuments an honourable
and ancient language capable of guiding and inspiring the present
from the past.

But more than ritual homage and ancestral veneration are entailed
in this revisiting. Henry is exhorted to 'invoke' the warrior spirits of
those martial grandsires, to raise them from the dead, as the
Archbishop immediately proceeds to do by citing the well-known
historical legend of Crécy, in which the battle is envisaged as little
more than an opportunity for the Black Prince single-handedly to
prove his chivalric prowess:

> invoke his warlike spirit,
> And your great uncle's, Edward the Black Prince,
> Who on the French ground play'd a tragedy,
> Making defeat on the full power of France.   (1.2.104–7)

'Look back into your mighty ancestors' combines several implications: look into your own lineage, and consider what responsibilities
it requires; look back at your ancestors as models for emulation and
imitation; and finally look back at them as they can be made to
appear, revivified, alive and present in narrative depiction and dramatic rehabilitation:

> Whiles his most mighty father on a hill
> Stood smiling to behold his lion's whelp
> Forage in blood of French nobility.   (1.2.108–10)

In a parallel passage (2.4) the French king himself reiterates this
legend point for point:

> Think we King Harry strong . . .
> . . . he is bred out of that bloody strain
> That haunted us in our familiar paths.

Witness our too much memorable shame
When Cressy battle fatally was struck,
And all our princes captiv'd by the hand
Of that black name, Edward, Black Prince of Wales;
Whiles that his mountain sire — on mountain standing,
Up in the air, crown'd with the golden sun —
Saw his heroical seed, and smil'd to see him.   (2.4.48–59)

That same precedent history that the Archbishop invoked to encourage Henry's heroic aspirations appears to the French as a 'haunting'. This hostile and grudgingly adulatory commemoration of the Black Prince goes far beyond respect for a past enemy, and the persistent sense of a national humiliation. Crécy has become a historical myth comparable to the myth that Agincourt is, in the play, yet to become. That extraordinary echo of the Baptism of Christ — 'And, lo, a voice from heaven, saying, This is my beloved Son, in whom I am well pleased' (Matthew, III.17) — elevates the battle into a great universal historical legend, and confers on such representatives of English chivalry and national pride as the Black Prince (and of course Henry V himself) some measure of divine approval. Henry's kindred, the French king reminds his followers in a highly-charged metaphor, 'hath been fleshed upon us' (2.4.50) — that is, their power has been inscribed in wounds on French flesh, 'blooded' as in hunting initiations; and their punishing force incarnated as the scourge of a providential retribution.

The challenge laid before Henry contains echoes of both 'renaissance' and haunting. He is exhorted to

Ely.   Awake remembrance of these valiant dead,
And with your puissant arm renew their feats.   (1.2.115–16)

To remember those dead is to reawaken the power of example, and to incur the heavy responsibilities of emulation. The responsibility envisaged here as personal is also national, a burden of historical destiny. In a strikingly evocative metaphor, the past is figured as the sea-bed, and history as the 'chronicle' that locates and enumerates its sunken treasures. Henry has the opportunity, he is told, to make England's

chronicle as rich with praise
As is the ooze and bottom of the sea
With sunken wreck and sumless treasuries.   (1.2.163–5)

The historical 'chronicle' is thus a lading-sheet of national achievements, an inventory of epic deeds. History is a remote, invisible world
of lost treasures and sunken cargoes, buried in the muddy ooze of
the past. Making history is conceived as a salvage operation that
can locate and identify those lost riches, which would otherwise
be destined to remain, in Dylan Thomas' phrase, 'dumb and deep'
(Thomas, 1952, 1966: 80), awaiting some cataclysmic exhumation, or
those last days when the sea shall, finally, give up its dead.

If Henry fails to achieve heroic distinction, he will have missed his
destiny, leaving his name to sink ignobly into the sea-bed's ooze. If he
does not achieve France, he must

> lay these bones in an unworthy urn,
> Tombless, with no remembrance over them.
> Either our history shall with full mouth
> Speak freely of our acts, or else our grave,
> Like Turkish mute, shall have a tongueless mouth.   (1.2.228–32)

This speech describes not a dilemma, but a 'catch-22'. If you're a
historical character, confronted with the vanished magnificence of
your heroic forebears, you have no alternative but to act historically.
There is no choice for Henry but that between a voluble history
of 'acts' which can be vocally proclaimed by the 'full mouth' of
documentary record (historical chronicle, or the memorial inscription
on an honourable funeral monument), and historical oblivion, a record
sealed to dumbness by mutilation, like the Turkish slave cruelly
silenced to preserve his master's secrecy. Nor, apparently, by this
stage, is there any real election of the basis on which Henry's
historical legend is to be founded. The only alternative to historical
oblivion is the conquest of France. The only alternative to the
conquest of France is historical oblivion.

III

Henry further develops these thoughts on kingship and destiny in his
response to the Dauphin's mocking present:

> we understand him well,
> How he comes o'er us with our wilder days,
> Not measuring what use we made of them.

We never valu'd this poor seat of England;
And therefore, living hence, did give ourself
To barbarous licence; as 'tis ever common
That men are merriest when they are from home.   (1.2.266–72)

Henry here identifies himself with his sovereignty, and his sovereignty in turn with his historical destiny. As a prince, he remained independent of his fate, maintaining his historical destiny at a distance, like the Prodigal Son (Luke, XV.12–13) giving himself to 'barbarous licence', for 'men are merriest when they are from home'. Absent in this way from his state, Henry was also alienated from himself, in a fundamentally existentialist sense self-absented, 'from home' (compare the Prince at the beginning of *Henry IV, Part Two*, promising to 'be himself', identifying his ontological identity with his historical destiny: see below, Chapter 7). In that shadow land of historical oblivion and self-alienation, he played the role of a common working man – 'plodded like a man for working-days'. But now it is time to reunite identity with state, self and kingship:

I will keep my state,
Be like a king . . .   (1.2.273–4)

Historical destiny is then decisively grasped and reformulated as political recovery, national rehabilitation and divine revelation:

I will rise there with so full a glory . . .   (278)

Henry will 'rise' from the nonentity of his prodigal youth, where he was, like Shakespeare himself, only 'a King among the meaner sort' (Davies, 1967: 26), to political eminence as a king. He will also 'rise' from the slothful peace of his hitherto uneventful and innocuous reign, 'rouse' himself from inactive slumber to emulate 'the former lions of [his] blood'. But the metaphor also links historical destiny with theological revelation, for Henry intends to 'rise' as the Saviour Himself rose on the third day, to re-enter his kingdom in 'full . . . glory'. In this Christian language Henry declares himself essentially and intrinsically godlike, even before he makes the claim of absolute conformity between his actions and the divine will:

But this lies all within the will of God,
To whom I do appeal; and in whose name,

Tell you the Dauphin, I am coming on,
To venge me as I may and to put forth
My rightful hand in a well-hallow'd cause.   (1.2.289–93)

The cause being thus 'hallow'd', God and king are inseparably fused:
or rather the King's divinely inspired will is reconciled with the will of
God. This unconditional conviction of 'God on our side' enables
Henry to reorientate his anxieties about the heavy costs of war. Earlier
concerned about the 'waste' inflicted by war on 'brief mortality', here
he attributes responsibility for war's 'wasteful vengeance' directly to
the Dauphin, indeed specifically to the Dauphin's 'mockery':

                                           his soul
Shall stand sore charged for the *wasteful* vengeance . . .
                                    (my italics; 1.2.282–3)

In constituting himself as this complex, inclusive being in whom
the plebeian, the royal and the divine natures are harmoniously intertwined, Henry enacts the kind of transformation previously identified
by the Archbishop of Canterbury as miraculous. The conversion of
Henry from prodigal and youthful wildness to mature sagacity and
gracious royalty is admitted as incredible by the very representatives
of that Christian faith that characteristically validates its authority
through stories of miraculous divine intervention and inexplicable
conversions such as that of St Paul:

                        miracles are ceas'd;
And therefore we must needs admit the means
How things are perfected.   (1.1.67–9)

The idea of such a 'sudden reformation' is surely no more incredible,
to a Christian, than the resurrection of the body (as St Paul says when
defending himself before Agrippa, 'Why should it be thought a thing
incredible with you, that God should raise the dead?', Acts, XXVI.8).
But the bishops, in their conspiratorial world of financial planning and
mercenary calculation, in one sense occupy a modern materialistic and
sceptical consciousness remote from their own historical realm of
mediaeval Christianity. They view the church not as the community
of Christ's faithful, or as a means of bringing men closer to God, but
as an administrative and political apparatus. From their perspective,

modern history is a social process which they can influence and manipulate, not an unfolding of God's providence: hence contact between the divine and human worlds, as manifested in the Incarnation, can no longer be imagined, for miracles are ceased.

While the clerics reason on secondary causes, Henry boldly affirms a new religion, in which God no longer becomes man, but man-king becomes God. In turn the human assumption of divinity becomes a manifestation of that which is unhistorical rising to the level of history. The whole process is, of course, as the Chorus initially explained, actually being managed by modern plebeian actors in a secular theatre. Hence, ironically, it is those anonymous and secular players, arrogating both aristocratic and sacerdotal functions, who are the instruments to administer this new historical sacrament, making the audience sharers in the miraculous transformation of action to character, present to past, theatre to history.

IV

In the form of the history play, the religion of this new secular church is, however, a gospel of war rather than one of peace: a sacrament of violence, not one of reconciliation. The key persona through which the play connects the demotic, the sovereign and the divine is that of the soldier. In the two key speeches of Act 3, Henry's address to his troops before Harfleur ('Once more into the breach'), and his speech to the Governor and citizens of the besieged town, the figure of the soldier becomes a constitutive embodiment of historical character and national destiny. The Christian virtues are acknowledged as appropriate to a pacific context –

> In peace there's nothing so becomes a man
> As modest stillness and humility   (3.1.3–4)

– but quite out of place in the theatre of battle. The 'blast of war' (3.1.5) which breaks that stillness is both *'nuntia vetustatis'*, the 'trumpet of chivalry', and the summons of history, requiring men to transform themselves into that grotesque collage of corporeal, animal, mechanical and natural forces that is celebrated in this epic exhortation, and that is finally posited as capable of conjuring the spirits of the past, raising the dead:

Then imitate the action of the tiger:
Stiffen the sinews, summon up the blood,
Disguise fair nature with hard-favour'd rage;
Then lend the eye a terrible aspect;
Let it pry through the portage of the head
Like the brass cannon ...
Now set the teeth, and stretch the nostril wide;
Hold hard the breath, and bend up every spirit
To his full height.   (3.1.6–17)

Literally the 'spirit' invoked here is simply that of military courage, a physiological property capable of inflating the body into an unstoppable war-machine. But the drawing up of the 'spirits' to superhuman effort is accomplished, the imagery reminds us, by the actor's capacity to breathe life into the 'flat unraised spirits' of the dead. The breath-stopping vigour of this violent poetry even implies a substitution, for ordinary human breath, of some supernatural afflatus invigorating the soldier's body, as God breathed life into the dry bones of Ezekiel's vision.

The provocation to undertake this metamorphosis is again the charge of responsibility for emulating past examples of paternal heroism:

On, on, you noblest English,
Whose blood is fet from fathers of war-proof –
Fathers that, like so many Alexanders
Have in these parts from morn till even fought.   (3.1.17–20)

Legitimate descent from the father links the nobility with a heroic dynasty traceable back much further than Crécy, back to one of the original progenitors of the epic tradition, Alexander the Great. The role of the mother in this process – 'Dishonour not your mothers; now attest / That those whom you call'd fathers did beget you' (3.1.22–3) – is a kind of 'quality assurance' function, that of legitimating by her chastity the honour of the father and of the son. Any failure on the part of the son to replicate the father's example will implicitly, by casting doubt on paternity, set a question mark against the mother's fidelity and secure custodianship of the male bloodline.

The nobility can thus look backwards towards their fathers and ancestors, incidentally honouring the unblemished chastity of their maternal transmission. But, of course, a fifteenth-century war is not fought in the chivalric poetry of the Accession Day tilt, or in the glamour of single combat between noble heroes. War also needs professional soldiers who have no such illustrious ancestry from which to claim their derivation.

> And you, good yeomen,
> Whose limbs were made in England, show us here
> The mettle of your pasture; let us swear
> That you are worth your breeding — which I doubt not;
> For there is none of you so mean and base
> That hath not noble lustre in your eyes.   (3.1.25–30)

Bred like cattle in the pastures of England, expected here to repay in loyal service the investment of their 'breeding', the common infantrymen stand as representatives of the anonymous and unhistorical. But here they have their own shot at entering history, a unique opportunity to join, by virtue of successful military action, the pantheon of heroes. Such inclusion is only possible, however, by possession of some trace of the patrician status that defines both military excellence and heroic reputation, some reflected glory, some faint glimmer of true nobility.

In his speech before the besieged city, however, Henry extends this mythologising further by numbering himself, as king, among the company of soldiers:

> as I am a soldier,
> A name that in my thoughts becomes me best.   (3.3.5–6)

Having already in the previous speech linked the figure of the noble chivalric knight with that of the dedicated warrior or modern trooper, all bound together by that gleam of shared nobility that is the unifying loyalty of the *comitatus*, Henry now instates into the heroic band the body of the king. The chivalric noble and the trusty *miles* are joined by the martial monarch as the soldier of Christ, crusader for a divine as well as royal patriotism:

> Cry 'God for Harry, England, and Saint George!'   (3.1.34)

This inclusive, composite figure of the noble and plebeian, divine and secular, hero-king allows for powerful effects of fragmentation and dissociation, as well as affirmations of unity. Henry represents that part of himself he names 'soldier' as an element that can readily be separated from the self, left to operate unilaterally and independently according to its own laws. Once the 'soldier' Henry is released, 'he' has no choice but to destroy Harfleur.

By this process of self-alienation and psychological splitting, Henry can represent himself as simultaneously the 'flesh'd soldier, rough and hard of heart' (3.3.11), and as a sovereign spirit of discipline, the 'cool and temperate wind of grace' (3.3.30) that holds this brutal and terrifying force within its control and command. 'Flesh'd' even suggests a process of incarnation, by which divine majesty, on a mission of national salvation, roots itself in the military body.

V

It may appear, as critics have often suggested, that Henry is simply disclaiming moral responsibility for the actions of his troops — 'What is it then to me' (3.3.15) — as he later exculpates himself from any share in the guilt of his soldiers' deaths. But it is specifically from the persona of the 'enraged soldier' that culpability is thus disclaimed; though later in the play, when Henry confronts his soldiers directly, it is adroitly reinstated. As a divine king, Henry can of course choose to maintain the inhibiting pressure of 'grace', but as a 'soldier', he can only relentlessly pursue his occupation of slaughter, rape, devastation and spoil.

The nightmare vision of warfare produced in this speech is of course entirely at odds with all the codes of chivalry. The emphasis throughout the speech is in fact on the likelihood of a systematic violation and destruction of exactly those members of society the chivalric hero is bound to protect — old men, women, virgins, infants.

> in a moment look to see
> The blind and bloody soldier with foul hand
> Defile the locks of your shrill-shrieking daughters;
> Your fathers taken by the silver beards,
> And their most reverend heads dash'd to the walls;
> Your naked infants spitted upon pikes,
> Whiles the mad mothers with their howls confus'd
> Do break the clouds, as did the wives of Jewry
> At Herod's bloody-hunting slaughtermen.   (3.3.33–41)

By virtue, however, of the complex and inclusive character Henry has established for himself, he is able to speak from different subject-positions within this composite totality. It is as a soldier that he threatens ('I will not leave the half-achieved Harfleur / Till in her ashes she lie buried' [3.3.8–9]), and as a pragmatic and secular monarch that he admonishes ('Will you yield, and this avoid?' [3.3.42]). But it is as a divine king or sovereign divinity that he promises, in the essential vocabulary of Christianity, mercy, pity and grace; alluding to 'The gates of mercy' (3.3.10), begging the citizens to 'Take pity on your town' (3.3.28), and figuring his own authority and command as 'the cool and temperate wind of grace' (3.3.30).

The idea of history as an unfolding of Divine Providence that structures many Tudor histories (such as that of Edward Halle), and that provided the initial framework for modern critical interpretations of the history plays, is here manifestly and visibly internalised within Henry's poetic language and theatrical role. He is the prime mover of this historical action, and within it his power is omnipotent. He is his own providence. His is the kingdom, the power, and the glory.

These pretensions to godlike status allow Henry virtually complete freedom and flexibility of action. He is able to act with all the confident power of divinity, or resign his will to that of God ('O God, Thy arm was here!' [4.8.104]); to initiate, control and finally legitimate processes that are transparently irreligious or anti-Christian (he even compares the imminent sack of Harfleur to the Massacre of the Innocents [Matthew, II], his own soldiers to 'Herod's bloody-hunting slaughtermen' [3.3.41]); to speak from the radically dissimilar subject-positions of common soldier, feudal warrior or divine monarch. It is therefore reasonable, as many critics have done, to interpret the speech before Harfleur as a transparent piece of bluffing, since at one level Henry is negotiating directly with representatives of a foreign government, on the basis of a mutual understanding (later identified as a 'Christian-like accord' [5.2.344]) deeper than the particular cause of conflict. He is in this sense vividly describing ravage and disaster that neither of the two ruling classes would wish to see (just as later he does not dissent from Burgundy's utopian vision of a pacified France, provided the French are prepared to 'buy' peace by submission to his demands). In this discursive frame, the ground of international affinity is a shared body of Christian values (mercy, pity, grace), against the background of which the 'soldier' becomes a monstrous alien force that Christian governments would naturally wish to suppress and control.

VI

Just as the plebeian actor is required to re-enact history, so the common soldier is needed to complete the historical action, accomplish the conquest of France and win a glorious English victory. As the action approaches this decisive testing, the play's investments in epic style and heroic convention intensify. The Chorus opening Act 4 is the most formally epic of all the Choric speeches. In a typically paradoxical conjuncture, a vivid poetry of action is used to describe a moment of inactivity – the tense stillness of the long night before Agincourt, the vague sounds and flickering lights of military preparation. In another subtle image for the nature of the historical drama, the Chorus sites itself in that empty space between encamped armies that later became known as 'no-man's-land': a marginal space between two embattled forces, between present and past, between audience and players, between us and them; a space about to be filled with the drama of history.

From this perspective the Chorus distinguishes, in traditional patriotic fashion, between the 'confident and over-lusty French' (18) and the 'low-rated English' (19) who wait in melancholy dejection 'Like sacrifices' (23) for the apparently inevitable defeat. Against this sombre background the figure of Henry appears in the full splendour of his own heroic myth:

> O, now, who will behold
> The royal captain of this ruin'd band
> Walking from watch to watch, from tent to tent,
> Let him cry 'Praise and glory on his head!'
> For forth he goes and visits all his host;
> Bids them good morrow with a modest smile,
> And calls them brothers, friends, and countrymen ...
>
> mean and gentle all
> Behold, as may unworthiness define,
> A little touch of Harry in the night.   (4, 'Prologue', 28–34, 45–7)

In this depiction Henry abundantly displays the expected heroic virtues of courage in the face of desperate odds, the gaiety and insouciance of a truly brave leader. But above all his presence inculcates a powerful sense of fraternity, of a common bond between himself and the common soldiers. The generosity of feeling extended to 'mean and gentle all' seems to construct an image of egalitarian leadership: as the socially diversified *comitatus* is bound together by a shared nobility, so Henry shares royalty liberally among all those who are to participate in the battle.

Beyond the battlefield itself there also lies an important political objective: which is that of transferring the majesty earned by the heroic 'ruin'd band' of Agincourt to the corporate body of the English nation. But the action of Act 4, far from sustaining or substantiating this impressive prologue, subjects the heroic vision of Henry and his army to an intensive interrogation. The dramatic device of the king's disguise is used to set up situations that explore the themes of equality and national unity propounded by the Chorus. In appearing as common man and disguised king, Henry is able to put into practice the idea of egalitarian majesty that is at the heart of the myth of Agincourt. The play, however, simultaneously presents history, and unpicks the fabric of its own representation, by exposing the nature of the process by which the king seeks, in his own body and in his triple role as king, captain and saviour, to unify the nation.

The idea of equality is interrogated particularly in Henry's conversation with the three soldiers (4.1). From the security of his disguise, Henry asserts the essential humanity of the king's person: 'I think the King is but a man' (4.1.101). The cold truth offered by plain John Bates, however, penetrates the armour of the king's disguise: this is how an ordinary man, who is not a member of any chivalric or aristocratic elite, feels on the night before battle:

> *Bates.*   He may show what outward courage he will; but I believe, as cold a night as 'tis, he could wish himself in Thames up to the neck; and so I would he were, and I by him, at all adventures, so we were quit here.
> *King.*   By my troth, I will speak my conscience of the King: I think he would not wish himself anywhere but where he is.
> *Bates.*   Then I would he were here alone; so should he be sure to be ransomed, and a many poor men's lives saved.   (4.1.112–22)

Bates' interrogation of Henry's purposes, and indeed of the whole expedition, offers to the audience an alternative position of intelligibility, in which it becomes possible to question the moral justice of the king's quarrel, and the political value of military success; and even to glimpse, in embryo, a popular pacifism that draws on the chivalric tradition to affirm that kings should fight their own battles, rather

than involve their peoples in bloody war. Bates argues that the king's
quarrel is so entirely the king's responsibility that the soldiers who
die in it are absolved of their guilt: 'If his cause be wrong, our obedience to the King wipes the crime out of us' (4.1.131–2). The soldier
Williams overtly rejects Henry's egalitarian ideology of a nation
organically bound into cohesive unity by a national quarrel with
a foreign enemy, and clearly identifies Henry's exculpatory arguments as a displacement of the problem, from the hierarchical realm
of history to the levelling kingdom of death. When Williams' insis-
tence on the essential inequality of king and common man becomes
unanswerable, Henry finds himself pushed into exactly the kind of
quarrel he has entered France to avoid: a civil conflict between subject
and king.

After the departure of the soldiers, Henry is able metaphorically
to cast off his disguise, and to relapse in soliloquy into a 'private',
royal identity. Kingship is a heavy responsibility, accompanied by
external signs of rank and power, unreal compensations for the
'hard condition' of greatness. By contrast the king's subjects, signified
throughout by terms of aristocratic contempt – 'fool ... wretched
slave ... peasant' (4.1.231, 264, 280) – live in bestial contentment.
This paternalistic diatribe against the common people is a response
to the uncomfortable common wisdom of the soldiers, against
which Henry defends himself by identifying it as ignorant prejudice
rooted in the 'gross brain' of the contemptible 'peasant' (4.1.278–80).
The soldiers themselves are hardly, in practice, immune from similar anxieties; and they scarcely at this moment benefit from the
king's 'peace'.

It has often been argued that Henry's egalitarianism represents an
effective challenge to the pre-eminently feudal ideology of war still
dominant in the French camp (Stribrny, in Kettle, 1964). The French
think only of the exploits and honour of their nobility, and regard
their common soldiers as 'superfluous lackeys'. Henry seeks to unite
his nation by incorporating his common soldiers into the majesty of
the realm: the earnest democratic heroism of his language differs
strikingly from the chivalric vaunting of the French nobles. And yet
what is the ground of this national unity?

> We few, we happy few, we band of brothers;
> For he to-day that sheds his blood with me
> Shall be my brother; be he ne'er so vile,
> This day shall gentle his condition.   (4.3.60–3)

The victors of Agincourt are to belong, not to a united nation, but to a crack military elite: the dissolution of hierarchy is envisaged only within the embattled ranks of an army, the ideal commonwealth invoked by a universalisation of the heroic language of chivalry. But this is a mere reaffirmation of the heroic tradition, not the construction of a new popular nationalism. The only ground for this unity of the English nation is the field of battle. 'England' is defined here simply in terms of this army: the few, the band of brothers whose occupation is to fight and kill. Here England is united in a spurious cohesion achieved by the channelling of feudal action into foreign war. The Welsh, Scottish and Irish officers obviously symbolise some political act of union: but they are professional fighting men, who talk only of war, and can hardly be held to represent a united kingdom.

The theatre is the ideal medium for the representation of such an image of national union, where a part is held to symbolise the whole: since a small group of characters can symbolise a nation as well as they can symbolise an army, and indeed can claim to be both at once. But a theatre which draws attention to the fabricated character of its own dramatic strategies can both present social reconciliation, and disclose the artifical character of the unity it enacts. While the spectator may be excited by the fighting camaraderie of this heroic body of men, the play insistently reminds him or her that such camaraderie of the battlefield can signify the unity of a nation only in a strictly limited and temporary sense.

Even within the strategic cohesion of this military unity, Henry's ideology remains too firmly attached to the values of the heroic tradition to become a genuine national sovereignty. The slaughter of the French prisoners, which arouses some conflicting sentiments in Holinshed's narrative, is presented in *Henry V* with similar ambivalence. Gower and Fluellen assume that the massacre is a reprisal for the killing of the boys left guarding the English supplies. In fact, we know from the previous scene, Henry knew nothing of this when he gave the order. In context, the command arises out of Exeter's highly charged chivalric account of the deaths of York and Suffolk.

> Suffolk first died; and York, all haggled over,
> Comes to him, where in gore he lay in-steeped,
> And takes him by the beard, kisses the gashes
> That bloodily did yawn upon his face,
> And cries aloud 'Tarry, my cousin Suffolk.
> My soul shall thine keep company to heaven;

Tarry, sweet soul, for mine, then fly abreast;
As in this glorious and well-foughten field
We kept together in our chivalry.' ...
So did he turn, and over Suffolk's neck
He threw his wounded arm and kiss'd his lips;
And so, espous'd to death, with blood he seal'd
A testament of noble-ending love.   (4.6.11–19, 24–7)

The chivalric emotion of this moment, as two noble warriors, dying in their own noble blood, seal a final knightly *Blutbrüderschaft*, is what provokes in Henry a response of intense personal grievance and swift ruthless reprisal which manifests him to be, not a consummate military strategist, but an incurable adherent of the heroic tradition, or rather his own particular consecration of it, in that linking of 'blood' and 'testament', to Christian theology: 'This is my blood of the new testament' (Mark, XIV.24). 'Sealed' also recalls the Sacrament of Baptism, as well as various legal and chivalric rituals. When the king reads the list of those killed on the English side he names only those with titles, from duke to esquire. The list of the dead contains 'None else of name' (4.8.103): though it might have contained, among those nameless common soldiers, Henry's companions of the previous night, John Bates and Alexander Court, whose names he never sought to know.

7

Henry IV

See that ye walk circumspectly, not as fools, but wise;
Redeeming the time, because the days are evil.
Ephesians, 5.15–16

I

So shaken as we are, so wan with care,
Find we a time for frighted peace to pant
And breathe short-winded accents of new broils
To be commenc'd in strands afar remote.
No more the thirsty entrance of this soil
Shall daub her lips with her own children's blood;
No more shall trenching war channel her fields,
Nor bruise her flow'rets with the armed hoofs
Of hostile paces. Those opposed eyes
Which, like the meteors of a troubled heaven,
All of one nature, of one substance bred,
Did lately meet in the intestine shock
And furious close of civil butchery,
Shall now in mutual well-beseeming ranks
March all one way, and be no more oppos'd
Against acquaintance, kindred, and allies.
The edge of war, like an ill-sheathed knife,
No more shall cut his master. Therefore, friends,
As far as to the sepulchre of Christ –
Whose soldier now, under whose blessed cross
We are impressed and engag'd to fight –
Forthwith a power of English shall we levy,
Whose arms were moulded in their mothers' womb
To chase these pagans in those holy fields
Over whose acres walk'd those blessed feet
Which fourteen hundred years ago were nail'd
For our advantage on the bitter cross.   (*HIV1*, 1.1.1–27)

Henry IV, Part One begins in a mood of revulsion against war, militarism, even masculinity. Although the violence of civil war is here initially figured as female, as the monstrous mother earth who devours her own children, the pattern of opposites is broadly the same as that deployed by Richard II in his 'pastoral' speeches (see below, Chapter 8) — the hard, violent instruments, the 'armed hoofs' of war, threaten an innocent, and implicitly feminine, landscape of pastoral 'fields' and vulnerable 'flow'rets'. But peace is again, as in *Richard III*, only a temporary suspension of the normal state of war: 'frighted peace' catches her breath merely to pant out news of another prospective battle.

The new military campaign Henry longs to undertake is, however, an alternative to the 'intestine shock' of civil war: it is a crusade, a vision of the nation united in the bonds of chivalric militarism, all marching in the same direction and against the same opponent. This potential unity is expressed in religious terms — the English military aristocracy are to become 'the soldiers of Christ' — but is also an implied effect of their common ethnic origin:

> All of one nature, of one substance bred ... (1.1.11)

By their breeding, as by their common faith, though many, they are all of one body, being of one substance 'with the Father, by whom all things were made' (Common Prayer, 1662: 'The Lord's Supper'). Yet though the nation's fighting men are made in the image of the heroic father, they are also shaped by their transmission through the vehicle of the mother:

> a power of English ...
> Whose arms were moulded in their mothers' womb ... (1.1.22–3)

Or as The Book of Common Prayer expresses it, while God is 'of the Substance of the Father, begotten before the worlds', Man is 'of the Substance of his Mother, born in the world' (Common Prayer, 1662: 'Quicunque Vult'). The true purpose of that shaping of masculine and military power ('arms' hints severally at 'limbs', 'weapons' and 'heraldic escutcheons') is certainly a heroic and patriarchal enterprise — 'to chase these pagans' — but one whose tutelary patron presents an image not of epic action, but of sacrificial passion; not of heroic aggression, but of voluntary subjugation; the Christ who, 'nail'd / For our advantage on the bitter cross', in the words of Venantius Fortunatus, 'immolatus vicerit' ('as a victim won the day' [New English Hymnal, 1986: 83]).

Henry is attempting here, therefore, not simply to unite the nation as a means of averting civil war, but to renew the heroic tradition by synthesising war and peace, male and female. He aspires to reconcile Christian values and heroic virtues, and to acknowledge the interdependence of male aggression and female creativity, feminine 'weakness' (as exemplified in Christ) and masculine force. The crusaders would thus be formed in the image of the heroic father and the creative mother: burning with individual heroic zeal, but drawn together by a common maternal origin; bearing arms against a foreign enemy, yet marching beneath the banner of a suffering and subjugated Christ.

II

The vision is immediately contextualised as a dream whose fulfilment is thwarted by the contradictory substance of which it forms the idealised shadow. The story told by current history-in-process is far 'more uneven and unwelcome news' (1.1.50) than Henry's gospel of war-in-peace, since it tells of a continuation, not a cessation, of the unresolved tensions and unreconciled uncertainties of civil war. The language of chivalric piety and *comitatus* cohesion, of dedicated troops all obediently marching together in unison, gives way to the more disturbing discourse used to describe Mortimer's failed expedition against 'the irregular and wild' (1.1.40) Glendower. The reported mutilation of the English soldiers' corpses by the Welshwomen (1.1.43–6) radically destabilises Henry's carefully constructed synthesis of male and female powers: the maternal creativity that in the womb moulds warriors in the image of their heroic fathers, is here perverted, by a 'shameless transformation', into a female form of violation that tears apart what has been so lovingly shaped and formed, the heroic male body.

Westmoreland also bears a tale of Hotspur's conflict with Douglas, in which the outcome is reported as dubious, and the clash of values within chivalry clearly delineated, since in terms of their heroic credentials both contendors are equally virtuous, the 'gallant Hotspur' (1.1.52) counterpoised against the 'brave Archibald' (1.1.53). The eyewitness who brings this information testifies to a continuing process of conflict, the 'pride of their contention' (1.1.60), which is and seems likely to remain unresolved. The emphasis on historical report as 'news', the transmission and construction of information, is as important as the stress on the internal contradictions and self-destructive tendencies of the heroic ethic. For this shows us precisely history in the making, as inconclusive and fragmentary reports are assimilated into a definitive interpretation:

> *King.* Here is a dear, a true industrious friend,
> Sir Walter Blunt, new lighted from his horse,
> Stain'd with the variation of each soil
> Betwixt that Holmedon and this seat of ours.   (1.1.62–5)

Cast in the comic role of the cod-Shakespearean 'hot-foot messenger', Blunt is 'new lighted from his horse', the bearer of immediate and up-to-date information. The authenticity of his report is also, however, guaranteed by physical signs, stained on his body, that confirm his status as a historical source: the variations of soil on his mud-splashed dress provide, like stratified geological layers, the means of tracing his passage directly back to the site of the battle.

As one would expect, the data available from such an immediate, eye-witness, and earth-coloured source is, as the play soon makes clear, an honest and accurate depiction of the uncertain and contradictory medium of historical process. It is the king who makes 'History' out of 'history', as he converts Blunt's discouraging message into 'smooth and welcome news', identifying Hotspur's victory as an 'honourable spoil' (1.1.74), and a 'gallant prize' (1.1.75); or as West-moreland phrases it, 'a conquest for a prince to boast of' (1.1.77). The true significance of the information is of course anything but 'smooth and welcome' (1.1.66): since as subsequent indications make clear, Hotspur's refusal to hand over his prisoners to the king has already clouded the brilliance of his victory. The chivalric language in which Henry attempts to relate this epic is as unstable as the feudal relation-ships it sought to express: in the same speech he both applauds Percy as 'sweet Fortune's minion and her pride' (1.1.83), and acknowledges that the young hero's 'pride', emanating in his resistance to the king's authority, is the principal source of disorder in the realm. The victory at Holmedon thus stands doubly for a triumph of the king's power over internal rebellion, and for an example of the internal divisiveness of chivalric values, the self-destructive energies of the heroic tradition.

III

The structure of the father–son interaction here differs from other examples we have studied, such as Hamlet's failure to conform to his heroic father's model, or Talbot's temporary renunciation of his son's heroic destiny in the interests of securing his survival. Here the heroic father has the opportunity to compare two sons, a young Talbot and a young Hamlet: Hotspur, 'a son who is the theme of honour's tongue' (*HIV1*, 1.1.81), and his own son Henry, who appears so signally to betray his historic inheritance. It seems at one level of no concern to Henry that the young Percy's chivalric pride here constitutes a dissident political energy: the king's heroic language betrays his admiration for the young hero even as it phrases expressions of resentment at his insubordination ('sweet Fortune's minion and her pride' — 'what think you, coz, / Of this young Percy's pride?' [1.1.91–2]). Or as Westmoreland expresses it to the king, Percy can be seen to 'prune' himself, like the aristocratic falcon preparing for flight, and to flout with his chivalric plumes the king's sovereignty, to 'bristle up / The crest of youth against your dignity' (1.1.98–9).

When the father, and the son he would wish to adopt as his own, actually meet, in Act 1, scene 3, the king appears more like the 'vile politician' of hostile propaganda than the 'most valiant gentleman in England' (*HIV2*, 4.1.132) we recall from *Richard II*, and quite unsympathetic to Hotspur's deployment of the heroic idiom. Clearly Percy seeks to invoke, in his satirical portrait of the courtier who approaches him after the battle, a warrior camaraderie he expects the king to share. That 'certain lord' (1.3.33), effeminately 'perfumed like a milliner' (1.3.36), who talks 'so like a waiting-gentlewoman' (1.3.55), is depicted as anathema to the tough man of action, leaning on his sword, smarting from his honourable wounds. Henry, however, is more concerned with issues of loyalty and betrayal, and sees the demand for ransom of Mortimer, Richard II's heir and now allied by marriage to Glendower, as covert treachery.

Hotspur responds with a miniature epic poem that seeks to isolate chivalric virtue from the tangled complexities of politics, to project all noble warriors into a fantasy realm where the poetry of action binds them in indissoluble camaraderie, and to rewrite disloyalty and betrayal as honourable combat:

> on the gentle Severn's sedgy bank,
> In single opposition hand to hand,
> He did confound the best part of an hour
> In changing hardiment with great Glendower.
> Three times they breath'd, and three times did they drink,
> Upon agreement, of swift Severn's flood;
> Who then, affrighted with their bloody looks,
> Ran fearfully among the trembling reeds
> And hid his crisp head in the hollow bank
> Bloodstained with these valiant combatants.   (1.3.98–107)

This vivid heroic style makes full use of poetic ornament, metaphor and personification, stirring rhythm and repetition, even rhyme – despite Hotspur's later disavowal of 'mincing poetry' (3.1.134) as irritating and worthless. But the king cuts across Percy's epic celebration with a flat denial that offers a diametrically opposed record and interpretation of history:

> He never did encounter with Glendower ...   (1.3.114)

The result is incontrovertible, yet secures no purchase on Percy's imaginative epic historiography – as well to claim that Hector never did encounter with Achilles. What is at issue here is not historical fact, but historical reconstruction: Hotspur's attempt to place heroic militarism at the centre of sovereignty and state power operates not by proving facts or demonstrating conclusions, but by creating an irresistibly compelling epic poetry that validates the hero as *sui generis*, and heroism itself as a *sine qua non* of virtue and power.

Hotspur's heroic conception of history is then further elaborated:

> O, pardon me that I descend so low
> To show the line and the predicament
> Wherein you range under this subtle king!
> Shall it, for shame, be spoken in these days
> Or fill up chronicles in time to come,
> That men of your nobility and power
> Did gage them both in an unjust behalf –
> As both of you, God pardon it! have done –

To put down Richard, that sweet lovely rose,
And plant this thorn, this canker, Bolingbroke?   (1.3.167–76)

Contemporary public opinion forms the basis of future historical tradition: that which is 'spoken in these days' may determine the subsequent interpretations contained in historical 'chronicles' not yet written. If the Percies, acknowledged as powerful agents within the aristocracy, allow themselves to be subjugated by Bolingbroke, they will permit the formulation of a Lancastrian dynastic history. Against that interpretation Hotspur opposes a Ricardian or proto-Yorkist reading, in which Richard, the 'sweet lovely rose', is unjustly destroyed by the usurping 'canker' Bolingbroke.

Heroic achievement is here tied closely to a concern with the verdict of history: the Percies need to 'redeem' their 'banish'd honours' (1.3.180–1) in heroic action, in order to secure an appropriate historical record, to be restored 'Into the good thoughts of the world again' (1.3.182). But Hotspur soon abandons history for epic:

By heaven, methinks it were an easy leap
To pluck bright honour from the pale-fac'd moon;
Or dive into the bottom of the deep,
Where fathom-line could never touch the ground,
And pluck up drowned honour by the locks;
So he that doth redeem her thence might wear
Without corrival all her dignities.   (1.3.201–7)

Heroic action becomes an end in itself, chivalric victory a paramount objective. The mental map of Hotspur's epic vision is one in which the social world dissolves, leaving the hero to grapple alone with the elements in a fantasy landscape where honour is sought in the skies or in the depths of the sea. True nobility, as always, is buried in the past: 'drowned honour' (1.3.205) has to be salvaged from the past, resurrected by the hero into contemporaneity. Worcester draws the familiar distinction between reality and dream, substance and shadow –

He apprehends a world of figures here,
But not the form of what he should attend ...   (209–10)

– where 'figures' are disembodied poetic creations, and 'form' the deep structure of reality. Yet in some ways Hotspur's vision is as real and substantial as many other interpretations of history.

IV

The version of history which will in the long run defeat Hotspur's is also already in the process of self-conscious construction. The Prince's well-known soliloquy in which he distances himself from his low-life companions, shows him deliberately and punctiliously constructing his own historical legend:

> I know you all, and will awhile uphold
> The unyok'd humour of your idleness;
> Yet herein will I imitate the sun,
> Who doth permit the base contagious clouds
> To smother up his beauty from the world,
> That, when he please again to be himself,
> Being wanted, he may be more wond'red at
> By breaking through the foul and ugly mists
> Of vapours that did seem to strangle him ...
>
> So, when this loose behaviour I throw off
> And pay the debt I never promised,
> By how much better than my word I am,
> By so much shall I falsify men's hopes;
> And, like bright metal on a sullen ground,
> My reformation, glitt'ring o'er my fault,
> Shall show more goodly and attract more eyes
> Than that which hath no foil to set it off.
> I'll so offend to make offence a skill,
> Redeeming time, when men think least I will.
>
> (1.2.188–96, 201–10)

Though Prince Henry formulates this process as one of transformation, the discarding of an assumed disguise and the re-emergence of a hidden identity, it is also a process of resurrection, as the image of the sun breaking through the clouds makes clear. At one level the 'reformation' is a moral transformation, a switch of characters, a change of heart; but more is involved here than individual moral growth. The predicted 'reformation' is also a reconstruction of royalty, a reuniting of sovereign authority with the heroic virtue it seems to be losing. At the same time the Prince's reputation will positively benefit from his dishonourable associations, just as God's glory is enhanced, not diminished, by His Son's Incarnation. The 'redemption' of time thus operates on at least three levels: it is a return of the prodigal, a vindication in strenuous moral reformation of time ostensibly wasted in 'riot and dishonour'; it is a conversion of historical tradition from a story of betrayal and usurpation, to a legend of heroic achievement; and it is a bold attempt to emulate the Redemption itself, by pursuing the Christian pattern of Incarnation and victorious Ascension: releasing the Lancastrian line from the contamination of its guilty past, showing the sun of majesty shining all the brighter against the obscuring clouds of hostile historical interpretation. 'See then that ye walk circumspectly, not as fools, but as wise; Redeeming the time, because the days are evil' (Ephesians, V.15–16).

At a critical point in the play the king returns to that comparison between Hotspur and Hal, but significantly revises its terms. Now Hal seems to resemble Richard, and Hotspur is the king's own younger self resurrected:

> For all the world
> As thou art to this hour was Richard then
> When I from France set foot at Ravenspurgh;
> And even as I was then is Percy now.
> Now, by my sceptre and my soul to boot,
> He hath more worthy interest to the state
> Than thou, the shadow of succession;
> For of no right, nor colour like to right,
> He doth fill fields with harness in the realm;
> Turns head against the lion's armed jaws;
> And, being no more in debt to years than thou,
> Leads ancient lords and reverend bishops on
> To bloody battles and to bruising arms.
> What never-dying honour hath he got
> Against renowned Douglas! whose high deeds,
> Whose hot incursions, and great name in arms,
> Holds from all soldiers chief majority
> And military title capital
> Through all the kingdoms that acknowledge Christ.   (3.2.93–111)

The king praises Percy's 'military title capital' (won from Douglas), his 'never-dying honour', his 'high deeds', his ability to 'fill fields with harness'; he is an 'infant warrior' (3.2.113), 'Mars in swathling clothes' (3.2.112). Yet Hotspur is prosecuting all this activity against the authority and sovereignty of the king: in an act of rebellion which Henry later calls 'pellmell havoc and confusion' (5.1.82), the 'churlish knot of all-abhorred war'. The chivalric values that here threaten the power and stability of the state are paradoxically celebrated by the head of that state. The explanation for that contradiction is to be found in the king's historical comparisons: for that younger Henry Bolingbroke, to whom Hotspur seems so near allied, was, in the historical moment recalled here, himself in opposition to the established sovereign authority, himself a rebel illegitimately returning from banishment to seek restitution of his expropriated inheritance.

The Prince defends himself against these accusations, and assures his father that he will be 'hereafter more myself'.

> I will redeem all this on Percy's head,
> And in the closing of some glorious day
> Be bold to tell you that I am your son.   (3.2.132–4)

Here then the son is reconciled to the father, and agrees to enlist in that heroic tradition that holds for him no less a destiny than to become its very apotheosis, Henry V. While the complexity of the Prince's social experience, and in particular his investment in those popular values – 'vulgar company' (3.2.41), 'popularity' (3.2.69), 'community' (3.2.77), 'participation' (3.2.87) – so bitterly despised by his father, may suggest that the assimilation to heroic chivalry is an arbitrary resolution, the Prince consistently shows himself conscious of the time-line that links him to the field of Agincourt. Hal is evidently capable of becoming a new kind of popular national monarch, like Elizabeth I (Stribrny in Kettle, 1964). But in the interests of healing the breach with the father, and of securing the uninterrupted forward transmission of the Lancastrian dynasty, he agrees opportunistically to acquire a heroic reputation, not by serving a hard apprenticeship in arms, but by taking the heavyweight title from its celebrated holder:

> for the time will come
> That I shall make this northern youth exchange
> His glorious deeds for my indignities.   (3.2.144–6)

The prince then immediately transforms himself from a complex and overdetermined dramatic character into a single-dimensional figure of heroic legend, mediated to the audience not through self-revelation or dramatic dénouement, but via a historical report couched in the language of chivalric romance:

I saw young Harry with his beaver on,
His cushes on his thighs, gallantly arm'd,
Rise from the ground like feathered Mercury. (4.1.104–6)

Hal issues a personal challenge to Hotspur which is cited by Vernon as a model of chivalric manners – 'I never in my life / Did hear a challenge urg'd more modestly' (5.2.52–3) – and which situates both contenders within a medium of heroic history, as Hal celebrates Percy's reputation in the manner of a 'chronicle', and Vernon identifies the Prince as the hope of a future national history:

England did never owe so sweet a hope ... (5.2.68)

The Prince's performance in the battle 'redeems' in the king's words, his 'lost opinion' (5.4.48), resurrecting his reputation to a heroic destiny. The other resurrection in this scene, Falstaff's rising from a pretended death, though a legitimate element of the dramatic totality, ultimately has no impact on the evolving continuity of the heroic tradition. The clown can rise in comic parody of the resurrected hero, just as the actor rises from a simulated death, and as the actor playing Percy will return from the dead for another performance. But here, at this moment of destiny, Percy will not, despite Falstaff's apprehension, rise again:

how if he should counterfeit too, and rise? (5.4.122)

The actor playing Percy might well adapt the Prince's own words in response to this question: 'I do, I will' (2.4.464). But as a historical character, Percy's heroic name, and his 'proud titles', have passed inexorably to the Prince, who is clearly determined to wear those dignities 'Without corrival' (1.3.207). As we have already seen in our discussion of *Henry V*, this reconcilation to the patriarchal tradition, the submission to the father and the killing of the adopted rival sibling, determine the growth of Henry's dramatic role and historical personality.

V

The opening scene of *Henry IV, Part Two* echoes the opening of its predecessor by approaching a key historical event – in this case the

Battle of Shrewsbury – through the medium of the various processes of communication by means of which historical fact and interpretation become established. The conflicting accounts of the battle's outcome provided by Lord Bardolph, Travers and Morton demonstrate both the difficulties involved in authenticating historical fact, and the ease with which historical interpretations spring so readily from such shifting and unreliable sources.

Lord Bardolph first reports the outcome of the conflict as success for the Percies, and the death of the Prince of Wales; and positions the battle immediately into the annals of historical success, the roll-call of famous victories:

> O, such a day,
> So fought, so followed, and so fairly won,
> Came not till now to dignify the times,
> Since Caesar's fortunes!   (*HIV2*, 1.1.20–3)

The only appropriate standard by which such heroic achievement is to be measured is that of the historical past, exemplified again in the critical figure of Julius Caesar. In this epic celebration, Shrewsbury serves as an instance of past glory revived, the spirit of an ancient chivalry reawoken to enrich the degenerate present, to 'dignify the times'.

Northumberland asks of his reporter some searching questions that test the authenticity of his observations:

> How is this deriv'd?
> Saw you the field? Came you from Shrewsbury?   (1.1.23–4)

What is the source of Bardolph's information – does it derive from eyewitness testimony or hearsay? Bardolph has to admit that his report is secondhand: though he trusts his source, on the basis of the man's evident breeding, and his positive assurance of accuracy:

> I spake with one, my lord, that came from thence;
> A gentleman well bred and of good name,
> That freely rend'red me these news for true.   (1.1.25–7)

The servant Travers, who left the battle before Bardolph, brings an account that more accurately reflects the uncertainties of the moment: each of his two witnesses gives a different testimony, either 'joyful tidings' (1.1.35) or the news that 'rebellion had bad luck' (1.1.41).

The truth is finally delivered by Morton, who appears to Northumberland as in himself a history book, current news already stabilised into printed and bound textuality:

> Yea, this man's brow, like to a title-leaf,
> Foretells the nature of a tragic volume.   (1.1.60–1)

The reporter's sorrowful countenance here becomes the historical chronicle's title-page, at a glance informing Northumberland of his son's death before it is formally recounted. Northumberland then also invokes classical history, but in an image of defeat, not victory; the sack of Troy rather than one of Caesar's triumphs:

> Even such a man, so faint, so spiritless,
> So dull, so dead in look, so woe-begone,
> Drew Priam's curtain in the dead of night
> And would have told him half his Troy was burnt.   (1.1.70–4)

Thus history has more than one story to tell, more than one model within which to shape contemporary experience and expectation. Historical parallels exist to articulate the equally possible outcomes of Hotspur's defeat or his triumph, his death or his victorious survival.

The play even provides in an 'Induction' a figure constructed to symbolise these history-making processes. Called simply 'Rumour' (though based on an image of Virgil's, 'Fama', who is both communication and reputation, both story and record [Virgil, 1950: 27]) the figure appears pentecostally *'painted full of tongues'* to indicate the multiplicity and plurality of the competing narratives which go into the making of history:

> I ... unfold
> The acts commenced on this ball of earth.
> Upon my tongues continual slanders ride,
> The which in every language I pronounce,
> Stuffing the ears of men with false reports.   ('Induction', 4–8)

Empowered, like the Apostles, to 'speak with other tongues' (Acts, II.4) Rumour can influence the present by planting misleading information, just as historical interpretations can, to some degree irrespective of their grounding in fact, shape present action and future development. Rumour positions itself directly within the theatre:

> But what need I thus
> My well-known body to anatomize
> Among my household?   (20–2)

So the clamour of tongues is the dialogic medium of the drama itself, and the 'acts commenced on this ball of earth' are simultaneously great events of the world, and dramatisations mounted in the microcosmic world of the theatre. Rumour's 'body' is sufficiently familiar to the audience, who actually constitute its 'household'. These theatrical metaphors indicate clearly that something more complex than a simple differentiation of truth from falsehood is at issue here. The theatre knows that 'truth' consists of a continual interaction of many competing tongues; that every historical 'action' can produce a multiplicity of different theatrical 'acts'; and that even the most solid historical fact cannot avoid entering some such process of transmission as that symbolised by 'Rumour'.

VI

The premature though probable death of the heroic son, Hotspur, and the anomalous survival of his father — a fate both feared and avoided by Talbot in *Henry VI, Part One* — conspire to produce a grotesque parody of the normal patriarchal pattern in which the example of the heroic father stirs the son to emulative achievement. Had Northumberland been well when receiving the news of his son's defeat and death, it would have made him ill; since he is already ill, the effect is reversed, and he is rendered by bad news paradoxically fit and healthy:

> these news,
> Having been well, that would have made me sick,
> Being sick, have in some measure made me well.   (1.1.137–9)

And where the tale of a father's legendary deeds would normally inspire a son to glorious enterprise, here the story of a son's tragic end energises his father into a burst of youthful chivalric energy:

> Hence, therefore, thou nice crutch!
> A scaly gauntlet now with joints of steel
> Must glove this hand ...
>
> Now bind my brows with iron ...   (1.1.145–7, 150)

In a later scene this process is amplified by Percy's widow, who paints a vivid picture of Percy as already an established figure of heroic legend, which in turn operates both to energise and enervate his father. Hotspur's honour, she claims,

> stuck upon him as the sun
> In the grey vault of heaven; and by his light
> Did all the chivalry of England move.   (2.3.18–20)

Reminded of his son's greatness and of his own failure to support him, Northumberland feels the familiar ebbing away of energy that we have seen exemplified in figures like Hamlet (and also Richard II, see below, Chapter 8), sons overwhelmed and weakened by the patriarchally imposed burden of responsibility:

> Fair daughter, you do draw my spirits from me
> With new lamenting ancient oversights.   (2.3.46–7)

On the other hand Northumberland does not look forward to a continuous and evolving chronicle history within which his deeds may be accorded appropriate prominence; but rather calls for a tragic holocaust, a universal reciprocal slaughter of brother by brother, an apocalyptic and final day of wrath in which history finally may reach its end:

> let order die!
> And let this world no longer be a stage
> To feed contention in a ling'ring act;
> But let one spirit of the first-born Cain
> Reign in all bosoms, that, each heart being set
> On bloody courses, the rude scene may end
> And darkness be the burier of the dead!   (1.1.154–60)

In this vision of apocalyptic violence, the drama provides the metaphors around which this desired historical dénouement is imaginatively formulated. The 'stage' is a location where historical conflict is drawn out into a lasting entertainment, perpetually recycled to prolong pleasure. But if every man could become a Cain, every heart set its course on mutually destructive violence, then history might be brought to an end, just as a 'rude scene' can be observed to reach its conclusion, and just as the silence following the close of performance can suggest that universal emptiness in which all the dead ultimately find their final resting-place.

VII

O God! that one might read the book of fate,
And see the revolution of the times
Make mountains level, and the continent,
Weary of solid firmness, melt itself
Into the sea; and other times to see
The beachy girdle of the ocean
Too wide for Neptune's hips; how chances mock,
And changes fill the cup of alteration
With divers liquors! O, if this were seen,
The happiest youth, viewing his progress through,
What perils past, what crosses to ensue,
Would shut the book and sit him down and die.   (3.1.45–56)

Henry's depressed and discouraging meditations on the progress of history describe a world in which radical change and revolutionary transformation are simultaneously to be expected, and yet quite unpredictable. Since 'changes fill the cup of alteration' in ways that cannot be foreseen, the pattern of change is perceived as the mockery of 'chance'. A study of that 'book', which interprets history in terms of the mutability he himself, throughout his 'unquiet reign', has consistently experienced, can teach only despair. As well to shut the book, sit down and die, as to go forward expecting all aspiration to be thwarted, all hope converted to despair.

The only access to a knowledge of future events is therefore through the inspired vision of the prophet. Henry recalls Richard II, confronted by the rebellion of which he himself was the leader, prophesying that Northumberland would eventually turn against him. Warwick seeks to rebut this belief in prophetic insight, arguing that the apparently unpredictable chances and changes of history can be reduced to certain general laws, and that from a thorough knowledge of the past can be derived a reasonable guess as to what the future holds:

> *War.*   There is a history in all men's lives,
> Figuring the natures of the times deceas'd;
> The which observ'd, a man may prophesy,
> With a near aim, of the main chance of things
> As yet not come to life, which in their seeds
> And weak beginnings lie intreasured.   (3.1.80–5)

Persuaded by this theory, Henry resolves to embrace Warwick's historical determinism:

> Are these things then necessities?
> Then let us meet them like necessities.   (3.1.92–3)

The action of the play does not, however, support this straightforward conventional view of history as a process in which past events broadly determine future developments, and which is therefore amenable to rational analysis and informed prediction. To begin with, as we have seen, 'the nature of the times deceas'd' is by no means a matter of established fact or uniform consensus. Consider the disagreement between the rebel Mowbray, son to that Duke of Norfolk banished by Richard II, and Westmoreland, about the combat between Bolingbroke and Mowbray, aborted by Richard II. The rebel and the state official are arguing about whether or not the disaffected aristocrats have or have not suffered injustice at the hands of the king.

> *Mowb.*   The King, that lov'd him, as the state stood then,
> Was force perforce compell'd to banish him,
> And then that Henry Bolingbroke and he,
> Being mounted and both roused in their seats,
> Their neighing coursers daring of the spur,
> Their armed staves in charge, their beavers down,
> Their eyes of fire sparkling through sights of steel,
> And the loud trumpet blowing them together –
> Then, then, when nothing could have stay'd
> My father from the breast of Bolingbroke,
> O, when the king did throw his warder down –
> His own life hung upon the staff he threw –
> Then threw he down himself, and all their lives

That by indictment and by dint of sword
Have since miscarried under Bolingbroke.
West. You speak, Lord Mowbray, now you know not what.
The Earl of Hereford was reputed then
In England the most valiant gentleman.
Who knows on whom fortune would then have smil'd?
But if your father had been victor there,
He ne'er had borne it out of Coventry;
For all the country, in a general voice,
Cried hate upon him; and all their prayers and love
Were set on Hereford, whom they doted on,
And bless'd and grac'd indeed more than the King.   (4.1.115–38)

In *Richard II*, this event is described from several different viewpoints before it even happens (see below, Chapter 8). Here in *Henry IV, Part Two* the historical narrative is rewritten to support two different and conflicting interpretations of history, two different and opposing present political loyalties. We need to remind ourselves, sorting through these multiple analyses and reconstructions, that the combat *never actually happened*: that it was a historical *non-event*, rather than an event. Had Richard not stopped the combat, Mowbray urges, his father would inevitably have won, Richard would not have been deposed, and the course of history would have been different. Westmoreland replies that the outcome, though necessarily remaining unresolved, would in all probability have been, one way or another, victory for Bolingbroke. The characters are arguing for competing understandings of the present, not conflicting interpretations of the past; or rather that non-event of the past is the chosen ground on which a contemporary conflict can conveniently be fought out.

VIII

In practice therefore arguments derived from an investigation of 'the times deceased' prove inconclusive, since the events of the past prove impossible to separate from their consequences in the present, and fact cannot be extricated from interpretation. Historical prediction meets no more success in the king's expectations of the succession.

The blood weeps from my heart when I do shape,
In forms imaginary, th' unguided days

And rotten times that you shall look upon
When I am sleeping with my ancestors.   (4.4.57–61)

Henry seeks here to 'figure' from the evidence of the past the likely outcomes of his son's reign, and naturally anticipates the rule of 'headstrong riot'. His error is to underestimate the capability of history to deliver that incongruous and unpredictable 'cup of alterations' so vividly figured in his earlier vision of history. If history consists of strange and bewildering transformations, then the miracle of Hal's conversion to royalty should in reality come as no surprise:

Presume not that I am the thing I was.   (5.5.57)

What the Prince tells his father, so the past declares to the present, clearly delineating then ('the thing I was') from now ('that I am'), sharply inscribing the parameters of historical difference.

8

Richard II

Thou sayest that I am a king. To this end was I born, and
for this came I into the world, that I should bear witness
unto the truth.
Pilate saith unto him, What is truth?

John, XVIII.37–8

I

Richard II is a historical drama in a self-conscious and metadramatic
sense, as well as a history play that purports to re-enact the past. The
emphasis of its opening lines is very clearly focused, as Richard
addresses his uncle, on the past –

> Old John of Gaunt, time-honoured Lancaster,
> Hast thou, according to thy oath and band,
> Brought hither Henry Hereford, thy bold son,
> Here to make good the boist'rous late appeal,
> Which then our leisure would not let us hear,
> Against the Duke of Norfolk, Thomas Mowbray? ...
>
> Tell me, moreover, hast thou sounded him
> If he appeal the Duke on ancient malice,
> Or worthily, as a good subject should,
> On some known ground of treachery in him?   (1.1.1–6; 8–11)

But this is a past-within-a-past, a history multiply situated in relation
to various different definitions of the present. Richard himself is
a ghost from the remote and alien past of the fourteenth century:
in the 1590s familiar, explicitly as a ghost, from such apparitions as
that which haunts *The Mirror for Magistrates*; and destined to haunt
Shakespeare's subsequent dramatisations of the history of his successors. Nonetheless, at the inception of his own play, as he characterises

his father's brother as inhabitant of a venerable antiquity, he declares himself the exponent of a vigorous and progressive modernity. Though he shares with his aristocratic subjects a formal language of feudalism and chivalry – invoking Gaunt's oath and bond of fealty, and acknowledging in technical phraseology Bolingbroke's legal 'appeal' – his speech distinguishes sharply between the 'inveterate' and 'ancient malice' (1.1.14, 19) of wounded and punctilious aristocratic honour, and a pragmatic apprehension of immediate and visible social disturbance, the 'known ground' and 'apparent danger' (1.1.11, 13) of present political peril.

The two 'knights' who confront one another in this antique quarrel stand squarely in the heroic tradition of military manliness. Ghosts from the past, they yet incorporate themselves in solid images of the body. The chivalric body is clearly the material instrument, the bone and muscle with which combat is undertaken and accomplished. The same body, apparelled in the gorgeous heraldic and military trappings of chivalry, symbolises aristocratic status and dynastic pride. But above all, within the coded ethics of chivalric trial by combat, the body is a sign and instrument of justice. Bolingbroke expresses this exactly:

> what I speak
> My body shall make good upon this earth,
> Or my divine soul answer it in heaven.   (1.1.36–8)

Speech, the honourable word of the noble warrior, is incarnated in the heroic body that alone gives it substance and authority. Just as word and body are inseparably combined, the one being the true and effective utterance of the other, so soul and body are not only linked but inextricably fused, the body here promising to express the soul's essential meaning. In another figure Bolingbroke reiterates this sense that the chivalric body is a kind of language, inscribing in its deeds a discourse of legality, speaking in its concrete actions an audible accent of honour and justice:

> What my tongue speaks, my right drawn sword may prove.
> (1.1.46)

Mowbray's speech of defiant antagonism affirms even more strongly the heroic ethic, dismissing language as an inferior and unreliable medium, within which the essential lineaments of chivalric justice can too easily become confused and obscured.

> Let not my cold words here accuse my zeal.
> 'Tis not the trial of a woman's war,
> The bitter clamour of two eager tongues,
> Can arbitrate this cause betwixt us twain;
> The blood is hot that must be cool'd for this.   (1.1.47–51)

'Cold words' are opposed against 'blood' that is both 'high' and 'hot': a vital substance that testifies both to aristocratic status and to military prowess (firstly the blood of noble lineage; and secondly the blood that energises the fighting body, and is spilt on the field of battle). The formal hearing over which Richard properly presides is contemptuously anathematised as 'the trial of a woman's war', 'the bitter clamour of two eager tongues'. The insult offered initially by Mowbray to Bolingbroke is a remonstrance against the use of words, and can be read as a simple 'macho' challenge: 'put up or shut up'. But that gesture of defiance also embraces the king, whose apparent reliance on debate as a means of conflict resolution places, from the knightly point-of-view, a question mark over his own masculinity.

The ostensible loyalty to the monarch exemplified by both combatants reinforces even more strongly that sense of a seamless heroic ethic, within which language and physical action, the poetry and violence of chivalry, are interfused. The language of loyalty is conceived not as a constitutive relationship between king and subject, but only as a constitutional check on the impetuous momentum of chivalric pride:

> First, the fair reverence of your Highness curbs me
> From giving reins and spurs to my free speech;
> Which else would post until it had return'd
> These terms of treason doubled down his throat.   (1.1.54–5)

Here the abstract conceptualisation of language ('cold words') is synthesised with the hot action of violent combat in a grotesque collocation. 'Free speech' (1.1.123) is imagined here as the knight's charger, which, given the incitements of rein and spur, would physically force Bolingbroke's accusations back where they came from, make him eat (in a comparable metaphoric conjuncture) his words. This is not just a poetic equivalent of a conceptual figure, but rather a clear indication that language is little more than an adjunct to the invincible righteous force of heroic action. The two combatants confront one another in a relationship formally constituted by antagonism, and thus both evade and seek to elude the sovereign authority of the king, united in their common affiliation to 'the rites of knighthood' (1.1.75), the 'chivalrous design of knightly trial' (1.1.81).

II

The key image of 'blood' has so far signified heroic mettle, aristocratic status, and royal authority. Although it is one common substance, its multiple capabilities of signification abundantly imply those conflicts of meaning that are employed by the characters to express difference and antagonism as well as unity and affiliation. Thus Bolingbroke at Mowbray's instigation is prepared to 'lay aside [his] high blood's royalty', his family ties with the king his cousin, in favour of deploying the sign of blood as a flag of chivalric honour. It is also within the symbolic medium of blood that the fundamental conflicts, political, dynastic and cultural, between Bolingbroke and Richard (the conflict that soon bifurcates along the branches of the Plantagenet family tree, and which I have identified elsewhere as the great constitutional struggle between a centralising mediaeval monarchy and the great aristocratic houses [Holderness, Potter and Turner, 1988: 32]) is disclosed. Bolingbroke accuses Mowbray (and through Mowbray the king) of having murdered Gloucester:

> he did plot the Duke of Gloucester's death,
> suggest his soon-believing adversaries,
> And consequently, like a traitor coward,
> Sluic'd out his innocent soul through streams of blood;
> Which blood, like sacrificing Abel's, cries,
> Even from the tongueless caverns of the earth,
> To me for justice and rough chastisement.   (1.1.100−6)

Here 'blood' becomes intertwined with associations of treachery, of murder, even explicitly of fratricide. The image is temporarily removed from the temporal and cultural dimensions of mediaeval chivalry, aristocracy and royalty, and reconfigured within a dark Old Testament world of blood-sacrifice and blood-revenge. The blood-sacrificing shepherd Abel's offering was more acceptable to the Judaic

God than Cain's vegetarian oblation; it was Abel whose own blood was consequently shed by a jealous brother's hand; and it was he who himself became a sacrificial victim in the first and prototypical murder. The blood of Gloucester, who was certainly, in the view of the Lancastrians, more favoured in God's sight than is Richard, becomes emblematic of an original and unforgivable offence, which in turn requires from Gloucester's blood-relatives a fundamental and apocalyptic commitment to judicial revenge. In that haunting image of the 'tongueless caverns of the earth', Bolingbroke draws on the Biblical text to produce a vivid image of history. Gloucester's secret murderer may hope, as Cain hoped, that his crime would remain undiscovered, as Abel's blood seeped unobtrusively into the soil:

> the earth, which hath opened her mouth to receive thy brother's blood from thy hand.   (Genesis, IV.11)

But the crying of Abel's blood was clearly audible to God: 'the voice of thy brother's blood crieth unto me from the ground' (10), and the voice of Gloucester's blood also cries to Bolingbroke for satisfaction. In the same way those 'tongueless caverns', though invisible and empty spaces, cannot be relied upon to remain sealed and inviolate. The lost meanings contained in those oubliettes of history will surface, reappear, return to daylight and consciousness. The past will return to haunt the present. The dead shall be raised.

In protesting his innocence, Mowbray counterpoises to this patriarchal affirmation of blood-vengeance nothing less than the Redemption itself (referring here not to the murder of Gloucester, but to a conspiracy against John of Gaunt):

>   ere I last received the sacrament
>   I did confess it.   (1.1.139–40)

The sacrament of the Eucharist invokes, of course, another fundamentally different meaning for 'blood': not the blood-sacrifice and revenge code of the Old Testament Mosaic culture, but the forgiveness and absolution entailed in that 'blood of the new testament' (Mark, XIV.24) shed in the Passion of Christ. Mowbray's sacramental allusion sets up a conflict between vengeance and forgiveness which is yet another formulation of the complex relations between past and present.

In this particular configuration, the past is strongly associated with family crime and vendetta, blood-guilt and blood-vengeance, encoded into the glamour of mediaeval chivalry; while the present is both Christian and pragmatic, realistic and forgiving. From that perspective of modernity Richard yet again revises the blood-metaphor, this time characterising himself as a doctor whose skill offers a cure for 'choler' without the harsh purgative extreme of blood-letting:

> Wrath-kindled gentlemen, be rul'd by me;
> Let's purge this choler without letting blood –
> This we prescribe, though no physician;
> Deep malice makes too deep incision.   (1.1.152–5)

Against the archaic values of the past – the blood that clamours for blood, the 'deep malice' that is so hungry for 'deep incision' – the king offers reconciliation and forgiveness, 'calm' (1.1.159) and 'peace' (1.1.160).

Though acceptable to the royalist baron Gaunt, this proffered solution finds no favour with the combatants, whose adherence to the heroic tradition relieves them of all responsibility to the monarch, or to the values of the modern world he is seeking to build. Mowbray sees such conciliation as a prospective betrayal of his historical memory:

>   my fair name,
> Despite of death, that lives upon my grave
> To dark dishonour's use thou shalt not have.   (1.1.167–9)

The wounds of 'inveterate malice' have already struck too deep. This speech continues to merge the technical vocabulary of chivalry with an appropriation of the Crucifixion image:

> I am disgrac'd, impeach'd, and baffl'd here:
> Pierc'd to the soul with slander's venom'd spear.   (1.1.170–1)

Humiliated and defenceless, Mowbray sees himself as the crucified Christ, pierced through the side. But where in Christian terms death is conquered by death, as the spilt blood of the Passion heals the fatal wound from which it is shed, here Bolingbroke's blood must be shed to cure the venom of his slander.

III

The potency of blood as the physical embodiment of aristocratic pride, chivalric honour, martial prowess and legitimate vindictiveness, continues to figure throughout the following scene, in which the Duchess of Gloucester remonstrates against her brother John of Gaunt's apparent reticence in the matter of Gloucester's murder. For the Duchess, the royal blood is sacred and indivisible. Edward III's seven sons were 'seven vials of his sacred blood', and also, like the sons of Jesse, seven branches of an original royal stem:

> But Thomas, my dear lord, my life, my Gloucester,
> One vial full of Edward's sacred blood,
> One flourishing branch of his most royal root,
> Is crack'd, and all the precious liquor spilt;
> Is hack'd down, and his summer leaves all faded,
> By envy's hand and murder's bloody axe. (1.2.16–21)

The indivisible royal blood demands an absolute and unconditional pathological loyalty: Gaunt is himself, by virtue of his consanguinity, personally injured by Gloucester's murder. If his blood is authentic, it will inevitably prompt his conscience with the correct impulses, generate from his natural instincts the authentic actions: 'Ah, Gaunt, his blood was thine! ... Hath love in thy old blood no living fire?' (1.2.22, 10). Where a base born brother might demonstrate the virtue of patience, a true noble will exemplify righteous and indignant anger:

> That which in mean men we entitle patience
> Is pale cold cowardice in noble breasts. (1.2.33–4)

In fact the blood shed by an act of murder that is figured as both religious sacrifice and mere animal slaughter, cries out to Gaunt as loudly as it did to Bolingbroke:

> Alas, the part I had in Woodstock's blood
> Doth more solicit me than your exclaims
> To stir against the butchers of his life! (1.2.1–3)

But Gaunt's actions are more strongly bound by the self-abnegating obligations of 'Christian service' than by the honourable promptings of 'true chivalry' (2.1.54). The hunger for vengeance that haunts his blood is not permitted to provoke the raising of an 'angry arm' (1.2.41) against the divinely appointed, ecclesiastically anointed sovereign. The duty of punishment lies, as did the responsibility for punishing Abel's murderer, only with God: 'since correction' [of the murderer] 'lieth in those hands / Which made the fault that we cannot correct' (1.2.4–5) [i.e. Original Sin].

The trial by combat that is decreed to follow ought to be, in principle, a godsent opportunity for resolving all these issues in a dénouement jointly subscribed by the conflicting ideologies of pagan heroism and Christian monarchy. The royal and aristocratic blood should, by virtue of its military capabilities and its incorruptible nobility, be competent both to secure victory and establish justice. Trial by combat was of course considered to be a referral of the cause back to the authority of divine justice. If indeed 'God's is the quarrel', this indicates not only that the issue is one of divine justice, but also that God can be assumed as personally in charge of the battle, the outcome of which would then inevitably be guaranteed as divinely determined.

An elucidation of the absence of that non-event that is the trial by combat has to entail an acknowledgement that it does in fact, 'happen', several times: but only in words. In its most graphic manifestation it becomes, literally, a 'woman's war', since it is realised only in the Duchess of Gloucester's would-be prophetic speech:

> O, sit my husband's wrongs on Hereford's spear,
> That it may enter butcher Mowbray's breast!
> Or, if misfortune miss the first career,
> Be Mowbray's sins so heavy in his bosom
> That they may break his foaming courser's back
> And throw the rider headlong in the lists,
> A caitiff recreant to my cousin Hereford!   (1.2.47–53)

What the Duchess vividly sees, in her mind's eye, is combat as the victory of justice, the fulfilment of revenge: Bolingbroke's spear strengthened by the truth of his cause, Mowbray's prowess enervated by his imputed guilt. Bolingbroke also has the same vision, seeing the trial played out as a moral victory, the instruments of war acquiring strength from family honour and dignity. 'O thou', he addresses his father,

> the earthly author of my blood,
> Whose youthful spirit, in me regenerate,
> Doth with a twofold vigour lift me up
> To reach at victory above my head,
> Add proof unto mine armour with thy prayers,
> And with thy blessing steel my lance's point,
> That it may enter Mowbray's waxen coat
> And furbish new the name of John o' Gaunt,
> Even in the lusty haviour of his son.   (1.3.69–77)

The noble blood of the family, inherited through the military-masculine heroic tradition, empowers the body; the justice of the cause both strengthens the hero's weapons, and enfeebles the adversary's defence. Gaunt foresees the same outcome:

> Be swift like lightning in the execution,
> And let thy blows, doubly redoubled,
> Fall like amazing thunder on the casque
> Of thy adverse pernicious enemy.   (1.3.79–82)

In his vision revenge assumes the supernatural properties of natural calamity, the thunder and lightning of divine justice. Even Mowbray, evidently far less certain of the future, anticipates at least a 'feast of battle' (1.3.92), in which his appetite for justice would presumably be satisfied.

IV

In these 'action (p)re-plays' we see the characters manufacturing history before it happens, preconfiguring the event in line with their own interpretative strategies. When Richard stops the combat, he does nothing less than rob the Lancastrians of 'their' history, stripping from their own dynastic chronicle a historical *exemplum* that would have manifested the truth and justice of their cause, the supremacy of their authority. The royal intervention also represents an emasculation of the combatants and their chivalric culture, since it leaves Bolingbroke and his supporters not merely disappointed of their expectations, but absurdly on record as voicing empty heroic boasts, fighting only a 'woman's war', the 'bitter clamour' of 'eager tongues'. The power to which their culture is subordinated, on the

other hand, makes no claim to masculinity, but rather declares itself a
feminised form of authority:

> Draw near,
> And list what with our council we have done.
> For that our kingdom's earth should not be soil'd
> With that dear blood which it hath fostered;
> And for our eyes do hate the dire aspect
> Of civil wounds plough'd up with neighbours' sword;
> And for we think the eagle-winged pride
> Of sky-aspiring and ambitious thoughts,
> With rival-hating envy, set on you
> To wake our peace, which in our country's cradle
> Draws the sweet infant breath of gentle sleep;
> Which so rous'd up with boist'rous untun'd drums,
> With harsh-resounding trumpets' dreadful bray,
> And grating shock of wrathful iron arms,
> Might from our quiet confines fright fair peace
> And make us wade even in our kindred's blood –
> Therefore we banish you our territories.   (1.3.123–39)

Richard identifies his sovereignty with a maternal realm which
'fosters' and 'nurses' both its progeny and the royal peace that
enfolds them into unity. The 'blood' image, which with its multiple
signifying capabilities has delineated the parameters of the preceding
ideological conflicts, is here decisively appropriated in a larger matriarchal metaphor. The king is both mother and nurse, both author and
custodian of the aristocracy's blood: it is for him to determine
whether it should be spilt or conserved. The fact that the decision to
stop the combat is made collectively by king and council only
strengthens this sense of a government subordinating traditional
masculinity to a modern, almost matriarchal authority prepared to
substitute peace for blood, words for swords, a 'woman's war' for the
'grating shock of wrathful iron arms'.

   Thus the trial by combat exists only in a kind of 'virtual history': it
is one of the things that might have been, one of the doors history
chose not to open. In one sense it dominates the play as a missed
opportunity for securing history as presence: the kind of critical
event that can be seen to have fulfilled a past and decisively shaped
a future. For Bolingbroke it represents a double disappointment: a lost
opportunity for testing and proving family honour, and a thwarted
aspiration to register his own memory in the pantheon of chivalric

heroes. As such the combat is shown to be essentially what all history is — words, visions, fantasies of what was or what might have been. In terms of theatrical representation, it has been suggested that the spectators as well as the characters must have been situated into that dimension of thwarted expectation and frustrated desire. If so, they would thereby have encountered this history, that great glamorous dream of mediaevalism, as always already and irrecoverably lost. On the other hand, as the Chorus of *Henry V* indiscreetly reminds us, a spectacle of the kind embodied in the characters' language could not have received adequate representation on the bare platform of the 'wooden O' (*HV*, 'Prologue', 13); or would at best have been reduced to an undignified tussle between poor players wielding vile and ragged foils. Elizabethan culture had to look elsewhere for a concrete re-enactment of such spectacles, to the fabricated antiquarianism of the Accession Day tilts, which, by their very authenticity of imitation, seem even more poignantly to invoke the irrecoverable loss of the world in which such rituals held very different capabilities of meaning.

V

John of Gaunt, as the play's first line emphasises, represents an apparently unbroken continuity with that ancient world. His England, the England of Edward III and the Black Prince, is a land of heroes, a kingdom of chivalry, crusades and imperial conquests. Gaunt's famous speech attributes to his imagined, remembered England majesty, military power and a paradisal security.

> This royal throne of kings, this scept'red isle,
> This earth of majesty, this seat of Mars,
> This other Eden, demi-paradise,
> This fortress built by Nature for herself
> Against infection and the hand of war,
> This happy breed of men, this little world,
> This precious stone set in the silver sea,
> Which serves it in the office of a wall,
> Or as a moat defensive to a house,
> Against the envy of less happier lands;
> This blessed plot, this earth, this realm, this England,
> This nurse, this teeming womb of royal kings,

> Fear'd by their breed, and famous by their birth,
> Renowned for their deeds as far from home,
> For Christian service and true chivalry,
> As is the sepulchre, in stubborn Jewry
> Of the world's ransom, blessed Mary's Son.   (2.1.40–56)

The heart of an empire, the island yet remained unviolated by its own violence, an isolated and protected fortified manor or moat-house, which sustained its own domestic peace by sending its heroes out to perform their 'deeds' in remote foreign lands.

The idealised England of this patriarchal vision is, however, even as Gaunt describes it, already in the past, its violence now turned self-destructively inwards. The vivid, radiant vision of a chivalric Eden is a vision of paradise lost, an elegiac lament for an England now betrayed and demoralised. Historical presence exists only in memory: the present is aware rather of immediate absence, since the 'teeming womb' of royal kings is already a 'hollow womb' that 'inherits naught but bones' (2.1.83). The space of uterine fertility becomes the space of mortal corruption, womb mutates into tomb. The place where history should be is revealed, on closer examination, to be yet another empty space.

The position Gaunt adopts is similarly paradoxical, as his language emphasises: he is both a live, surviving embodiment of that past, and its dying memory; a corporeal link between present and past, and a ghost hopelessly dedicated to bringing the past home, as haunting memory, to an oblivious present. The painful contradictions are exemplified in his desperate effort to choose the precise moment at which his voice will be heard, the exact historical conjuncture where the past can inscribe its record ineffaceably on the present:

> they say the tongues of dying men
> Enforce attention like deep harmony ...

> More are men's ends mark'd than their lives before.
> The setting sun, and music at the close,
> As the last taste of sweets, is sweetest last,
> Writ in remembrance more than things long past.
>
> (2.1.5–6, 11–14)

At the precise interface of life and death, *in articulo mortis*, Gaunt aspires to testify from a knowledgeable past to an ignorant and doom-directed future. But clearly 'remembrance' consists only of 'things long past', and there can be no guarantee that history will retain in its records any fixed hierarchy of priorities. Gaunt speaks of his 'death's sad tale' (2.1.16) as, to paraphrase, 'the sad tale told by his death', the chastening testimony of his dying counsel; but as if aware that another story may well supervene — 'the sad story *of* his death' — the depressing account of an unheeded demise, the lost voice of an ineffective witness.

Richard too, in Gaunt's speech, is another 'dead man held on end' (Hardy, 1912, 1952: 319), his sovereign authority already occupying the deathbed of its own demise. The crown, ostensible symbol of power, is in fact an empty space — as its physical shape, circumscribed by a rich, but soft and vulnerable metal, declares — and is only as strong as the substance that space contains. In Richard's case, since its content is the vacancy of self-delusion, the emptiness of the crown is coterminous with the 'waste' (2.1.103), the desolation and devastation, of the whole kingdom. 'Possession' and 'deposition' occur here as linked terms: power at once possessed and abnegated, occupied and surrendered in a single action. Anticipating the dynastic discontinuity of a subsequent history, Gaunt rewrites in wish-fulfilment fantasy the 'fair sequence and succession' (2.1.199) that brought Richard to the throne. If Edward III had 'with a prophet's eye' (2.1.104) foreseen the history of interfamilial violence that is here already in the past, he might have pre-empted that process by aborting his grandson's reign, dismissing him from that office he should ideally never have inherited, 'Deposing thee before thou wert possess'd' (2.1.107) . Richard's patriarchal ancestor would ironically have better served his own royal and heroic tradition by perverting its natural linear progression. Since this precise eventuality is, in the future-past of the play, to occur through the actions of Gaunt's own son, Bolingbroke, the powerful ghost of Edward III seems here not to have been invoked in vain.

This pattern of ideas is then repeated by Gaunt's brother York, 'the last of noble Edward's sons' (2.1.171), who also sees Richard's succession as a perverted inheritance, a lineal descent that paradoxically inverts the true patrilinear succession. Richard appropriately displays a physical resemblance to his father the Black Prince: but such facial replication belies a birthright betrayed by a systematic inversion of all his father's values and achievements:

> His face thou hast, for even so look'd he,
> Accomplish'd with the number of thy hours;

But when he frown'd, it was against the French
And not against his friends. His noble hand
Did win what he did spend, and spent not that
Which his triumphant father's hand had won.
His hands were guilty of no kindred blood,
But bloody with the enemies of his kin.   (2.1.176–83)

Richard has substituted internecine violence for imperial conquest, reckless profligacy for territorial accumulation, clandestine assassination of his kin for open confrontation with his kingdom's enemies. Richard is king, it is true, by legitimate progeniture ('fair sequence and succession' [2.1.199]): yet his action in 'wrongly' confiscating his cousin's inheritance throws his legitimacy into question. If Richard is prepared to break that dynastic line for the aristocracy, then his own descent from Edward III and the Black Prince is morally annulled: as if his grandfather had indeed, in another 'virtual history' scenario, deprived him of the crown before he could take possession, stripped him of what, in this imagined 'time-line', he would never have had. York, like Gaunt, attributes to the patriarchal ancestor an awe-inspiring power to call in his inheritance, to truncate the line of succession when he sees the degeneration of his heroic lineage. Richard, hopelessly overwhelmed by the overbearing authority of that patriarchal past, simply rejects history altogether: his seizure of the patrimony, an action which clearly attempts to obliterate the principal law of this historical tradition, is accompanied by a clear and overt disrespect for the characteristic signs of that history, those monuments of remembrance and rituals of adulation. His epitaph on the death of John of Gaunt – 'so much for that' (2.1.155) – really is a 'Brief abstract and record' (*RIII*, 4.4.28), that flattens out the landmarks of traditional history as effectively as any postmodernist historiography.

VI

Gaunt had described the past as a 'teeming womb of royal kings', degenerated to a sterile present in which the 'womb' has become a hollowness of corruption, in effect a tomb. The play then strikes at the heart of this uterine metaphor by focusing directly on a woman, wife to a king, the queen whose youthful fertility ought to be the medium for protraction of the patriarchal dynasty. Her womb, however, is not filled with the plenitude of procreation, but is more like Gaunt's 'hollow womb', empty, or at best nurturing an imminent calamity, 'some unborn sorrow'. Richard's ostensible emotional callousness, as he unceremoniously assists his dying uncle from 'bed' to 'grave', is matched by an intense sensitivity of the female organs, as if the space of that hollow womb can perceptively pick up lingering echoes of a future yet uncreated:

> Some unborn sorrow, ripe in fortune's womb,
> Is coming towards me, and my inward soul
> With nothing trembles.   (2.2.10–12)

'Nothing', that lack or defect that is the female condition in this imagined patriarchal universe (Holderness, 1991: 177), is also the creative space of uterine productivity, the *chora* (Kristeva, in Moi, 1986: 94) which, even though empty of foetal development, is capable of moulding knowledge, language and emotion, and with its infinite plasticity shaping the contours of a history not yet enacted.

This paradox of the womb as an empty space that is yet capable of reproduction is expanded through a play on the terms 'nothing' and 'something', initially located as a simple opposition, but ultimately co-positioned as a binary dualism in which one term can pass imperceptibly and impossibly into the other. As we have seen, Isabella's prescient intuition, which accurately foresees disaster, is located in the specifically female property of the womb. Just as the 'hollow womb' seems a vacant space, so this prophetic emotion feels like 'nothing', and finds no natural equivalent in external reality. The Queen's foretaste of calamity seems entirely disproportionate to its ostensible cause, the pain of separation:

> my inward soul
> With nothing trembles. At something it grieves
> More than with parting from my lord the King.   (2.2.11–13)

The courtier Bushy then explains this apprehension with an elegant and urbane conceit:

> Each substance of a grief hath twenty shadows,
> Which shows like grief itself, but is not so;
> For sorrow's eye, glazed with blinding tears,
> Divides one thing entire to many objects,

Like perspectives which, rightly gaz'd upon,
Show nothing but confusion – ey'd awry,
Distinguish form. So your sweet Majesty,
Looking awry upon your lord's departure,
Find shapes of grief more than himself to wail;
Which, look'd on as it is, is nought but shadows
Of what it is not. Then, thrice-gracious Queen,
More than your lord's departure weep not – more is not seen;
Or if it be, 'tis with false sorrow's eye,
Which for things true weeps things imaginary.   (2.2.14–27)

Just as Isabella naturally thinks of 'nothing' as something's poor relation, its defect or absence, so Bushy posits a positivistic philosophical hierarchy in which only 'substance' has reality, while its multiplying shadows are mere delusions, 'shadows / Of what it is not'. Things are either 'true' or 'imaginary'. The figure through which this position is explicated ends up, however, saying more than Bushy intends. Using the perceptual paradox of a 'perspective' (a visual representation in which form can be coherently descried only from a certain angle of vision, while from any other position it appears fragmented and formless), he argues that Isabella is viewing her experience from the wrong angle ('awry') and seeing 'form' and 'substance' where they do not exist. If she would only perceive from the correct angle ('rightly gaze'), she would apprehend her expanded and multiplied grief as a mere confusion of shadows. It does not seem to occur to Bushy that the de-centred and marginal position from which a perspective has 'form' is in fact the 'true' and 'right' way of looking at it. Evidently 'sorrow's eye, glazed with blinding tears', is not a distorting lens scattering formal coherence into unintelligible fragments, but a glass in which the future can accurately be descried.

Placed in its narrative context, this scene therefore re-evaluates the 'inward soul' that perceives in its 'shows', 'shadows', and 'shapes' an imaginary composition corresponding more closely to the real than Bushy's commonsense Aristotelean faith in 'substance', 'truth', 'what is'. The point is reinforced by Bushy's glib dismissal of the queen's whole perceptual universe as 'nothing but conceit'. While he uses the term to mean 'whimsical fancy', Isabella lights on its substantive meaning:

conceit is still deriv'd
From some forefather grief.   (2.2.34–5)

Here 'conceit' is reconnected to its semantic origin in 'conception', and the capacity to imagine truth again related back to the womb, the female capacity for reproduction. Conception must have a father, as grief must have an underlying cause. But Isabella's term *fore*father' extends the scope of her thinking backwards to precedent and origin, her curiosity 'searches past and future' (Eliot, 1963: 212). She is quite correct, of course: the past and future of the history in which she is implicated is indeed, as the play has abundantly demonstrated, all a matter of fathers and sons. Her 'natural' function in that history would be to father Richard's heir, Edward III's great-grandson, to act as medium for the forward transmission of that heroic line. As Richard is to die childless, her 'hollow womb' operates instead as a space for the conception of knowledge, an arena in which history is envisioned and formulated. Acutely aware of how the present will inherit the past, Isabella confesses to the limitations of her knowledge, which consists of a history currently 'in reversion' (2.2.38) (a legal term defining an inheritance not yet claimed or confirmed), lying in a transitional space between testator and beneficiary. As such, though apprehended, it cannot yet be 'named'; like an unborn foetus, it is anonymous and unformed; though a form of knowledge, it remains undefined: ''tis nameless woe, I wot' (2.2.40).

By focusing on the process of reproduction in which she, as a vessel for transmitting the royal line, ought to play a critical role, and on these metaphors of inheritance and naming, Isabella's language links her female story of personal sorrow to a tragic vision of history. Richard, from his vantage-point of masculine centrality and apparent ideological security, seems incapable of such intuitive prescience, and equally cavalier in his attitude to dynastic history. But Isabella, from her position on the margins (as a woman who has no formal role to play in the play's central events), and from the creative potency of her 'hollow womb' (which like the 'wooden O' of the theatre itself can mould the 'shapes', shadows' and 'forms' by means of which history is apprehended) can clearly see the 'something' that lies on the other side of 'nothing'.

These diverse threads of metaphor are finally caught up and resolved into a single clear explication. The message brought by Green —

> The banish'd Bolingbroke repeals himself,
> And with uplifted arms is safe arriv'd
> At Ravenspurgh ... (2.2.49–51)

— is a matter of clear and straightforward historical information: arms and power, authority and rebellion, loyalty and treason. Isabella assimilates this raw data into a fulfilment of her metaphors and an explanation of her grief: the 'unborn sorrow' that is the fruit of her conception, the 'prodigy' of Bolingbroke's rebellion, is born:

> So, Green, thou art the midwife to my woe,
> And Bolingbroke my sorrow's dismal heir.
> Now hath my soul brought forth her prodigy;
> And I, a gasping new-deliver'd mother,
> Have woe to woe, sorrow to sorrow join'd.   (2.2.61–5)

She is right, after all. Her emotion was no mere 'conceit', but a 'conception' of history, sired by a 'forefather' past; culminating in the offspring of a tragedy yet to unfold. Her grief for the past has become a sorrow for the future; woeful loss meets woeful expectation; and in an elegiac present, a regretted past poignantly interfaces with a tragic future.

VII

By the time Richard reappears, in Act 3, scene 2, he has come to display more affinity with that feminine dimension of language and metaphor inhabited by his queen, than with the masculine heroic tradition from which he derives, and into which he ought to be located. In his opening words he compares himself to a mother, and the kingdom to his child:

> I weep for joy
> To stand upon my kingdom once again.
> Dear earth, I do salute thee with my hand,
> Though rebels wound thee with their horses' hoofs.
> As a long-parted mother with her child
> Plays fondly with her tears and smiles in meeting,
> So weeping-smiling greet I thee, my earth,
> And do thee favours with my royal hands.
> Feed not thy sovereign's foe, my gentle earth,
> Nor with thy sweets comfort his ravenous sense;
> But let thy spiders, that suck up thy venom,
> And heavy-gaited toads, lie in their way,

Doing annoyance to the treacherous feet
Which with usurping steps do trample thee;
Yield stinging nettles to mine enemies.   (3.2.4–18)

The unmanly excess of emotion disclosed here – 'I weep for joy' –
seems to link him more closely to Isabella's world of female emotion
than to the tough masculinity of his competitor, Bolingbroke, who
shortly before this has invested himself firmly into the heroic tradition. When York chides Bolingbroke by invoking the examples of
John of Gaunt and the Black Prince, discharging their historical
destiny of heroic military action in France –

when brave Gaunt, thy father, and myself
Rescued the Black Prince, that young Mars of men,
From forth the ranks of many thousand French ...   (2.3.100–2)

– Bolingbroke adroitly explains his position within that tradition,
invoking both its legendary past and its capacity for rebirth and
future action:

You are my father, for methinks in you
I see old Gaunt alive.   (2.3.117–18)

The patriarchal heroes of his ancestry must surely rescue their heir
from his enemies, as Gaunt and York rescued their brother the Black
Prince: 'Will you permit that I should stand condemn'd?' (2.3.119).
Richard, by contrast, claims a maternal relation to the kingdom,
thus confessing to a relationship of emotional intimacy and weakness.
As a mother, playing with her child, he occupies a ludic world of
infancy, and his imagination populates itself with childlike fantasies
of omnipotence. This 'fond' play is therefore both affectionate and
foolish; the 'favours' he offers to his beloved earth link royal patronage to a childish megalomania. In this fantasy the creatures of the
earth – toads, adders, stinging nettles – can be relied upon to guarantee the loyalty so manifestly refused by Richard's human subjects.
  The different historical functions of Richard and Isabella here determine the dramatisations of their historical experience. Once Isabella's
function as medium of dynastic reproduction is removed, a space
is cleared for her to act as a medium of historical knowledge. But
Richard is designated by the great patriarchal heroic tradition to
occupy and defend his kingship, not to renounce it in favour of

alienation, prophecy and visionary art. The kind of 'power' Richard has here been exercising — that *force majeur* of absolutist autocracy — remains to be exercised, if not by the king, then by his opponents. The Bishop of Carlisle distinguishes sharply between that practical 'power' of military and political duress, and the kind of 'Power' Richard's imagination is now seeking:

> that Power that made you king
> Hath power to keep you king in spite of all. (3.2.27–8)

What Richard has succeeded in doing is engineering a split between 'Power' and 'power', which on the one hand disempowers his own cause, and on the other robs his opponents of any language of value; this puts him on the losing side in political and military terms, yet in possession of an immensely powerful and tragic historical narrative and legend. Within that discourse of absolutist royalty, later to be designated as the 'Divine Right of Kings', issues of practical legitimacy and pragmatic authority fade into insignificance, eclipsed by the majestic poetry of divine kingship. 'knows't thou not', he says to Bolingbroke,

> That when the searching eye of heaven is hid,
> Behind the globe, that lights the lower world,
> Then thieves and robbers range abroad unseen
> In murders and in outrage boldly here;
> But when, from under this terrestrial ball
> He fires the proud tops of the eastern pines
> And darts his light through every guilty hole,
> Then murders, treasons, and detested sins,
> The cloak of night being pluck'd from off their backs,
> Stand bare and naked, trembling at themselves? (3.2.37–46)

Here Richard echoes the stern remonstrances of the Old Testament prophet: his malefactors, like the adulterer, the murderer and the thief in Job's admonition, 'know not the light. / For the morning is even to them as the shadow of death' (Job, 24, 16–17).

VIII

As Walter Pater noted, a characteristic poetic strategy of this play is to set discordant textures and sensations into incongruous collocation – soft against hard, metal against flesh, feminine against masculine – as if to convey a sense of distasteful revulsion, a physical shrinking from the tough insensate priorities of militarism (Pater, 1889, 1907: 192). This comes across clearly in one of Richard's best-known aphorisms:

> Not all the water in the rough rude sea
> Can wash the balm off from an anointed king.   (3.2.54–5)

The gentle emollient caress of that sacramental 'balm', the oil of Chrism with which the king is 'anointed' at his coronation, is contrasted sharply with the boisterous force of the 'rough rude sea' that threatens to remove it. Richard goes on to draw a further contrast between the 'shrewd steel' (3.2.59) of Bolingbroke's naked force, and the 'golden crown' (3.2.59) of divinely appointed kingship; and then between the men 'press'd' (3.2.58) by Bolingbroke, as if coerced into unwilling insurrection, and the legions of angels who loyally serve the appointed deputy of their Lord:

> For every man that Bolingbroke hath press'd
> To lift shrewd steel against our golden crown,
> God for his Richard hath in heavenly pay
> A glorious angel. Then, if angels fight,
> Weak men must fall; for heaven still guards the right.   (3.2.58–62)

The image may echo the scene depicted on the Wilton Diptych, where a young and effeminately beautiful Richard is presented to a figure of the Virgin surrounded by particularly feminine angels. The line drawn by this formulation of the gender divide thus represents nothing less than a cleavage between the natural and divine worlds; and Richard's attempt here is to impose on one the values of the other. In that heavenly kingdom illustrated on the Wilton Diptych, a world of glorious angels and golden crowns, femininity reigns supreme, and divine glory emanates its unmistakable 'Power'. But in Bolingbroke's world of conscripted armies and the 'shrewd steel' of weaponry, the man who relies on divine aid proves to be the 'weaker' man, who inevitably 'must fall' (3.2.62).

The play goes on to acknowledge clearly the extent to which the space of this substantial mythology, which in this scene fills the stage and will in the play's future dominate history, is in a sense a space of 'nothingness'. To some degree this is a negative and reductionist realisation – deprived of 'power' Richard tries to imagine an alternative realm of 'Power' in which he can remain omnipotent despite worldly defeat. But from another point of view, this pragmatic and materialist explanation seems parochial: for in the *longue durée* of history the myth of the deposed king will live far longer than the practical achievements of his enemies. Here, for once, history is not written by the victors, but unforgettably formulated by the dispossessed, in a poignant poetry of defeat and inconsolable loss.

Once again it is the hollow space that has throughout the play signified those empty vessels of sterile vacuity and extraordinary productivity: the womb, that contains both past and future (like Hopkins' vast darkness, 'womb-of-all, home-of-all, hearse-of-all night' [Hopkins, 1996: 157]) and the tomb that seals and yet releases the meanings of the past. Richard's erstwhile supporters, executed by Bolingbroke, lie interred in such a space, 'grav'd in the hollow ground'. It is those dead, ineffectual enough when alive, whose remembered names provide Richard with that morbid eloquence of despair that so often in this play seems to represent history's last word:

> Let's talk of graves, of worms, and epitaphs;
> Make dust our paper, and with rainy eyes
> Write sorrow on the bosom of the earth.
> Let's choose executors and talk of wills;
> And yet not so – for what can we bequeath
> Save our deposed bodies to the ground?
> Our lands, our lives, and all, are Bolingbroke's.
> And nothing can we call our own but death
> And that small model of the barren earth
> Which serves as paste and cover to our bones.
> For God's sake, let us sit upon the ground
> And tell sad stories of the death of kings:
> How some have been depos'd, some slain in war,
> Some haunted by the ghosts they have depos'd,
> Some poison'd by their wives, some sleeping kill'd,
> All murder'd – for within the hollow crown
> That rounds the mortal temples of a king
> Keeps Death his court; and there the antic sits,
> Scoffing his state and grinning at his pomp;
> Allowing him a breath, a little scene,
> To monarchize, be fear'd, and kill with looks;
> Infusing him with self and vain conceit,

As if this flesh, which walls about our life,
Were brass impregnable; and humour'd thus,
Comes at the last, and with a little pin
Bores through his castle wall, and farewell, king!   (3.2.145–70)

This macabre fantasy is not merely a gesture of despair, or even a
vision of death as the inevitable end of all human striving. The speech
is as much about 'epitaphs' as 'graves' and 'worms': the signs of death
recorded, the inscriptions of commemoration, the traces of a vanished
past. Richard's proposal is to use dust and tears as paper and ink, to
'write sorrow' on the earth, so it will bear the traces and retell the
story of a royal tragedy.

Again the emphasis falls naturally on inheritance as the natural and
primary mechanism of dynastic continuity. Richard, however, has
no heir of his own body, no continuance of his own line – his only
bequest is that of his corpse to the inheriting ground. Without material property to bequeath, Richard is conscious of possessing nothing
except his own body, which in funereal effigy will commemorate his
physical being while the more poignantly marking the contrast
between its simulated shape, and the corruption breeding within.
Richard is here operating, as many critics have seen him, in the roles of
poet and actor: but he is also acting as a historian. The action of
manufacture, of 'telling' these 'sad stories', replaces the active making
of history. This vision of history is certainly a narrow and exclusive
one, a lineage of deposed and murdered kings, occupants of that
'hollow crown' that proves ultimately to be a symbol of vulnerability
rather than of power, and generates from its open space only a richly
tragic historical mythology. The image of the body as a wall of flesh
which in the protected and privileged position of kingship seems as
impregnable as brass, provides yet another image of a hollow space,
apparently full of life, yet vulnerable to the fatal wound of a mere 'pin',
that can pierce the circumambient armour. 'Is my strength', asks Job,
'the strength of stones? or is my fleshe of brasse?' (Job, 6.12).

When Richard finally encounters Bolingbroke, his language shifts
from poetry to prophecy:

well we know no hand of blood and bone
Can gripe the sacred handle of our sceptre,
Unless he do profane, steal, or usurp.   (3.3.79–81)

Richard is no longer seeking here to describe the superior force of a
divine 'Power' he can hope to command, but rather prospectively

predicting the inevitable consequences of his anticipated deposition. His fantasies of omnipotence have matured, in other words, into the vision of history identified by modern critics as 'the Yorkist myth' (Kelly, 1970). In a single image Richard expresses both the possibility and the impossibility of usurpation – 'no hand of blood and bone / Can gripe the sacred handle of our sceptre' – the brute physical strength of 'blood and bone' at once validates the superior authority of legitimate possession – 'sacred handle' – yet also renders that divine 'Power' as a singularly abstract entity by comparison with the fierce tenacity of natural force. It is abundantly obvious, in other words, that physical force *is* capable of grasping power; and in response to that inevitability Richard's imagination conjures a vision not of divine assistance, but of divine revenge:

> Yet know – my master, God omnipotent,
> Is mustering in his clouds on our behalf
> Armies of pestilence; and they shall strike
> Your children yet unborn and unbegot,
> That lift your vassal hands against my head
> And threat the glory of my precious crown.   (3.3.85–90)

Again, the dynastic associations of lineage and inheritance provide the framework for a vision of history, a past, present and future inextricably linked by interpretative continuity. Bolingbroke has come to 'open / The purple testament of bleeding war' (3.3.94) – his usurpation will ensure that his subjects and successors inherit a history of chaotic violence and civil war. The aggressive and appetitive terms of usurpation – 'gripe', 'steal', threat' – collide roughly with an image of the kingdom as both pastoral and feminine, a place of 'pastures' quietly ruled by 'maid-pale peace'; a grassy land with the feminine delicacy of a 'flower-like face' (3.3.98–100).

Northumberland's defence of Bolingbroke again invokes the heroic tradition of 'honourable tombs' and 'royalties of blood', in order to vindicate Lancaster's limited ambition to recover his own 'lineal royalties' (3.3.113). Satisfaction of that demand would guarantee conciliation, a laying aside of weapons: 'His glittering arms he will commend to rust' (3.3.116). All that the play has already said of 'blood' and 'honour', of the demanding memory of heroic fathers, makes clear that no simple definition of 'lineal royalty' is available. That term clearly encompasses legitimate restitution, sovereign ambition and patriarchal domination. The action required by Gaunt's 'honourable tomb' is more than the recovery of an expropriated birthright. The 'buried hand of warlike Gaunt' (3.3.109), the hand that was raised in heroic action against the French, has already returned as the 'blood and bone' of Bolingbroke's rapacious fist.

Once Richard has acknowledged the inevitability of the historical process in which he is implicated, his language again gravitates more closely towards that previously employed by Isabella:

> O, that I were as great
> As is my grief, or lesser than my name!
> Or that I could forget what I have been!
> Or not remember what I must be now!   (3.3.136–9)

Just as Isabella recognised an apparently insignificant sensation of sorrow as a substantial monitor of historical process, so Richard now sees the reality of his existence in grief, not sovereignty. The grief of his impending loss now fills the space formerly occupied by his sovereign being, just as his historical myth is beginning to replace the actuality of his power. His own name has become a paradox, like the term 'deposed king': humiliation would be more tolerable were he not falling, like Phaeton, from so great a height. That name, however, the name of fallen King Richard, is the name that will enter history. Richard cannot 'forget' what he has been, or prospectively fail to 'remember' what he must become. Were he 'lesser than' his name, a welcome historical oblivion might obscure his downfall. But a king who has fallen, though fallen only to the level of his subjects ('subjected thus'), cannot seek the obscurity of a common destiny. Historical memory casts the shadow of his humiliation across a glamorous past and a bitter future.

In the fantasy of renunciation that follows, Richard envisages himself seeking the consoling obscurity of a pilgrim's life, an existence of innocuous vagabond piety:

> I'll give my jewels for a set of beads,
> My gorgeous palace for a hermitage,
> My gay apparel for an almsman's gown,
> My figur'd goblets for a dish of wood,
> My sceptre for a palmer's walking staff,
> My subjects for a pair of carved saints,
> And my large kingdom for a little grave.   (3.3.147–53)

Anticipating the more formal ritual of 'undecking' that Richard invents for the subsequent 'deposition scene', the 'palmer' speech enumerates the details that go to compose royal power, and are here exchanged for the trappings of anonymity: jewels, palaces, decorated goblets, the sceptre, are traded for a rosary, a hermitage, a beggar's gown, a wooden platter. The 'name' of a king is renounced in favour of anonymity, and the kingdom itself swapped for

A little little grave, an obscure grave ...   (3.3.154)

The monumental tomb that would naturally commemorate a distinguished, glorious and heroic reign, is renounced in favour of a nameless grave that will tell no story. While the tombs of the ancestors loudly proclaim, by their monumental magnificence, all the pomp and circumstance of glorious war, Richard craves the anonymity of a subject's death, a pauper's grave; or even to be buried in 'the king's high way' (3.3.155), to mingle his dust with the traffic of common life. And while the deeds of the fathers are sternly inscribed on their monuments, Richard hopes rather to be swallowed back, through an aperture carved out by his own unmanly tears, into the tender and forgiving womb of his mother earth.

IX

The scene that dramatises 'the deposing of King Richard' (4.1) is a critical element in this analysis, since it clearly shows historical agents attempting to compose a particular construction of history; trying to align historical process, in advance of the event, with an appropriate future retrospective interpretation. The 'deposition' scene is set up by Bolingbroke in order to demonstrate his accession as a process of smooth, uninterrupted, natural dynastic progression. It is intended that Richard voluntarily 'surrender' (4.1.156) the crown, and do so 'in common view' (4.1.155); so that no apparent disturbance would be visible in the continuity of the crown — 'so we shall proceed / Without suspicion' (4.1.156–7). Northumberland's intervention, in which Richard is required openly to confess his crimes, brings the procedure closer to the modern 'show trial'; the power of established legitimacy, of the status quo, is such that the incumbent monarch must be seen not only voluntarily to surrender the crown, but willingly to discredit himself, subvert his own reputation, and thereby openly and conclusively vindicate his successor.

Richard, however, manipulates the public ritual to produce very different effects, varying from a disclosure of the political mechanisms masked by this cosmetic formality, to a rewriting of the 'woeful pageant' (4.1.321) as a re-enactment of the trial and condemnation of Christ. The physical handover of the crown is designed to enact this voluntary 'resignation':

> Give me the crown. Here, cousin, seize the crown.
> Here, cousin,
> On this side my hand, and on that side thine.
> Now is this golden crown like a deep well
> That owes two buckets, filling one another;
> The emptier ever dancing in the air,
> The other down, unseen, and full of water.
> That bucket down and full of tears am I,
> Drinking my griefs, whilst you mount up on high.   (4.1.181–9)

Although the crown is used symbolically, it is constituted by the terms of the ritual as emblem rather than image, as a theatrical prop of kingship rather than as an embodiment of kingly authority. For if sovereignty can be ceded, legitimacy transferred, then the crown is merely a badge of office, worn as well by a usurper as by a rightful king.

It is towards this hypostatisation of the crown as a commodity capable of exchange (Richard himself has in any case, according to his supporters, delivered it into 'broking pawn' [2.1.293]), that Richard begins to direct his powerful poetic imagination. According to the pretender's carefully scripted intentions, the crown should simply be handed over. Richard has, after all, agreed; the symbol of authority should function as a prop in a performance. But Richard instead elects to use the crown as instrumental to an alternative agenda, and in doing so regains the initiative, in a theatrical if not in a political sense. By retaining his grip on the crown, he forces Bolingbroke to perform a duet with him, in which the king presents himself as despoliated victim, and the 'natural' successor finds himself forced into the public role of rapacious contender. The crown should simply figure a transfer of power: but Richard uses it as a metaphor for representing a royal tragedy.

The hollow circle of the crown becomes a space in which an emblematic and figurative representation of history can be constructed. The image of the 'deep well' in which the two contenders are counterpoised in unequal balance, is another image of history. The crown ceases to be a solid object, an intrinsically empty insignia of power. Its hollow circle becomes an aperture through which the historical process being enacted can be viewed. Appropriately positioned, a spectator can gaze through that circle and discern the two contenders, no longer complicit in a willing negotiation, but rather involved in a struggle for power in which the loser retains both the moral advantage, and the privilege of writing his own history. The victorious bucket, Bolingbroke, dances into public visibility through lightness, not weight; while the loser, descending into the obscurity of the past, testifies with potent and compelling eloquence to his tragic Passion.

Previously it has been Bolingbroke who is associated with a practical and naturalistic view of the world, concerning himself with matters of protocol and procedure, of legal right and title, of military advantage and political contingency. Here, however, it is Richard who, confronted with Bolingbroke's attempt to elide, in a ritual of abdication, the real mechanics of this transfer of power, uses poetic expression to disclose the true character of the struggle. This strategy is fully realised in Richard's formal speech of abdication:

> Now mark me how I will undo myself:
> I give this heavy weight from off my head,
> And this unwieldy sceptre from my hand,
> The pride of kingly sway from out my heart;
> With mine own tears I wash away my balm,
> With mine own hands I give away my crown,
> With mine own tongue deny my sacred state,
> With mine own breath release all duteous oaths;
> All pomp and majesty I do forswear.   (4.1.203–11)

As Walter Pater pointed out (Pater, 1889, 1907: 198), Richard is literally inventing a ritual unavailable to his culture. There is no ceremonial rite of 'de-coronation', as there are rites to represent, for instance, the deconsecration of the clergy. In addition to drawing painfully focused attention on the detail of his abdication, Richard makes clear what is entailed in this process of 'undoing' himself. What is the existential nature of a de-crowned king? The oxymoron 'unking'd Richard' (4.1.220) says it all: if 'kingship' is not simply the occupation of an office, but a condition of being, then a king whose kingly status is removed from him is, literally, nothing – 'for I must nothing be'. There is no intermediate status between king and not-king, King Richard and 'unking'd Richard'. Denuded of royalty, he is stripped of his defining character, his very being, and reduced to an alienated anonymity:

> I have no name, no title –
> No, not that name was given me at the font –
> But 'tis usurp'd.   (4.1.255–7)

Nameless, powerless, Richard represents himself as an existential zero, an elimination of all that he has been. In one sense this trajectory is defined as a fall from political eminence to social dispossession: his abdication has

> Made glory base, and sovereignty a slave,
> Proud majesty a subject.   (4.1.251–2)

In the play's closing moments, in the isolation of his imprisonment, Richard will discover the existence of others, and realise the illusion of believing that the only alternative to royalty is 'nothing' (5.5.64–6). But in the process of abdication he elects to position himself precisely on 'nothingness', exactly at 'the point of intersection of the timeless / With time' (Eliot, 1963: 212), by aligning himself with the simultaneous incarnation and transcendence of the Christian Passion.

The analogy is made first of all by the Bishop of Carlisle, who warns that the usurpers will turn the kingdom into 'the field of Golgotha and dead mens' skulls' (4.1.144); then by Richard himself, who compares his opponents to Judas, and then calls them so many emulators of Pontius Pilate:

> you Pilates
> Have here delivered me to my sour cross.   (4.1.240–1)

'Then delivered he him therefore unto them to be crucified' (John, XX.16). Renouncing the natural power of 'wordly men', Richard assumes the divine Power of a very different type of king, becoming a man of sorrows , a king of 'griefs' (4.1.193), a sacrificial victim whose power is paradoxically established through the subjugation of martyrdom.

X

The ceremony with the mirror belongs to the same philosophical and metaphoric discursive dimension. Richard wants to view his own natural face, 'bankrupt of his majesty':

> I'll read enough,
> When I do see the very book indeed
> Where all my sins are writ, and that's myself.
> *Re-enter attendant with a glass*
> Give me that glass, and therein will I read.
> No deeper wrinkles yet? Hath sorrow struck
> So many blows upon this face of mine
> And made no deeper wounds? O flatt'ring glass,
> Like to my followers in prosperity,
> Thou dost beguile me! Was this face the face
> That every day under his household roof
> Did keep ten thousand men? Was this the face
> That like the sun did make beholders wink?
> Is this the face which fac'd so many follies
> That was at last out-fac'd by Bolingbroke?
> A brittle glory shineth in this face;
> As brittle as the glory is the face;
> *[Dashes the glass against the ground*
> For there it is, crack'd in a hundred shivers.
> Mark, silent king, the moral of this sport –
> How soon my sorrow hath destroy'd my face.   (4.1.273–91)

The mirror is of course one of the key images of history:

> in recalling to mind the truth of things past, which otherwise would be buried in silence, [Historie] setteth before vs such effects ... and layeth vertue and vice so naked before our eyes ... that it may rightly be called an easie and profitable apprentiship or schoole for euerie man to learne to get wisedome ... Hence it is, that Historie is tearmed of the auncient Philosophers, the ... looking glasse of mans life.   (Beard, 1597)

As 'the looking glasse of mans life', history is assumed truly to reflect the reality of human experience, an exact imitation which in turn produces 'wisdome'. In Hamlet's neo-classical dramatic theory, it is drama that 'holds the mirror up to nature', and thereby produces the age's own self-consciousness. The metaphor of the 'looking glasse' seeks to establish an unproblematical continuity between appearance and knowledge: on the one hand, accurate reflection or precise imitation of the object ('setteth before us ... the truth of things past'), and on the other, a wisdom or understanding acquired via that process of reflection ('the light of truth' [Cicero, 1962: 224]).

When Richard calls for a looking-glass to reflect back to himself a climactic moment of his own historical drama, what he sees is not an accurate reflection, but a distortion, or even inversion, of the truth. Richard expects the mirror to act not just as an agent of reflective wisdom, but as a confessional record of his own soul. The glass is assumed to be capable of not merely reflecting a surface reality, but of disclosing a hidden truth, depicting an underlying reality, presenting as accurately and as openly as in a book the literature of his own 'sins'. What Richard sees in the glass is, however, the very opposite of what he feels himself to be. The mirror shows an image of beauty, power and brightness, where the subject knows only sorrow, weakness and an overshadowing abnegation.

Bolingbroke attempts to explain away Richard's fantasy, just as Bushy tried to console the Queen by questioning the reality of her grief:

The shadow of your sorrow hath destroy'd
The shadow of your face.   (4.1.292–3)

Bolingbroke recognises two types of 'shadow': the darkness of Richard's sorrow, that has provoked him to this action; and the mere 'shadow' of reality. The image in the mirror can be destroyed without affecting the substance it reflects. What Richard saw in the mirror was after all nothing but the shadow of his face. Richard seizes the opportunity of positing an alternative view of reality, using language very close to that earlier employed by Isabella:

my grief lies all within;
And these external manner of laments
Are merely shadows to the unseen grief
That swells with silence in the tortur'd soul.
There lies the substance ...   (4.1.295–9)

Shadow *is* substance; nothingness *is* something; and the true representation of history resides, not in objective imitation of material fact, but in intuitive apprehension of an 'unseen' reality.

XI

Act 5, scene 1 takes us again down one of those mysterious corridors of 'what might have been', to one of those passages history chose not to take, a door 'we never opened' (Eliot, 1963: 189). Nothing else can explain the dramatic oddity of this scene, which prepares the audience for Richard's interment in the Tower, and which enables him under its walls to utter the crowning declaration of his tragic philosophy of history, and yet then twists to remove him from this heavily symbolic site to the relative obscurity and marginality of Pomfret Castle in Yorkshire.

Plate 4 Richard II in the Tower of London, from MS Hart, 4380, f. 181v in the British Library. Reproduced by kind permission of the British Library.

The propriety of the Tower as the final scene of Richard's 'woeful pageant' lies precisely in the ancient lineaments and grim precedents of its long history.

> Ah, thou, the model where old Troy did stand;
> Thou map of honour, thou King Richard's tomb ...   (5.1.11–12)

Identified by popular mythology as 'Julius Caesar's ill-erected tower' ([5.1.2] not badly built, so much as built to bad ends), the edifice is redolent of an even longer historical vista, regarded by historical legend as the site of Britain's original colonisation by the Trojans, 'the model where old Troy did stand'. Richard's contemporary tragedy is thus historicised by contextualisation in that long historical perspective that looks back to Julius Caesar and beyond to the mythical foundation of Britain by Brutus, supposed grandson of Aeneas. The Tower thus represents, with its appropriately 'flint bosom' (5.1.3), a product of the heroic patriarchal past. Its 'hard-favour'd' (5.1.14) masculinity becomes a 'tomb' for the pitifully unmanly Richard, the 'fair rose' (5.1.8) who, because dissociated from his true heritage, is no longer himself, 'not King Richard' (5.1.13).

Here Richard assumes the persona of the living dead, prematurely a ghost of himself, to voice his clear perception of the historical tradition he is himself in the process of making:

> Think I am dead, and that even here thou takest,
> As from my death-bed, thy last living leave.
> In winter's tedious nights sit by the fire
> With good old folks, and let them tell thee tales
> Of woeful ages long ago betid;
> And ere thou bid good night, to quit their griefs
> Tell thou the lamentable tale of me,
> And send the hearers weeping to their beds;
> For why the senseless brands will sympathize
> The heavy accent of thy moving tongue,
> And in compassion weep the fire out;
> And some will mourn in ashes, some coal-black,
> For the deposing of a rightful king.   (5.1.38–50)

Northumberland's unceremonious arresting of this dénouement –

> My lord, the mind of Bolingbroke is chang'd;
> You must to Pomfret, not unto the Tower   (5.1.51–2)

— is, like Richard's earlier stopping of the combat, a deliberate nipping in the bud of a flowering historical legend. On no more plausible pretext than a change of mind, Richard is removed from a manifestly historical site, to one of relative obscurity.

The objective is presumably to eliminate the deposed king from history altogether. But the attempt is a failure. Richard's history has already been made. It can certainly be rewritten; but it cannot be effaced. Though the historic portrait may be pinned to the backside of a base room door, its tragic story will inevitably be told and retold. Whether publicly executed in the Tower, or secretly murdered at Pomfret Castle; whether restored to a rightful place among his ancestors and successors, or discarded in some dusty lumber-room of lost historical knowledge — Richard has proved too competent a manufacturer of history for his vivid historical presence to be permanently forgotten.

Conclusion

I

Through the 1960s and 1970s most critical work on Shakespeare's history plays countered the providential interpretations of Tillyard with an alternative promotion of Italian humanism as a counterpoised or even dominant intellectual influence. Machiavelli, rather than Edward Halle, became the key point of reference (see Prior, 1973; Sanders, 1968). Subsequent work has tended to offer a different view, arguing that in practice Italian humanism, innovative though it may have been, ultimately shared common cause with mediaeval providentialism; that early modern historical thinkers were capable of a much more 'modern' grasp of the pastness of the past than that produced by humanist historical writing; and that Shakespeare's historical plays were more concerned with reconstructing and mediating such alien pasts, than with innocently reflecting their own familiar and contemporary present. It became generally accepted that Shakespeare's history plays self-consciously and strategically manipulated a wide range of historical perspectives, including providentialism, machiavellianism, quasi-scientific positivism and a popular tradition of 'comic history', and thereby situated themselves into an ideological contest between conflicting ways of knowing and explaining the past (Kastan, 1982; Thayer, 1983; Holderness, 1985; Wikander, 1986; Marcus, 1988; Rackin, 1990; Hodgdon, 1991; Hawley, 1992).

Historiographers long ago began to identify that period during which the historical drama of the Renaissance developed and died, as a transitional space between two great epistemological 'breaks' in historical theory – that of the Reformation, which isolated Christian providential history from its mediaeval and European heritage, and encouraged local applications of Italian humanism; and that represented by the birth in the early seventeenth century of a proto-modern, positivistic and quasi-scientific historical practice (see Pocock, 1957; Fussner, 1962; Holderness, 1985) . In the early 1980s, approaches to Shakespeare's histories were strongly influenced by a sense that the discipline of history was (or at least ought to have been) radically destabilised by such powerful intellectual influences as poststructuralism and deconstruction, Althusserian marxism and the various theories of 'postmodernism'. An acute consciousness of that disciplinary crisis seemed readily to facilitate new perspectives on those earlier paradigm shifts, already identified by historiographers, in the conceptual fields of early modern historical thinking:

> Historians today, working at the end of the modern period, like their predecessors, working at its beginning, are impelled by a cultural and intellectual revolution that forces us to revaluate the nature of history.   (Rackin, 1990: 34)

But to speak now of a 'revolution' in historical practice is surely to some degree premature. For although it is clear that literary and cultural studies *have* since 1970 been both intensively historicised and thoroughly penetrated by those theoretical influences that insistently call for new historical approaches to the past, it could scarcely be argued that the practices of writing *history* have in the period between 1970 and 1990 been genuinely 'revolutionised' in the way they were, say, in the period between 1590 and 1610. A 'historical revolution' that has as yet neither fully involved the historians, nor thoroughly destabilised the dominant practices of historical writing, cannot with any confidence be described as an accomplished 'revolution' (see Sharpe, 1994).

The challenges to history from psychology, linguistics and philosophy have certainly in those two decades been issued, if history has not as yet definitively given satisfaction (see Burgess, 1996; Toews, 1987). Poststructuralist views of language and perception have challenged 'objective' and 'value-free' perspectives, and problematised positivist notions of 'fact' and 'interpretation'; and in philosophy theories of postmodernism have demanded a review of traditional ideas about 'reality' (Megill, 1987; Goldstein, 1994; Rorty, Schneewind and Skinner, 1984). Simultaneously, the political initiatives of marxism, feminism and postcolonialism have had their impact on the way in which contemporary societies look back to the past (see Southgate, 1996: 86–107; Holderness, 1992). Perhaps we may, being optimistic, look forward to a historical practice consisting no longer mainly of 'facts', 'dates' and 'interpretations', but also of poetry, narrative and postmodern stylistic innovation. But in the *writing* of history this is certainly not as yet happening (see Easthope, 1993; Davies, 1987; Burke, 1992).

This book has attempted to revisit early modern 'history' with an intensified awareness of the contemporary 'historical revolution' in process, and with a distinct consciousness of the provisionality of contemporary disciplinary parameters. Though I have tried throughout to retain a consciousness of the contemporaneity of my own preoccupations, I remain confident that these 'postmodern' views of history would, if returned to the early modern period, afford its inhabitants few surprises.

II

One of the commendatory poems affixed to the 1632 Folio edition of *Mr William Shakespeare's Comedies, Histories and Tragedies*, under the superscription 'I.M.S.' (Wells and Taylor, 1987: xli) praises Shakespeare's achievement in a manner appropriate both to the occasion, and to the editorial structuring of the volume into the three major dramatic 'kinds'. In celebrating generic diversity, however, the poet concedes a definite preferential emphasis to History:

> The buskined muse, the comic queen, the grand
> And louder tone of Clio ... (44–5)

Although full of admiration for Shakespeare's comic and tragic successes, it is on the capacity of drama to enact *history* that the poem particularly dwells.

The dramatist's mind is, first of all, figured as a mirror. Like the mirror deployed as a key image in Hamlet's exposition of dramatic theory, this one is also less a medium for the transmission of information, and more a primary source of knowledge (see Grabes, 1982: 202–20):

> A mind reflecting ages past, whose clear
> And equal surface can make things appear
> Distant a thousand years, and represent
> Them in their lively colours' just extent. (1–4)

The mirror is identified as both flat and clear: so it is neither a distorting convex mirror, nor a semi-opaque 'flattering glass'. But neither is it simply a mechanism of reflection, as is the mirror in Lucian of Samosata's exhortation to the historian to 'bring a mind like a mirror, clear, gleaming bright, accurately centred, displaying the shape of things just as he receives them, free from distortion, false colouring, and misrepresentation' (Lucian, in Kelley, 1991: 66–7). For this mirror is, like virtually all mirrors in this Renaissance aesthetic tradition, a 'magic' mirror that is useful precisely because it does *not* simply reflect what passes before it. The mirror of Shakespeare's mind distorts and restructures reality in two important ways: firstly by making available to present vision images of a remote past, to cause things that are 'distant a thousand years' to *appear*; but secondly by simulating a past reality out of a contemporary performative medium – to make present things *appear to be* distant a thousand years. Contrary to Lucian's stipulation that the historian should use no 'misrepresentation' or 'false colours', the mirror of the historical dramatist's mind can only 'represent' (re-present and imitate) historical objects in 'colours' that only appear to be 'lively'. Mirror-minded Shakespeare can make things from a thousand years ago appear before his audience; but he can do so only by making what is, in present actuality, before that audience – stage and actors – take on the convincing appearance of a thousand-year-old reality.

The poem thus grasps immediately the two-way process of historical reconstruction, in which the past has to be made to be remade, its reconstruction being also its initial construction. The historical imagination is here equipped with a power of resurrection exceeding even those images already considered of the dead revived in contemporary presence. For this grand reawakening of departed souls mingles antique myths of the descent into the underworld, with a Christian vision of the Last Judgement:

> To outrun hasty time, retrieve the fates,
> Roll back the heavens, blow ope the iron gates
> Of death and Lethe, where confused lie
> Great heaps of ruinous mortality.   (5–8)

What that powerful imagination finds in the past is a humanity as indiscriminately mingled in universal decay as the jumbled contents of the churchyard at Elsinore. Its particular gift, is however, from that homogenised ruin, to isolate and identify the historically significant:

> In that deep dusky dungeon to discern
> A royal ghost from churls.   (9–10)

Once the memorable character has been recognised, however, historical reconstruction involves more than merely drawing it forth from
the 'ruinous' mortality' of historical oblivion to the light of common
day. The poet's emphasis falls more strongly here on the artistic skills
needed to create a contemporary presence out of the disembodied
spirits of history:

> by art to learn
> The physiognomy of shades, and give
> Them sudden birth.   (10–12)

Historical figures are in this conception not so much reborn, as born
for the first time, and newly equipped with a physiognomy bestowed
by 'art'. The poet then defines historical drama in precisely the language we have seen deployed by Nash, Heywood and Shakespeare:

> To raise our ancient sovereigns from their hearse.   (19)

But as in the more self-reflexive formulations of this image, the raised
spirit is firmly subjected to the power of the conjuring writer who can:

> *Make kings his subjects.*   (20, my italics)

However sovereign their historical status, the 'subjects' of the plays
are also in some sense 'subject' to the dramatist who creates them.
The poem goes on to further explore some of the doubling and inverse effects of drama in characterising the responses of the audience:

> fearful at plots so sad,
> Then laughing at our fear; abused, and glad
> To be abused, affected with that truth
> Which we perceive is false.   (25–8)

If history is 'that truth / Which we perceive is false' then truly the
truest history is the most feigned.

The author of this process is clearly recognised by the poem as
a potent force, as a power that can genuinely invoke the dead,
recuperate a vanished past, or reconstruct a lost history. There are
other emphases, however, on magic, playfulness, and on the social
and political radicalism of the dramatist's art:

> While the plebian imp from lofty throne
> Creates and rules a world.   (33–4)

The implicit republicanism of these sentiments is contextually focused by their sharing a page with Milton's poetic tribute, 'An Epitaph on the Admirable Dramatic Poet, William Shakespeare', which forcefully asserts the moral superiority of the popular dramatist's reputation over that of his royal and historic 'subjects':

> kings for such a tomb would wish to die.
> > (Milton in Wells and Taylor, 1987: xli)

Despite its base origins on the common and popular stage, historical drama is nonetheless the power that *makes* history: engenders and directs, shapes and governs, 'creates' and 'rules' a retrospective but unprecedented historical 'world'.

III

Both the historical drama and the historiographical theory of the Renaissance can therefore be perceived as particularly responsive to our contemporary historical and historiographical preoccupations. Though the Ciceronian vocabulary of Truth, Memory and Instruction has been replaced by a critical language that would substitute, for these same concepts, terms such as representation, narrative and ideology, it is apparent from the preceding analysis that early modern thinkers and writers struggled in analogous ways with comparable problems. If, however, for Renaissance intellectuals, as for post-modern historians, historical truth could in substantial part be reduced to contemporary acts of narration and representation, that still need not necessarily point towards the conclusion reached by Phyllis Rackin, who describes:

> Shakespeare's emplotment of history as an obsessive circling around a lost and irrecoverable center ... the Renaissance sense of history constitutes a similar pre/postfiguration of a historiographic project driven and finally disappointed by an intensified sense of the distance and difference that separate the history-writing present from the historical past it seeks to recover.   (Rackin, 1990: x)

But this is to reverse the discovery that there existed, within early modern culture, competing historiographical methodologies, and to return to an assumption that there was only one History: not, certainly, the providentialism of Tillyard, but the great neo-classical tradition of heroic achievement, masculine supremacy and *Res Gestae*. In the preceding pages we have seen that tradition subjected to an intensive critical scrutiny that in turn discloses a powerful recognition of its ideological character. But we also find in Shakespearean historical drama a much stronger and more optimistic emphasis on the history-making powers of the 'plebeian' theatre. The condition of that shift is that the struggle between competing historiographies offered both historian and historical dramatist genuine moral, cultural and political *choices*. *Hamlet*, for example, absorbs that classical historical tradition, and reproduces it as tragedy: the past appears to be capable only of hurting, not liberating, the present. But in the saturnalian comedy of the grave-digging clowns, the theatre found its own creative historiographical medium: plebeian rather than aristocratic, demotic rather than epic; open to new possibilities of historical method, but radically dissenting from the dominant historical tradition.

In making this argument I am consciously aligning myself with a 'democratic' tradition of Shakespeare criticism developed and consolidated by Robert Weimann, Michael Bristol, Walter Cohen, Leah Marcus, Annabel Patterson and Kiernan Ryan (Weimann, 1978; Bristol, 1985; Cohen, 1985; Marcus, 1988; Patterson, 1989; Ryan, 1990); and equally dissenting from what seems an increasingly influential tendency, exemplified in the work of Richard Helgerson (Helgerson, 1992), to identify the Shakespearean drama with an aristocratic and authoritarian culture. Helgerson places Hamlet, his author, and the dramatic text that contains him, firmly on the upstage terrain of authority and order, while the 'disruptive and discordant improvisation' of the clown occupies a rapidly shrinking, audience-contingent area of 'unauthorized' speech and action (Helgerson, 1992: 224). But Hamlet, whether he is expounding neo-classical dramatic theory to the actors, or exploring philosophies of history with the grave-diggers, continually shares the downstage territory of common player and clown. In many respects he himself enters into the roles of player and clown, resisting authority, disrupting established order, both acting and speaking more than is set down for him: it is not for nothing that he describes himself as a 'rogue and peasant slave' (2.2.543). Nor is this realisation, in the light of the preceding analysis, at all surprising. In so far as both history, the events of time past, and 'history', the contemporary narrative, were considered the exclusive province of sovereign authority (the history, as Holinshed defined it, of 'kings and Queens', in 'thier orderlie successions') then Hamlet's place is not in the pantheon of sovereignty, but among the wretched and dispossessed of the earth. He has more in common with those writers and actors who irreverently 'make kings their subjects', than with the king who complains bitterly, in a self-fulfilling prophecy, that his royalty is 'subject to the breath / Of every fool' (*HV*, 4.1.230–1).

In that creative space of the public theatre, history could be made, in full awareness of its true status as a contemporary process of cultural production. The clowns in *Hamlet* formally link the retrospective narrative of history with the contemporary medium of cultural production, referring as they do to a place called 'England': a country that for Claudius represents a real historical territory, the tributary of early Denmark (4.3.58); to Hamlet remains a fictive location, an 'undiscover'd country, from whose bourn / No traveller returns' (3.1.79–80); but which was, for actors and audience, the immediate environment of the play's manufacture. For the early modern English audience, watching a play whose historical content purports to have been recuperated from a remote mediaeval past, history is clearly visible as a contemporary narrative representation: 'History is now and England' (Eliot, 1963: 222).

Bibliography

Agrippa, Henrie Cornelius (1575) *Of the Vanitie and Uncertaintie of Artes and Sciences*, Englished by Ia. San. Gent. (London: Henrie Bynneman).

Alberti, Leon Battista (1966) *On Painting (Della Pittura)*, trans. John R. Spencer (New Haven and London: Yale UP).

Amiot, James (1579, 1928) 'Amiot to the Readers', in *The Lives Of The Noble Grecians And Romanes, Compared together by that grave learned philosopher and historio-grapher, Plutarke Of Chaeronea*, translated by Thomas North (Oxford: Basil Blackwell).

Anderson, Perry (1974) *Lineages of the Absolutist State* (London: New Left Books).

Aristotle (1965) *Classical Literary Criticism*, trans. T. S. Dorsch (Harmondsworth: Penguin).

Ascham, Roger (1970) 2nd prefatory letter, 'R. Ascham, to Iohn Astely' in 'A Report and Discourse of the Affaires and State of Germany', Roger Ascham, *English Works*, ed. William Aldis Wright (Cambridge: Cambridge UP).

Attridge, Derek (1987) *History, Post-structuralism and the Question of Theory*, with Geoff Bennington and Robert Young (Cambridge: Cambridge UP).

Avery, Charles (1970) *Florentine Renaissance Sculpture* (London: John Murray).

Bacon, Francis (1605, 1973) *The Advancement of Learning* (London: J. M. Dent).

Bamber, Linda (1992) *Comic Women, Tragic Men: A Study of Gender and Genre in Shakespeare* (Stanford, CA: Stanford UP).

Banks, Carol (1998) ' "Mother-England": finding the female in Shakespeare's Histories' (PhD Thesis: University of Hertfordshire).

Barclay, Alexander (1520) 'The preface of Alexander Barclay preest unto the right hye and mighty prince. Thomas duke of Northfolke', in *Sallustius Crispius, Jugurtha*, trans. Alexander Barclay (London: n.d.).

Barker, Francis (ed.) (1991a) *Uses of History: Marxism, Postmodernism and the Renaissance*, with Peter Hulme and Margaret Iverson (eds) (Manchester: Manchester UP).

Barker, Francis (1991b) 'Which Dead? *Hamlet* and the ends of history', in Barker (1991a).

Barker, Francis (1993) *The Culture of Violence: Essays on Tragedy and History* (Manchester: Manchester UP).

Barrie and Jenkins (eds) (1989) *William Shakespeare: The History Plays* (London: Barrie and Jenkins).

Batho, G. R. (1983) *Thomas Harriot and the Northumberland Household* (London: Historical Association).

Baxandall, Michael (1988) *Painting and Experience in Fifteenth Century Italy* (2nd edn, Oxford: Oxford UP).

Beard, Thomas (1597, 1612) *The Theatre of Gods Iudgements* (London: 1612 edn), 'The Preface'.

Belsey, Catherine (1991) 'Making histories then and now: Shakespeare from *Richard II* to *Henry V*' in Barker (1991a).

Berger, Harry, Jr (1985) 'Psychoanalyzing the Shakespeare text: the first three scenes of the *Henriad*', in *Shakespeare and the Question of Theory*, ed. P. Parker, G. Hartman (New York and London: Methuen).

Bevington, David (1966), 'The domineering female in *1 Henry VI*', *Shakespeare Studies*, 2.

Blundeville, Thomas (1574) *The True Order and Methode of Wryting and Reading Hystories* (London: William Seres, unpaginated).

Boris, Edna Z. (1974) *Shakespeare's English Kings, the People and the Law: A Study in the Relationship between the Tudor Constitution and the English History Plays* (Cranbury, NJ: Associated UPs).

Brende, John (1602) *The Historie of Quintus Curtius, conteining the Actes of the great Alexander*, translated out of Latine, into English, by *Iohn Brende* (London: Thomas Creede), 'The Preface'.

Bristol, Michael D. (1985) *Carnival and Theatre: Plebeian Culture and the Structure of Authority in Renaissance England* (London: Routledge).

Brooks, Perry (1992) *Piero della Francesca: the Arezzo Frescoes* (New York: Rizzoli).

Bullough, Geoffrey (1960) *Narrative and Dramatic Sources of Shakespeare*, Vols III and IV (London: Routledge and Kegan Paul).

Burgess, Anthony (1993) *A Dead Man in Deptford* (London: Vintage).

Burgess, Glenn (1996) 'Renaissance Texts and Renaissance Republicanism', *Renaissance Forum*, 1, uttp://www.hull.ac.uk:80/Hull/EL-Web/renforum.

Burke, Peter (1992) *New Perspectives on Historical Writing* (Cambridge: Polity Press).

Burke, Peter (1969) *The Renaissance Sense of the Past* (London: Edward Arnold).

Cairncross, A.S. (ed.) (1962) *Henry the Sixth, Part One* (London: Methuen).

Calderwood, James L. (1979) *Metadrama in Shakespeare's Henriad* (Berkeley, CA: California UP).

Campbell, Lily B. (1947) *Shakespeare's Histories: Mirrors of Elizabethan Policy* (San Marino, CA: Huntingdon Library Press).

Cecil, David (1975) *The Cecils of Hatfield House: Portrait of an English Ruling Family* (London: Constable).

Chatman, Seymour (1978) *Story and Discourse: Narrative Structure in Fiction and Film* (Ithaca, NY: Cornell UP).

Cicero (1962) *De Oratore*, trans. E. W. Sutton (London: Heinemann), vol. 1, Book II.

Cohen, Derek (1988) '*Henry IV*: Carnival and History', *Shakespearean Motives* (London: Macmillan).

Cohen, Walter (1985) *Drama of a Nation* (Ithaca, NY: Cornell UP).

Cohen, Walter (1987) 'Political criticism of Shakespeare', *Shakespeare Reproduced*, ed. Jean E. Howard, Marion F. O'Connor (London: Methuen).

Colie, Rosalie (1974) 'Reason and need: *King Lear* and the "Crisis of the Aristocracy"', in Colie and F.T. Flahiff (eds) *Some Facets of 'King Lear': Essays in Pragmatic Criticism* (Toronto: Toronto UP).

Common Prayer, Book of (1662) (Cambridge: Cambridge UP, unpaginated, n.d.).

Cressy, David (1991) 'Foucault, Stone, Shakespeare and social history', *English Literary Renaissance*, 21.2.

Davies, Sir John (1967) *The Complete Works of Sir John Davies of Hereford,* ed. A. B. Grosart (New York: AMS Press), vol. 2.

Davies, Martin L. (1987) 'Orpheus or Clio? reflections on the uses of history', *Journal of European Studies,* 17.

Derrida, Jacques (1994) *Specters of Marx: the State of Debt, the Work of Mourning and the New International,* trans. Peggy Kamuf (London, Routledge).

Dictionary of National Biography (1887) vol. IX, ed. Leslie Stephen (London: Smith, Elder & Co.).

Dictionary of National Biography (1895) vol. XLIV, ed. Sidney Lee (London: Smith, Elder & Co.).

Dollimore, Jonathan, and Sinfield, Alan (1985) 'History and ideology: the instance of *Henry V*', *Alternative Shakespeares,* ed. J. Drakakis (London: Methuen).

Dusinberre, Juliet (1975) *Shakespeare and the Nature of Women* (London: Macmillan).

Eagleton, Terry (1986) *William Shakespeare* (Oxford: Basil Blackwell).

Easthope, Anthony (1993) 'Romancing the Stone: history-writing and rhetoric', *Social History,* 18.

Edwards, Philip (ed.) (1985) *Hamlet* (Cambridge: Cambridge UP).

Elias, Norbert (1982) *State Formation and Civilization,* vol. 2 of *The Civilizing Process,* trans. Edmund Jephcott (Oxford: Basil Blackwell).

Elyot, Sir Thomas (1531, 1907) *The Boke Named the Governour* (London: J. M. Dent).

Elyot, Sir Thomas (1538) *The Dictionary* (London: Thomas Berthelitus).

Eliot, T. S. (1963) *Collected Poems 1909–1962* (London: Faber and Faber).

Emerson, R.W. (1841–4, 1907) *Essays and Other Writings* (London: Cassell).

Ferguson, A. B. (1979) *Clio Unbound: Perceptions of the Social and Cultural Past in the Renaissance* (Durham, NC: Duke UP).

Foucault, Michel (1977, 1979) *Discipline and Punish: the Birth of the Prison,* trans. A. Sheridan (Harmondsworth: Penguin).

Frye, Susan (1992) 'The myth of Elizabeth I at Tilbury', *Sixteenth Century Journal,* 23, 1: 95–114.

Fukayama, Francis (1992) *The End of History and the Last Man* (London: Hamish Hamilton).

Fussner, F. Smith (1962) *The Historical Revolution: English Historical Writing and Thought 1580–1640* (London: Routledge).

Garber, Marjorie (1986) ' "What's past is prologue": Temporality and prophecy in Shakespeare's history plays', *Renaissance Genres: Essays on Theory, History and Interpretation,* ed. Barbara Kiefer Lewalski (Cambridge, MA: Harvard UP).

Goldberg, Jonathan (1988) 'Rebel letters: Postal effects from *Richard II* to *Henry IV*', *Renaissance Drama,* 19.

Goldstein, Jan (ed.) (1994) *Foucault and the Writing of History* (Oxford: Blackwell).

Gosson, Stephen (1579, 1973) *The Schoole of Abuse* (New York and London: Garland).

Grabes, Herbert (1982) *The Mutable Glass: Mirror-imagery in Titles and Texts of the Middle Ages and English Renaissance,* trans. Gordon Collier (Cambridge: Cambridge UP).

Grady, Hugh (1991) *The Modernist Shakespeare* (Oxford: Clarendon Press).

Greenblatt, Stephen (1988) *Shakespearean Negotiations: The Circulation of Social Energy in Renaissance England* (Oxford: Clarendon Press).

Greenblatt, Stephen (1990) *Learning to Curse: Essays in Early Modern Culture* (London: Routledge).

Greene, Robert (1592, 1997) *Groats-worth of Wit*, reprinted in *The Norton Shakespeare*, ed. Stephen Greenblatt et al. (New York and London: Norton).

Greene, Thomas (1982) *The Light in Troy: Imitation and Discovery in Renaissance Poetry* (New Haven, CT: Yale UP).

Hackett, Helen (1995) *Virgin Mother, Maiden Queen: Elizabeth I and the Cult of the Virgin Mary* (London: Macmillan).

Halle, Edward, (1548, 1809) *The Union of the Two Noble and Illustre Famelies of Lancastre & Yorke* (rpt. London: J. Johnson et al.).

Hardy, Thomas (1912, 1952) *The Collected Poems of Thomas Hardy* (London: Macmillan).

Hawkins, Sherman (1982) 'Henry IV: the structural problem revisited', *Shakespeare Quarterly*, 33.3.

Hawley, William M. (1992) *Critical Hermeneutics and Shakespeare's History Plays* (New York: Peter Lang).

Helgerson, Richard (1992) *Forms of Nationhood: The Elizabethan Writing of England* (Chicago: Chicago UP).

Herodotus (1910) *The History*, trans. G. Rawlinson (London: J. M. Dent). vol. 1.

Heywood, Thomas (1612, 1973), *An Apology for Actors* (facsimile, New York and London: Garland Publishing).

Hibbert, Christopher (1990) *The Virgin Queen: the Personal History of Elizabeth I* (London: Penguin).

Hodgdon, Barbara (1991) *The End Crowns All: Closure and Contradiction in Shakespeare's History* (Princeton, NJ: Princeton UP).

Holderness, Graham (1985) *Shakespeare's History* (Dublin: Gill and Macmillan).

Holderness, Graham (1986) 'Radical potentiality and institutional closure', *Political Shakespeare*, ed. J. Dollimore, A. Sinfield (Manchester: Manchester UP).

Holderness, Graham, with Nick Potter and John Turner (1988) *Shakespeare: the Play of History* (London: Macmillan).

Holderness, Graham, with Nick Potter and John Turner (1990) *Shakespeare Out of Court: Dramatizations of Court Society* (London: Macmillan).

Holderness, Graham (1991) ' "A woman's war"; a feminist reading of Richard II', in *Shakespeare Left and Right*, ed. Ivo Kamps (New York and London: Routledge).

Holderness, Graham (ed.) (1992) *Shakespeare's History Plays: 'Richard II' to 'Henry V'* (London: Macmillan).

Holderness, Graham and Loughrey, Bryan (eds) (1992) *The Tragicall Historie of Hamlet, Prince of Denmarke* (1603) (Hemel Hempstead: Harvester Wheatsheaf).

Holinshed, Raphael (1587, 1965) *Chronicles 'of England, Scotland and Ireland*, 6 vols (London: J. Johnson et al., 1808 edn reprinted New York: AMS Press).

Homer (1946) *The Odyssey*, trans. E. V. Rieu (Harmondsworth: Penguin).

Hopkins, G. M. (1996) *Selected Poetry*, ed. Catherine Phillips (Oxford: Oxford UP).

I.M.S. (1632, 1987) 'On Worthy Master Shakespeare and his Poems', in Wells and Taylor (1987).

Jackson, Gabriele B. (1988) 'Topical ideology: witches, Amazons, and Shakespeare's Joan of Arc', *English Literary Renaissance*, 18.

James, Mervyn (1978) 'English politics and the concept of honour 1485–1642', *Past and Present*, Supplement 3 (London: The Past and Present Society).

Kahn, Coppélia (1981) *Man's Estate* (Berkeley, CA: California UP).

Kamps, Ivo (1991) *Shakespeare Left and Right* (London and New York: Routledge).

Kantorowicz, E.H. (1957) *The King's Two Bodies* (Princeton, NJ: Princeton UP).

Kastan, David Scott (1982) *Shakespeare and the Shapes of Time* (Hanover, NH: New England UP).

Kelly, Henry A. (1970) *Divine Providence in the England of Shakespeare's Histories* (Cambridge, MA: Harvard UP).

Keneally, Thomas (1974) *Blood Red, Sister Rose* (London: Collins).

Kernan, Alvin B. (1970) '*The Henriad*: Shakespeare's major history plays', *Modern Shakespeare Criticism*, ed. Alvin B. Kernan (San Diego, CA: Harcourt Brace Jovanovich).

Kernodle, George R. (1944) *From Art to Theatre: Form and Convention in the Renaissance* (Chicago: Chicago UP).

Knight, G. Wilson (1944) *The Olive and the Sword* (Oxford: Oxford UP).

Kristeva, Julia (1986) 'The revolution in poetic language', trans. Margaret Waller, in Toril Moi (ed.), *The Kristeva Reader* (Oxford: Blackwell).

Laurence, Anne (1994) *Women in England 1500–1760: A Social History* (London: Weidenfeld & Nicolson).

Leone, Mark (1981) 'The relationship between artifacts and the public in outdoor history', *Annals of the New York Academy of Sciences*, 376, xxiv.

Lowenthal, David (1985) *The Past is a Foreign Country* (Cambridge: Cambridge UP).

Lucian of Samosata (1629) quoted in Thomas Hobbes, *The History of the Grecian War* (3rd edn, London: D. Brown, 1723), 'Preface'.

Lucian of Samosata (1991) quoted by D. R. Kelley in his edition, *Versions of History* (New Haven, CT: Yale UP).

Lucretius (1951) *On the Nature of the Universe* (*De Rerum Natura*), trans. R. E. Latham (Harmondsworth: Penguin).

Macherey, Pierre (1978) *A Theory of Literary Production*, trans. G. Wall (London: Routledge and Kegan Paul).

Marcus, Leah (1988) *Puzzling Shakespeare: Local Reading and its Discontents* (Berkeley, CA: California UP).

Marx, Karl (1963) *Selected Writings in Sociology and Social Philosophy*, ed. T. Bottomore (Harmondsworth: Pelican).

Megill, Allan (1987) 'The reception of Foucault by historians', *Journal of the History of Ideas*, 48.

Milton, John (1623, 1987) 'An Epitaph on the Admirable Dramatic Poet, William Shakespeare', in Wells and Taylor (1987).

Milton, John (1674, 1961) 'Paradise Lost' (2nd edn) *The Poems of John Milton*, ed. Helen Darbishire (Cambridge: Cambridge UP).

Miner, Madonne M. (1983), ' "Neither mother, wife, nor England's queen": the roles of women in *Richard III'*, in *The Woman's Part: Feminist Criticism of Shakespeare*, ed. C. R. S. Lenz, G. Greene, C. T. Neely (Urbana and Chicago, IL: Illinois UP).

Montrose, Louis Adrian (1986) 'Renaissance literary studies and the subject of history', *English Literary Renaissance*, 16.

Moretti, Franco (1982) ' "A huge eclipse": tragic form and the deconsecration of sovereignty', *Genre*, 15.

Nash, Thomas (1592, 1969) *Pierce Pennilesse His Svpplication to the Divell* (facsimile edn, Menston: Scolar Press, 1969).

Neale, J. E. (1934, 1960) *Queen Elizabeth I* (Harmondsworth: Pelican).

New English Hymnal (1986) (Canterbury: Norwich Press).

Newman, John Henry (1857) 'The Second Spring', in *Sermons Preached on Various Occasions* (London: Burns, Oates and Co., 3rd edn, 1870).

Nuttall, A. D. (1983) *A New Mimesis: Shakespeare and the Representation of Reality* (London: Methuen).

Ong, Walter J. (1988) *Orality and Literacy: the Technologizing of the Word* (London: Routledge).

Ornstein, Robert (1972) *A Kingdom for a Stage: The Achievement of Shakespeare's History Plays* (Cambridge, MA: Harvard UP).

Parker, Patricia (1996) *Shakespeare from the Margins: Language, Culture, Contexts* (London and Chicago: Chicago UP).

Pater, Walter (1889, 1907) *Appreciations* (3rd edn, London: Macmillan).

Patterson, Annabel (1989) *Shakespeare and the Popular Voice* (Oxford: Basil Blackwell).

Peck, Linda Levy (1995) 'Peers, patronage and the politics of history', in *The Reign of Elizabeth I: Court and Culture in the Last Decade*, ed. John Guy (Cambridge: Cambridge UP).

Platter, Thomas (1599, 1995), reprinted in Peter Razell (ed.) *The Journals of Two Travellers in Elizabethan England* (London: Caliban Books).

Pocock, J. G. A. (1957) *The Ancient Constitution and the Feudal Law* (Cambridge: Cambridge UP).

Pocock, J. G. A. (1987) 'The sense of history in Renaissance England', *William Shakespeare: His World, His Work, His Influence*, ed. J. Andrews (New York: Charles Scribner's Sons).

Prior, Moody E. (1973)*The Drama of Power* (Evanston, IL: Northwestern UP).

Pugliatti, Paola (1996) *Shakespeare the Historian* (London: Macmillan).

Puttenham, George (1589, 1904), *The Arte of English Poesie*, in G. Gregory Smith (ed.) *Elizabethan Critical Essays* (Oxford: Clarendon Press).

Rackin, Phyllis (1990) *Stages of History: Shakespeare's English Chronicles* (London: Routledge).

Raleigh, Sir Walter (1614) *The History of the World In Five Books* (London: Walter Bvrre).

Raleigh, Sir Walter (1984) *Selected Writings*, ed. Gerald Hammond (Manchester: Carcanet Press).

Ribner, Irving (1957) *The English History Play in the Age of Shakespeare* (Princeton, NJ: Princeton UP).

Riggs (1970) *Shakespeare's Heroical Histories: Henry VI and its Literary Tradition* (Cambridge, MA: Harvard UP).

Rorty, Richard (1984) with J. B. Schneewind and Quentin Skinner (eds) *Philosophy in History: Essays on the Historiography of Philosophy* (Cambridge: Cambridge UP).

Rossiter, A. P. (1961) *Angel With Horns and other Shakespeare Lectures*, ed. G. Storey (London: Longmans Green).

Roston, Murray (1987) *Renaissance Perspectives in Literature and the Visual Arts* (Princeton, NJ: Princeton UP).

Rous Roll, British Library Add. Ms. 48976.

Ryan, Kiernan (1990) *Shakespeare* (Hemel Hempstead: Harvester Wheatsheaf).

Sanders, Wilbur (1968) *The Dramatist and the Received Idea: Studies in the Plays of Marlowe and Shakespeare* (Cambridge: Cambridge UP).

Sellars, W. C. and R. J. Yeatman (1930, 1933) *1066 and All That* (Stroud: Sutton).

Shakespeare, William (1605, 1969) *The Tragicall Historie of Hamlet, Prince of Denmarke* (London: I.R. for N.L., 1605) (facsimile, Menston: Scolar Press).

Sharpe, Kevin (1994) 'Religion, rhetoric and revolution in seventeenth-century England', *Huntington Library Quarterly*, 57.

Shaw, G. B. (1924) *St Joan* (London: Constable).

Sidney, Sir Philip (1595, 1966) *A Defence of Poetry*, ed. Jan Van Dorsten (Oxford: Oxford UP).

Sidney, Sir Philip (1591, 1962) 'Astrophil and Stella', in *The Poems of Sir Philip Sidney*, ed. William A. Ringer (Oxford: Clarendon).

Sinfield, Alan (1986) 'Royal Shakespeare', in *Political Shakespeare*, ed. J. Dollimore, A. Sinfield (Manchester: Manchester UP).

Smithe, Sir John (1595, 1966), quoted in Geoffrey Bullough (ed.) *Narrative and Dramatic Sources of Shakespeare* (London: Rouledge and Kegan Paul), vol. IV.

Smith Fussner, F. (1962) *The Historical Revolution: English Historical Writing and Thought 1580–1640* (London: Routledge and Kegan Paul).

Southgate, Beverley (1996) *History: What and Why?* (London: Routledge).

Spiegel, G. M. (1990) 'History, historicism and the social logic of the text in the Middle Ages', *Speculum*, 65.

Stanyhurst, Richard (1577, 1965) 'Epistle Dedicatory' to 'The Description of Ireland', in Holinshed (1577, 1965).

Stribrny, Zdenek (1964) '*Henry V* and history', *Shakespeare in a Changing World*, ed. A. Kettle (London: Lawrence and Wishart).

Strong, Roy (1984) *The English Renaissance Miniature* (London: Thames and Hudson).

Taylor, Gary (1989) *Reinventing Shakespeare: a Cultural History 1642–1986* (New York: Weidenfeld and Nicolson).

Tennenhouse, Leonard (1986) *Power on Display* (London: Methuen).

Thayer, C. G. (1983) *Shakespearean Politics: Government and Misgovernment in the Great Histories* (Athens, OH: Ohio UP).

Thomas, Dylan (1952, 1966) *Collected Poems 1934–1953* (London: J. M. Dent).

Thucydides (1954) *The Peloponnesian War*, trans. Rex Warner (Harmondsworth: Penguin).

Tillyard, E. M. W. (1941) *The Elizabethan World Picture* (London: Chatto & Windus).

Tillyard, E. M. W. (1944, 1980) *Shakespeare's History Plays* (London: Chatto & Windus).

Tillyard, E. M. W. (1949) *Shakespeare's Problem Plays* (London: Chatto and Windus).

Toews, J. E. (1987), 'Intellectual history after the linguistic turn: the autonomy of meaning and the irreducibility of experience', *American Historical Review*, 92.

Traversi, D.A. (1957) *Shakespeare from 'Richard II' to 'Henry V'* (London: Hollis & Carter).

Traversi, D.A. (1963) *Shakespeare: the Roman Plays* (London: Hollis and Carter).

Trill, Suzanne et. al. (eds) (1997) *Lay by Your Needles, Ladies, Take up the Pen: Writing Women in England 1500–1700* (London: Edward Arnold).

Ure, Peter (ed.) (1961) *King Richard II* (London: Methuen).

Vasari, Giorgio (1550, 1965) *Lives of the Artists*, vol. 1, trans. G. Bull (Harmondsworth: Penguin).

Virgil (1950) *Aeneid IV*, ed. A. Sidgwick (Cambridge: Cambridge University Press).

Virgil (1956) *The Aeneid*, trans. W. F. Jackson Knight (Harmondsworth: Penguin).

Watson, Curtis B. (1960) *Shakespeare and the Renaissance Concept of Honour* (Westport, CN: Greenwood Press).

Weimann, Robert (1978) *Shakespeare and the Popular Tradition in the Theatre*, trans. R. Schwarz (Baltimore, MD: Johns Hopkins UP).

Wells, Stanley and Taylor, Gary (eds) (1987) *William Shakespeare: the Complete Works* (Oxford: Oxford UP).

White, Haydn (1978) *Tropics of Discourse: Essays in Cultural Criticism* (Baltimore, MD: Johns Hopkins UP).

Wikander, Matthew H. (1986) *The Play of Truth and State: Historical Drama from Shakespeare to Brecht* (Baltimore, MD: Johns Hopkins UP).

Woolf, Virginia (1958) 'Women and fiction', in *Granite and Rainbow* (London: Hogarth Press).

Wordsworth, William (1805) *The Prelude: A Parallel Text*, ed. J. C. Maxwell (Harmondsworth: Penguin, 1971).

Yates, Frances A. (1975) *Astraea: the Imperial Theme in the Sixteenth Century* (London: Routledge and Kegan Paul).

Yeats, W. B. (1933, 1978) *Collected Poems* (London: Macmillan).

Index

NOTE: Page numbers in *italic* indicate a plate. Page numbers in **bold** indicate major discussion of a subject.

228

Index

history
    ambiguity of term, 57, 58
    and antiquity, 73–5
    and character, 79–83
    Cicero's definition, 42, 54, 58, 205
    construction of, 163–6
    critical movements and, 209–11
    Elizabethan concept of, **42–56**
    historical destiny, 143–5
    historical determinism, 171–4
    as instruction, 46, 47, 49, 51–2, 53,
        54–6, 92; in *Hamlet*, 67–73
    masculinisation of, 16, 55–6
    as memory, 46, 51–4; in *Hamlet*, 64–7
    as mirror, 204–5, 211–12
    postmodernist view of, 8, 210, 211
    as reawakening, 139–43, 212
    theatrical representation of *see* historical
        drama; histories; theatre
    and truth, 46–50, 213, 214; historical
        testimony, 58–64, 187; reporting
        of events, 158–60, 166–9
Holinshed, Raphael, 5, 46, 112, 154,
    215–16
    on Joan of Arc, 124, 125–6, 129
Homer, 46
    The Odyssey, 43, 61–2
Hopkins, Gerard Manley, 139, 196
hour-glass image, 138–9
humanism, 75, 209
    in *Hamlet*, 72

I.M.S. (poet), 53, 73, 138, 211–14
instruction *see* education
intelligence gathering, 29–30, 31–3
Isabella, Infanta of Spain, 32, 38

Jackson, Gabrielle B., 128, 133
James I, King of England (James VI of
    Scotland), 6, 19, 27–8, 32–3
James, Mervyn, 74
Joan of Arc in *Henry VI, Part One*, 38, 110,
    118, 124–35
Job, 194
John (gospel), 203
Johnson, Samuel, 16
Jonson, Ben, 43
Julius Caesar, 4, 45, 66

Kahn, Coppélia, 17
Kelly, Henry A., 198
King Henry VI see Henry VI
King John, 4, 6, 7, 38
King Lear, 6
Knollys, Sir William, 26
Kristeva, Julia, 189

Lambarde, William, 12
language
    female *see* female, language of
    in *Richard III*, 176–8
'late romances', 5
Laurence, Anne, 38
Leicester, Robert Dudley, Earl of, 24, 25,
    27, 37
Leone, Mark, 72–3
Life and Death of Julius Caesar, The, 4
Life and Death of King John, The, 4, 7
literary criticism
    'democratic' tradition, 215–16
    and genre categories, 4–5
    and histories, 7–9, 209–11
Lowenthal, David, 76
Lucian of Samosata, 46, 211–12
Luke (gospel), 127
    Prodigal Son imagery, 131, 144

Macbeth, 6, 14, 36–7, 43, 62
Macherey, Pierre, 14, 15
machiavellianism, 209
Marcus, Leah, 215
Mark (gospel), 99, 155, 179
Marlowe, Christopher: *Edward II*, 5
Marx, Karl, 14, 53, 67, 108
marxism, Althusserian, 210
Mary I (Mary Tudor), Queen of England,
    19, 20, 22, 38, 55
Mary, Queen of Scots, 29, 30, 31,
    32, 38
Matthew (gospel), 142
Medici, Catherine de' *see* Catherine
    de'Medici
Melville, Herman, 133
memory, 46, 51–4, 186–7
    in *Hamlet*, 64–7
Merry Wives of Windsor, The, 7